Spirituality

OTHER BOOKS BY ROGER S. GOTTLIEB

History and Subjectivity: The Transformation of Marxist Theory

Marxism 1844–1990: Origins, Betrayal, Rebirth

A Spirituality of Resistance: Finding a Peaceful Heart and Protecting the Earth

Joining Hands: Politics and Religion Together for Social Change

A Greener Faith: Religious Environmentalism and Our Planet's Future

Engaging Voices: Tales of Morality and Meaning in an Age of Global Warming

Edited by Roger S. Gottlieb

An Anthology of Western Marxism: From Lukacs and Gramsci to Socialist-Feminism

A New Creation: America's Contemporary Spiritual Voices

Thinking the Unthinkable: Meanings of the Holocaust

Radical Philosophy: Tradition, Counter-Tradition, Politics

This Sacred Earth: Religion, Nature, Environment (First and Second editions)

The Ecological Community

*Deep Ecology and World Religions: New Essays on Common Ground
(with David L. Barnhill)*

Liberating Faith: Religious Voices for Justice, Peace, and Ecological Wisdom

The Oxford Handbook of Religion and Ecology

Religion and the Environment

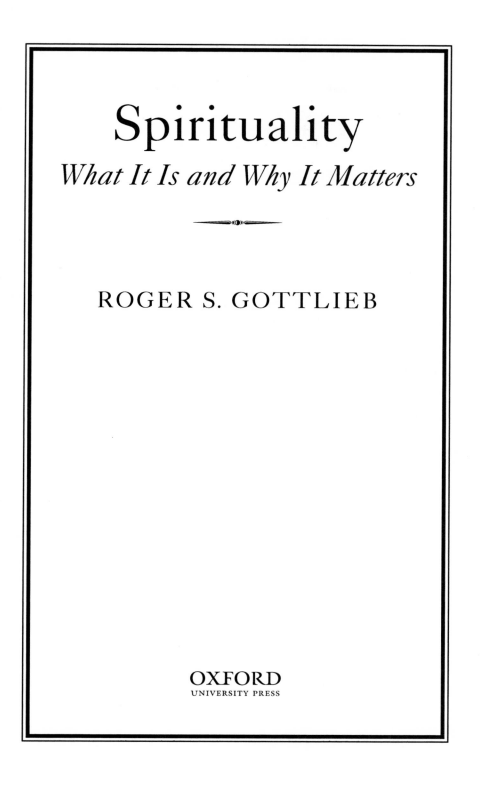

Spirituality
What It Is and Why It Matters

ROGER S. GOTTLIEB

OXFORD
UNIVERSITY PRESS

OXFORD
UNIVERSITY PRESS

Oxford University Press is a department of the University of Oxford.
It furthers the University's objective of excellence in research, scholarship,
and education by publishing worldwide.

Oxford   New York
Auckland   Cape Town   Dar es Salaam   Hong Kong   Karachi
Kuala Lumpur   Madrid   Melbourne   Mexico City   Nairobi
New Delhi   Shanghai   Taipei   Toronto

With offices in
Argentina   Austria   Brazil   Chile   Czech Republic   France   Greece
Guatemala   Hungary   Italy   Japan   Poland   Portugal   Singapore
South Korea   Switzerland   Thailand   Turkey   Ukraine   Vietnam

Oxford is a registered trademark of Oxford University Press
in the UK and certain other countries.

Published in the United States of America by
Oxford University Press
198 Madison Avenue, New York, NY 10016

© Oxford University Press 2013

Library of Congress Cataloging-in-Publication Data
Gottlieb, Roger S.
Spirituality : what it is and why it matters / Roger S. Gottlieb
p. cm.
Includes bibliographical references and index.
ISBN 978-0-19-973875-5—ISBN 978-0-19-973874-8
1. Spirituality. I. Title.
BL624.G675 2013
204—dc23
2012018340

ISBN 978-0-19-973875-5
ISBN 978-0-19-973874-8

For all my teachers

Thank you

Contents

Contents

PART III: *End/Beginning*

Preface

I would not talk so much about myself if there were anyone else
whom I knew so well.

THOREAU[1]

I WAS A high school senior, and though I was doing well in my classes and had friends and a wide range of interests, I was also bitterly disappointed that after three years on the wrestling team I simply wasn't good enough to make the varsity. An unexpected sophomore, tutored by his star athlete older brother, arrived at practice one day and promptly beat me out for the 145-pound spot. Like pretty much everything else in my life, I'd worked hard at wrestling. But unlike some other things, mainly those concerned with books, it hadn't come easy. I wasn't very strong, and no matter what I did, I couldn't seem to get that much stronger. But wrestling meant something to me, something it took me years to fully understand. It was a way to prove that even though I was an intellectual who loved reading and classical music, I, too, was a real man, as tough as the other types of guys—not just a soft Jewish kid with thick glasses. And here, in my third year of grueling 2½-hour practices, I was failing. I obsessed over my failure, tried to lick my wounds and get over it, but felt it as a relentless, nagging unease.

Fortunately, at the same time, I was rereading Thoreau's *Walden*. While in my first encounter with the book, I had been taken by his celebration of nature and, perhaps even more, the way he thumbed his nose at what a few years later I would disdainfully call "The Establishment," this time something else struck me. "Live as deliberately as nature," he counseled, and instead of seeking wealth or success or status, find a center of awareness and serenity that no accomplishment or possession can replace, and no social failure dislodge. Dig deep into your soul and reach out to the universe, and you will find contentment.[2]

And so my first encounter with spirituality's wise and healing response to the pains of life came to me from Thoreau. I would like to say that his soothing insights calmed my disappointment and insecurity, but they did not. Although I sensed that he was, in the deepest sense, "right" about how to live, I still held a burning hunger for achievement and recognition, a painful belief that I deserved love only if I succeeded, over and over again.

Eighteen years later, after encounters with Zen Buddhism, Kierkegaard, psychedelics, Hasidic mystical stories, yoga, meditation, and Jewish Renewal and a yearlong trip through India vastly enlarged my sense of what spirituality could be, I faced a much darker and more demanding test. My first child, Aaron, was born a month early with severe brain damage, never left the hospital, and lived only 65 days. My hopes for bonding with an infant and raising a son or daughter turned into the nightmare of Aaron connected to tubes and beeping machines, tormented by the hospital's well-meaning and near-endless tests. In his final moments— lungs and immune system overwhelmed by pneumonia—he died in our arms.

What was I to do with my grief? My rage at fate and bitter envy of people who had normal, healthy children? No psychotherapy could cure this malaise, nor could the banal pieties (all of which my wife and I actually heard) of "God took Aaron's spirit," "You must have done something bad in a previous life," or "You're better off."

Only a "spiritual" response could even temporarily sooth my aching heart. I would think of the love that, despite everything, we had been able to show Aaron and of a similar desperate love against all odds I saw from other parents on the neurology floor of Children's Hospital. The ways I would usually distance myself from those other parents—who weren't leftists, or educated, or counterculture types—were erased by a commonality of shared suffering and compassion. I tried to see the miracle of life that was in all children, even if none of them were mine. I realized that unless I faced both the depth of my grief and my crushing sense of failure over my inability to protect my son, I was doomed to endless heartache.

And I began to understand that the radical politics I had been part of for a decade, the hyperintellectualized techniques of academic philosophy in which I'd earned a doctorate, and my conventional pursuit of pleasure and career success simply paled in front of Aaron's death. This other thing, spirituality, was my only hope.

Spirituality

Introduction

Not God but life, more life, a larger, richer more satisfying life,
is in the last analysis the end of religion.

WILLIAM JAMES[1]

AMERICA IS FILLED with people who say they are "spiritual but not religious," a news story tells us, as if the two ideas repel each other.[2] Yet a leading Catholic publisher advertises extensive offerings in Jewish, Christian, and Islamic "spirituality."[3] Amazon lists 282 books in the general area of "spirituality and aging" and 14 on "spirituality and art therapy" alone. A casual Internet search turns up a listing of more than 400 "spiritual retreat centers." Alabama's Blessed Trinity Shrine Retreat Center offers "Ongoing Spiritual Direction," in which a person "meets with a director on a regular basis to share one's journey of faith and to discern the direction in which the Lord is leading the person in prayer and daily life."[4] Alaska's Stillpoint at Halibut Cove, by contrast, provides guests a chance "to create a safe contemplative environment to rekindle their spirit and re-connect with themselves, nature, and a source beyond themselves."[5]

These examples could be multiplied indefinitely—into politics and art, medicine and poetry, exercise and gardening; into virtually every religious tradition and into contexts where the ideas of God, church, or scripture do not appear at all.

What is spirituality, and is there any coherent way to understand it? How can we make sense of ideas like "a spiritual center," "a spiritual director," or a "spiritual experience" or know what a person is doing when she responds to a life crisis "spiritually" instead of some other way, taking a "spiritual lesson" from a disappointment that might otherwise be a crushing setback?

But first, is it so important that people use *spirituality, spiritual,* and *spiritually* in a wide variety of often contradictory ways? Is that not just like the ways people talk about religion or marriage?

True enough. But it is also true that our understanding of an idea is not something that interests only authors of dictionaries, but is an embodiment of our values and ideals. That is why differences over what *religion* or *marriage* really means lead to intense conflicts. How we understand something shapes how we live it.

But why should we want to understand—or live—spirituality?

This deserves two answers.

For a large group of people in today's world (including myself), spirituality is essential to who we are. What it asks of us is a, perhaps *the*—central task in life, and therefore it is important that we understand it as best we can.

But what of those people whose focus in life is traditional religion, art, the military, career advancement, or economic success; who seek social status, political power, cutting-edge scientific knowledge, or simply a good time—why should any of them care about what spirituality is or isn't?

The rest of the book is an answer to this question, but here is the highly condensed version. In the early 1970s, I was a somewhat hard-nosed philosophy graduate student but had also begun to study Kundalini Yoga, a practice involving dynamic postures, intense breathing, chanting, and meditation. One evening I went to a lecture by the guru of Kundalini, Yogi Bhajan, a cheerful, bearded Sikh with a booming laugh and a big belly. He offered what I would later recognize as the basics of nondenominational spirituality: make a fundamental change in your life by letting go of your ego, surrendering your attachments, doing away with greed, and manifesting kindness and compassion. When he asked for questions, I stood up and, in a slightly pretentious "I'm an academic philosopher" tone, asked him: "I see what you are saying, but tell me why I *ought* to do any of these things." In other words, why *should* I live a spiritual life? Where were the justifications and the motivations? Undaunted by either the question or my manner, Yogi Bhajan was relaxed and clear in his response: "I am not saying you ought to, I am simply saying you will never be happy, never have real peace of mind or serenity, unless you do."

This, in essence, is the point. For all their association with soothing music, peaceful country settings, and nonjudgmental love, spiritual teachings are actually quite radical. They propose a sweeping transformation in how we live and assert that only through such a transformation are lasting happiness and true contentment possible.

Of course, if things are going really well for you—if you are healthy and good-looking and smart, successful and well taken care of—you might not take up spirituality on its offer to make your life better. Spiritual values typically enter our lives when something goes wrong or at least isn't working right. When a beloved child is hopelessly disabled by a drunk driver, a husband walks out on a 20-year marriage, you get everything you thought you wanted and are still unsatisfied, go to church and wonder what you're doing there, or find out that modern industrial society is extinguishing a species every 10 minutes—then it is to the spirit that you may turn.

Or spirituality can come into our lives as something unexpected and miraculous. We feel a source of joy so profound, a connection to everyone and everything so complete, that our usual goals, pleasures, and sense of self dwindle in comparison. Some people call these moments of God or truth or the real self; Freud talked of an "oceanic feeling"; an 11-year-old boy excitedly asks his older brother, "Does everyone really know they are alive?"[6] We may be awed by the wonder of birth, an unexpected kindness, music that for a few moments makes life seem utterly complete, or a universe of stars in a night sky. So powerful and true are these moments, we tell ourselves, that we will do anything to hold on to them, so we can live in their light.[7]

In the face of sorrow, in response to joy, with or without organized religion and belief in God, in tight-knit communities or in silence and solitude, in disciplines of our minds or bodies or hearts—in all these ways, spiritual life beckons, offering incomparable rewards and (as we shall see) an equally extreme set of demands.

PART I

What It Is

Open yourself, create free pace; release the bound one from his bonds. Like a newborn child, freed from the womb, be free to move on every path.

ATHARVA VEDA 6.121.4

What is God? He is the breath inside the breath.

KABIR[1]

IN ITS BROADEST terms, spirituality is an understanding of how life should be lived and an attempt to live that way. A spiritually oriented life gives rise to certain characteristic experiences, and certain characteristic experiences may prompt the adoption of a spiritual perspective and motivate a spiritually oriented life. Spiritual teachings contain some perplexing paradoxes; and have significant connections to and differences with morality, mysticism, and traditional religion. Overall, the attempt to live spiritually is a lifelong striving beset with a variety of challenges and long-term labors (including, ironically, the labor of learning how to stop laboring too hard).

Chapters 1 and 2 discuss fundamental beliefs, experiences, and difficulties described by a broad range of spiritual perspectives. Chapter 3 offers examples of spiritual teachings contained in religious tradition, and Chapter 4 provides an account of the development of distinctly modern forms of spirituality. Chapter 5 explores why many people say they are "spiritual but not religious," and Chapter 6 examines some common spiritual practices. Chapter 7 concludes part I by briefly sketching some historical reasons that there is so much contemporary interest in spirituality.

To vary my sentences, I use a variety of terms and phrases—*spirituality, spiritual teachings, spiritual perspectives*, and the like—to refer to pretty much the same thing: an understanding of life, the attempt to live by that understanding, and the experiences to which that attempt gives rise. Certain themes appear a number of times, particularly questions of attachment, truth, discipline, selflessness, and social justice. With each reappearance (hopefully), the thread of the discussion will go a little deeper and draw on a greater amount of supporting and clarifying material.

Most of what follows, even when informally or casually expressed, is rooted in more than 25 centuries of spiritual writings. What is original stems from the peculiarities of my historical situation, the contours of my life history, and the particular way I combine spiritual ideas and progressive politics. I often make statements about the universality of human experience, the psychological consequences of certain forms of behavior, and what works and what doesn't in life. These ideas derive from a wide array of spiritual teachings, which this book attempts to summarize, synthesize, and analyze.[2]

Because this book is not only an account but also an expression of spirituality, its frequently direct and personal tone and the use of my own life for an occasional example are necessary. From Christian mystics to thirteenth-century Islamic Sufis to the Dalai Lama in today's bookstores, spiritual teachers share lessons based in their own experience and believe that what they are saying is of immediate practical importance. Although spiritual insights may be many things, they are never abstract, academic, theoretical, or impersonal. Ultimately, they are about the meaning and value of each of our lives. To represent them in any other way would be to misrepresent them.

I

Spirit in Motion

*To be a Sufi is to give up all worries and there is no worse worry
than yourself. When you are occupied with self you are separated
from God. The way to God is but one step: The step out of yourself.*

ABU SA'ID IBN ABI-L-KHAYR[1]

*For me to be a saint means to be myself. Therefore the problem
of sanctity and salvation is in fact the problem of finding out
who I am and of discovering my true self.*

THOMAS MERTON[2]

*The Infinite is the source of joy. There is no joy in the finite.
Only in the Infinite is there joy. Ask to know the Infinite.*

CHANDOGYA UPANISHAD 7.23

SPIRITUALITY BEGINS IN movement—away from what we come to see as unreal, painful, disappointing, trivial, or meaningless and toward the ultimate, true, vital, real, or sacred. This movement can be illustrated by what might be called "spiritual" responses to a number of difficult or painful situations.

- If you are constantly distracted or anxious, turn off your computer–cell phone–iPad-TV and sit in silence for a time, every day, for the rest of your life.
- If you are angry, develop some empathy for the people you are angry at, learn to honestly admit your own failings, and face the grief or fear your anger may be obscuring.
- If you are consumed by wanting things you do not have, begin to see the endlessness of desire—how wanting gives rise to only more wanting.
- If you discover that pursuing status or career is empty and unfulfilling, find forms of love that are meaningful.

- If you are in despair because of what you have lost—your spouse, your eyesight, your career—feel the depth of your sorrow and then find faith in the simple goodness of life.
- If you are chronically ill, see how your attachments, refusal to accept reality, or inability to shape your mind toward wellness is making you worse.
- If people you love are ill, self-destructive, or in trouble, and you are tormented by their pain, learn to accept the inevitability of human suffering, to love them despite their problems, and to be a source of peace for them no matter what they are going through.
- If you are addicted to alcohol or drugs, sex or gambling, turn over your obsession to a Higher Power, get honest about who you are, and make amends to all the people you've hurt.
- If you are grieving your child's multiple disabilities, face the depth of your loss and learn to value him for what he is and for the love you can give him.
- If your relation to God has slipped into a boring routine, reawaken your devotion by slowly exploring the meanings of each word of a familiar prayer. Ask yourself, for example, what it means to "forgive them that trespass against us."
- If you practice your spirituality with arrogance or competitiveness, realize that reproducing your ego in a "spiritual" setting will get you nowhere.
- If your spirituality is a search for the pleasant—elegant retreat centers, beautifully decorated meditation spaces—develop your capacity for spirituality as service. Learn to maintain your spiritual calm volunteering in a hospital, serving meals at a homeless shelter, trying to end a war.
- If you are a victim of oppression, honor your suffering but learn compassion and forgiveness lest you destroy your own peace of mind.
- If you are trying to change the world for the better and are constantly overcome with rage at all the oppressors, reflect on how much violence there is inside your own heart.
- If you are trying to change the world for the better and find yourself desperate and overwhelmed, perilously close to burnout, learn to accept the limits of what you can do, and remember the love that still exists in the world.
- "If you are hungry, look for someone to feed; when you are sad, look for someone to cheer; when you need understanding, find someone who needs yours; and when you need to be looked after, find someone to care for."[3]

In all these settings of suffering, disappointment, or emotional unease, we are instructed to practice what I call the "spiritual virtues": mindfulness or awareness, acceptance and equanimity, gratitude and generosity, compassion, and loving connection to other people, nature, and God. The core spiritual belief is that these virtues are the only way to achieve enduring contentment and goodness in the face of life's challenges and that they will benefit both the person who manifests them and everyone around her. Spiritual virtues have this power, it is taught, because they are in some deep sense right for who we are. As the oak tree needs a particular combination of sunlight, water, soil, and climate, as fish need the ocean, so human beings need spiritual virtues.

The Basic Idea

From a spiritual perspective, who we are and what happiness is take a distinct and highly unconventional form. As taught by virtually every religious tradition (though not always as their dominant message) and as embraced by countless individuals who are "spiritual but not religious," this is what we hear:

You are not who you think you are, and you do not have to live the way you think you do. You carry within yourself a capacity for self-understanding, acceptance of whatever life offers, generosity, spontaneous moral behavior, and love. These are the essential promises, the gifts, of a spiritual life.

However, in order to realize these gifts you will have to give something up, something which right now you seem to believe is the most important thing you have. Spiritual development is not possible without a transformation so intense that it may feel like a sacrifice of your very identity, a kind of death. Which, in some sense, it is.

You need to surrender your attachment to what Taoists call the "ten thousand things," meaning all the world's attractive and repulsive physical objects and human relationships; what Buddhists call *samsara*, the illusion that getting what you want will make you happy; what Christians sometimes describe, not approvingly, as "the things of this world," (1 John 2:15); and what we secular moderns might call your normal social self, ego, or personhood.

Consider what is on your mind when you wake up in the morning, where you direct your energy, what you use to evaluate how good or successful a person you are, what you think is truly important. It might be career, bank account, house or car, the way you look in the mirror, your health, how many people came to your last birthday party, intense emotions like grief over a parent's death or anger at a friend's betrayal, the quality of your love life, family relationships, what you do for fun on Saturday night, ending world hunger, whether you voted for Obama or despise him, what country you live in, even what you believe about God. In truth, these things are not who you are. And your attachment to them and the sense of separation from other people and the world based in that attachment will leave you frustrated, anxious, and disappointed.

It is not involvement with the world that is mistaken. It is spiritually appropriate to have work and family, political ties, aesthetic interests, and communities to which you belong. But if you want to live with contentment and inner peace, to be self-aware and deeply compassionate, you will need to change *how* you have them.

Let us try a simple, almost trivial, example. Walk through a large park in any major city on a spring weekend, and you will see people running. Most of them will have surprisingly cheap, multitasking chronographs on their wrists—handy gizmos that tell the time, count down to zero, serve as alarm clocks, and also function as stopwatches. Periodically, the runners—superslim teenage girls with ponytails bouncing behind them, gray-bearded overweight middle-aged men wearing old T-shirts and grim faces, weight lifter types with perfect abs—will look at their watches to see how they are doing. By "see how they are doing," they mean "see how fast (or slow) they are running," how close or far away they are from some arbitrary but quite definite good time.

In and of itself, there is nothing wrong with noting one's running times, but listen to this:

SPIRITUAL TEACHER: "What difference does it make how fast you are running? What's your hurry?"[4]
RUNNER: "Well, obviously, faster is better!"
ST: "Why?"
R: "Silly question, but if you must know, I like to do things well. And besides, my times tell me what kind of shape I'm in."
ST: "Why don't you think simply running until you want to stop is doing it well? And wouldn't you know you were in fine shape if you could do that? And if you felt good afterward?"
R: "You mean just run for the sheer pleasure of it, without any objective measurement of success? That's crazy!"

And to those of us who (like me)[5] keep records of every workout for decades, this indeed might sound a little strange. Yet attachment to a formula for success usually leads to a compulsion to perform. We know it is a compulsion because (ask any sports medicine clinic) the need to do well all too often turns into running too many miles, too often, too fast—and to injury.[6] Then we have the inevitable anger and frustration because the pleasure, emotional uplift, and sense of accomplishment of aerobic exercise must be put on hold. The vast majority of injured runners get hurt because they do not pay attention to the early warning signs: a little twinge gradually getting worse, an ache that doesn't go away after a night's rest. But the compulsive attachment to a goal drives the runner on anyway. "I can't miss a workout, my times have been lousy, or "Now I'm getting closer to my goal. I'll just run through it." Obsession, we might say, always wears something out—in this case, a foot, a knee, or a back.

From a spiritual point of view, there is nothing wrong with running (or, of course, with not running either). The mistake is in the attachment, the compulsion, the obsession, in the way an arbitrary and abstract measure becomes essential to a person's self-evaluation: *arbitrary* because there is no rational need to run seven-minute rather than nine-minute miles and *abstract* because the value of the running is not based in how it feels or how it connects to overall health, but in a measure external to the actual lived experience. In serious cases, the measurement becomes linked to the runner's self-definition. I am a *good* (adequate, successful, worthy, lovable, manly) person when I run well. If this is what is at stake, no wonder there is a compulsion, and no wonder there are injuries. And the price paid for the obsession is not only heel pain and shredded knee cartilage but also the simple enjoyment of one's strength and grace sacrificed to an external calculation of "how good am I?"—a question that must be answered by the stopwatch over and over again.

For people whose attitude to exercise is more leave it than take it, we can replace the numbers on the chronograph with other numbers: for some men and a lot more women, the numbers on the bathroom scale or the dress label; the numbers on your paycheck; the number of friends you have on Facebook; how many times you had sex last month; the letters on your daughter's report card. In each case, there is an attachment to an external measure of your identity and worth. In each case, the attachment to this measure often leads to compulsive, even self-destructive, behavior. In the realm of weight, this behavior can be on-and-off dieting, eating disorders, an inability to enjoy food or one's body, or a nagging, energy-depleting sense that there is something wrong. In the realm of money, it can be overwork that destroys health and personal relationships, continual self-criticism because one has too low level a job, or willingness to do anything to succeed, no matter what the moral cost. In the realm of love or family, it can be a self-defeating attempt to control, a desperate need for external validation of one's worth, and a crushing depression when things do not work out.

But what else can I do? cries the successfully socialized self. Isn't it important how fast and far I run? How I look? How much money I make? Whether I'm loved or how well my kids do in school? If I am not to obey the imperatives of the normal social ego—*do, accomplish, control, measure, measure up, possess*—how else can I live?

Out of Reach?

The spiritual response is that a self that clutches at external proof of its worth or grasps at pleasures, possessions, accomplishments, or even relationships is only temporarily satisfied. Like the mad dog chained up in the basement, it might sleep after a eating a large steak, but sooner or later it will be pulling at its chain, so hard the house shakes, wanting more. The entire pattern of attachment is a fundamental mistake. And though a spiritual life does not require faith in the conventional sense of belief in God, reincarnation, or revelation, it does require faith that it is possible to overcome this pattern, that—as is said in 12-step circles—the "obsession" (with whatever it is that you obsess about) "can be lifted."

We can toss away the chronograph and just enjoy a morning's three-miler, commit ourselves to our work in the world with or without fame and fortune, take delight in our body whatever our dress size, be grateful for the family we have even if they are far from perfect, say a peaceful good-bye to a departed loved one or a genuine good luck to a divorced spouse. We can face the dark truths of our lives and still thank God that we are here.

How far this message is from what we have been taught by our schools, TV sets, politicians, and leading corporations! And how many drastic changes will be necessary if we decide to detach from the addictive consumerism, competitiveness, hyperindividualism, aggressive nationalism, emotional codependence, and greed that pass for normality. So much would have to be overcome that even if spiritual teachings appeal, they might seem far out of reach.

Realizing spiritual values will be a daunting task for followers of traditional religion as well. Such people may believe that God's love is all they need or that complete Enlightenment is possible. But an abstract belief in spiritual ideals is very different from actually experiencing them. We pray to God on Sunday, but Monday 10 A.M. finds us following the movement of the stock market as if our lives depended on it. We say that our dead son will be with Jesus, but in the middle of yet another sleepless night, we are tortured by unhealed grief and relentless bitterness. We say that God heals all wounds, but when the oncologist clears his throat and talks about bad news, we feel abandoned to a bitter fate. We want to think that the world is perfect, but pictures of starving children reveal a reality that is absolutely wrong.

Regardless of whether we consider ourselves religious, we may be impressed by exemplary spiritual teachers—the Dalai Lama, Mother Teresa, the neighborhood priest whose humility and generosity inspires. Yet at the same time, they seem so unlike ourselves that it is hard to trust that we could ever resemble their wisdom and compassion.

Thus while spiritually oriented ideas may seem to offer a ray of hope in a dark night, they may also seem impossible to realize. As we aspire to spiritual

contentment, our anxious, obsessively goal-oriented, selfish selves keep intrud-
ing. We are all too conscious of our limitations and yearn for an enlightenment,
spiritual truth, and connection to God that should be ours but so clearly is not.
Even when we tell ourselves that we really are enlightened (pure, holy, faithful,
successfully on the spiritual path), a discomfortingly unspiritual personal reality
keeps surfacing.[7]

Ordinary Spirit

Is it possible to see beyond our current limited existence and have a taste of what
spirituality promises? Perhaps that taste is closer than we realize if we recall times
from our own lives when contentment, fulfillment, and even joy did not depend
on the ability to control, possess, evaluate, or own, that is, did not depend on a
conventional ego or sense of personal identity. It might have been a particularly
intense sexual encounter, walking through a grove of redwoods, or going into the
zone of unself-conscious, spontaneous performance of sports or music. Perhaps a
childhood memory of the world becoming suddenly mysterious and illuminated
by love,[8] the mind-opening revelation of how similar you are to someone you
hate,[9] or how, despite regrets about the past or anxieties about the future, you
really have no time at all except this precious present instant. It could come as
you face your beloved mother's death and move beyond the desperate desire to
save her, the dread of what life will be like when she is gone, and even the fear of
your own mortality. Instead, you feel nothing but gratitude for her presence and
compassion for her suffering. As unlikely as it seems, it might even come in a concentration camp: "In a last violent protest against the hopelessness of imminent
death, I sense my spirit piercing through the enveloping gloom. I felt it transcend
that hopeless, meaningless world, and from somewhere I heard a victorious 'Yes'
in answer to my question of the existence of an ultimate purpose."[10]

There are countless other ways in which spiritual illumination may enter our
lives. But despite the different circumstances in which they arise, they all share
some common features: acceptance of reality rather than resistance to it, gratitude rather than greed for more, compassionate connection to other people rather
than isolation, and a profound, joyous, nongrasping enjoyment of life. If you have
ever extended a simple kindness when you are suffering yourself, chosen to feel
grateful rather than deprived, understood how much we share despite our differences of culture or ideology, then even if you have never used the word, you have
a firsthand experience of *spirituality*, which simply *is* the manifestation of such
spiritual virtues. And these virtues are natural to human beings (though, sadly,
many other things are natural as well). That is why spirituality is universal, why it
can, and does, happen at any time and to anyone. "We can experience intimations
of the divine," suggest two contemporary writers, "in a lover's embrace, a rainbow,

a baby's smile, a bird's flight overhead, a friend's forgiveness, a dolphin's leap, or the self-service of a volunteer."[11] To be a spiritual person, then, is simply to see the value of spiritual virtues and seek to make them increasingly important in your life.

The immediacy and accessibility of spirituality are illustrated in the following three examples.

The Baal Shem Tov (1698–1760) was the mystically oriented founder of Hasidic Judaism. His teachings inspire not only a sizable percentage of contemporary Orthodox Jews but also other Jews and non-Jews. He tells us: "The world is filled with wonders and miracles. Yet we take our little hands and cover our eyes and see nothing."[12] This is a remarkable idea, especially from someone whose religious tradition celebrates decidedly uncommon miracles: God's voice from the burning bush, the parting of the Red Sea. Yet clearly the Baal Shem Tov is not talking about *those* miracles, since the world is not filled with such momentous, one-of-a-kind events. He is talking about what is right in front of our eyes: birds magically ascending from earth to sky, children playing in the yard, the sound of a musician practicing scales on his flute, my ability to see the brilliant reds of the tulips I pass on my way to the bus stop.

Ivan is the main character in Christian writer Leo Tolstoy's (1828–1910) masterpiece short novel *The Death of Ivan Ilych*, a classic tale of spiritual awakening. Ivan loses the spontaneous authenticity of childhood and is socialized into late-nineteenth-century upper-class Russia's cultural milieu of sexual license, careerism, professional distance, and interpersonal selfishness and dishonesty. He gets married as much for convenience as love, is unsupportive to his wife during both failed and successful pregnancies, and distances himself from his family through attention to work and male camaraderie. His passions, to the extent he has them, are career advancement, a nice house, and keeping things pleasant.

All this falls apart when he develops a mysterious, eventually fatal, illness. Treated by the doctors with the same uncaring professional distance that he employed in his legal career, emotionally abandoned by his family as he had abandoned them, and surrounded by people who will not name his condition for what it is, he experiences profound loneliness. Out of that loneliness is born a sudden doubt about his whole life. "Perhaps," he thinks, "I did not live as I should have. Perhaps all the time I thought I was going up, I was really going down."[13] He wrestles with this terrifying prospect during his last days, initially resisting it as simply too crushing. But eventually he realizes that his life had been shaped by values that were self-destructive and terribly hurtful to others. During his last moments, he breaks through to "the light."

Suddenly it grew clear to him that what had been oppressing him and would not leave him was all dropping away at once from two sides, from ten sides, and from all sides. He was sorry for them, he must act so as not to hurt them: release them and free himself from these sufferings. "How good and how simple!" he thought. "And the pain?" he asked himself. "What has become of it? Where are you, pain? He sought his former accustomed fear of death and did not find it. "Where is it? What death?" There was no fear because there was no death.

In place of death there was light.

"So that's what it is!" he suddenly exclaimed aloud. "What joy."

If only for a moment, Ivan thought of the welfare of someone else, something that, in Tolstoy's narrative, he has not done a single time before. In that moment of commonplace compassion, his suffering disappears, replaced by acceptance and exaltation.

Consider the words of Lewis Randa, a peace, disability, and animal rights activist: "Each of us has our limitations, our disabilities, our brokenness—and it is through those that we can each make our special contribution to the world."[14] Therefore, despite our many flaws, we can feel an essential personal value that can be the basis of spiritual virtues such as gratitude and compassion.

Thus while spirituality may initially seem unattainable, it is, many teachers tell us, right before our eyes: rooted in an acceptance of who we are, including our faults and frailty, and in the discovery of the miraculous nature of the ordinary. "Ring the bells that still can ring," poet Leonard Cohen counsels, "Forget your perfect offering. There is a crack in everything. That's how the light gets in."[15] This lesson can often be found in traditional religious literature, where the most advanced saints and sages are, like us, somehow maimed, flawed, or resistant to God's call. Moses had a speech defect and tells God to choose someone else to liberate the Jews from slavery. Jacob could not heal his fractured family relationships—fractured by his own actions—until he became lame from wrestling with an angel. Arjuna, hero of the *Bagavad Gita*, shrinks from his duty. Even Jesus, nailed to the cross, feels abandoned by his Father.

Yet even with our limitations, we can still experience, and share, the beauties of life. Buddhist Thich Nhat Hanh suggests: "The miracle is not to walk on water but on the earth."[16]

Sacrifice

Although gifts like seeing miracles when we walk down the street are available to everyone, they do require a sacrifice: a fundamental shift in what we think of as important and how we understand ourselves. Above all, we will have to surrender the part of us that seeks to control, possess, and separate. From the founder of the Sikh religion: "Ego is the greatest malady of humankind and nations, and forgiveness and self-surrender the greatest virtues."[7]

Think of the runner: for his exertion to be an exuberant celebration of life, rather than recalcitrant service to a tyrannical ego, he must surrender his attachment to a measurable success. If any of us wish to experience the Baal Shem Tov's daily miracles, we will have to give up our hunger for the special, unique, or very expensive. And we will have to forfeit our sense of being entitled to all the things we take for granted to see all of them, no matter how familiar, as gifts. The Ivans of this world must sacrifice attachment to career, pleasure, and social conformity and the illusion that position and wealth can banish all that is unpleasant. Until Ivan can accept the inevitability of illness, aging, and death, he will close off the comfort he might receive from people who can face these inevitable facts of life and nevertheless offer loving consolation to their fellow sufferers.

Spirituality also raises critical questions about aspects of human life that have been sources of personal and collective identity and pride. They include science and technology's goal of the unrestrained domination of nature and identities such as nationality, ethnicity, gender, or religion that often support hierarchies of power, privilege, and aggression to protect "us" at the expense of "them." It is not that spiritual ideas are in conflict with scientific theories, technical expertise, nations, or ethnic heritage. It is a question of how attached we are to them and of how unthinking, selfish, or violent we are in their service.

Three Questions about Attachment

Those slain by the sword of acceptance are given a new life at
every moment.

AHMAD JAM[18]

Virtually all spiritual perspectives tell us that getting what we want through a compulsion to achieve, possess, or control will lead to suffering.

This strange idea seems to be obviously mistaken. "Getting what I want," someone might reply, "doesn't make me *unhappy*, it makes me *happy*. That's what life, or at least a lot of it, is all about. The problem is not with wanting, but with not getting what I want."

In perhaps the most striking of their denials of common sense, spiritual teachings disagree. They suggest instead that if we are attached to anything—money, possessions, fame, romantic love, negative goals like revenge or positive ones like helping others, any kind of socially constructed identity (being an American, a man, a liberal)—we are liable to suffering. We will get what we want and be disappointed that we still feel empty inside, become bored and soon want something else, become frightened of losing it or sad when it changes, keep contrasting the real life we have with the fantasy of some other life where our desires are met, or simply not get what we want and feel deprived. Our attachment to "being" an American, or a Christian, or a man can lead us to unthinking obedience, arrogant self-congratulation, anxiety because we do not measure up to some ideal, or self-imposed blindness to the suffering our group inflicts on others.

In and of itself, the object of desire means little, for what is really going on is the psychological pattern of wanting. In its extreme form, we might think of heroin addiction. Each shot produces immense pleasure but also promises that in a few hours the addict will experience a monstrous craving he will do anything to satisfy. As Krishnamurti (1895–1986), a widely read, nondenominational teacher, stated: "You may ask why then should life not be guided by pleasure? For the very simple reason that pleasure must bring pain, frustration, sorrow and fear, and, out of fear, violence."[19]

Spiritually, the heroin addict is not so different than you or me—he has just simplified his life so that he wants only one thing. Those of us whose desires take multiple forms (love, career, possessions, healthy children, being really masculine or feminine) are simply less focused in what we pursue. In the words of Thomas Merton (1905–1968), perhaps the best known of American Catholic spiritual writers, "All sin starts from the assumption that my false self, the self that exists only in my own egocentric desires, is the fundamental reality of life to which everything else in the universe is ordered."[20] As long as we feel that we cannot be happy until something else happens, we will never stop searching for "something else" to make us feel better.

This idea that true contentment comes with lessening attachment rather than fulfilling desires raises (at least) three difficult questions.

First, what motivates people who no longer have desires? If I don't want, why will I act? If I am not passionate about my social identity (such as nationality or religion), will I have anything to care deeply about?

Spiritual teachers answer by distinguishing between typically compulsive, self-oriented, and unaware action prompted by the normal ego and the creative and spontaneous movement of which we are capable when we are not driven by craving or blind identification with a group. Once the ego is taken out, or at least reduced, we can engage in life more clearly and creatively and with a lot less anxiety, overperformance, and greedy clinging to results. We will choose tasks and social roles compatible with our abilities and our situation, shaped by a fully internalized moral sensibility that manifests itself in generosity, compassion, and an ability to face the truth.

Here's a story on this theme: A Chinese Buddhist monk deeply desired to found a new monastery. He spent fifteen years walking through poor villages,

collecting thousands of minuscule contributions from peasants. When he had
enough money to start building, there was a terrible famine, so he gave all that
he had saved to provide food for the hungry. Another fifteen years passed, and
once again the monk had saved enough for the monastery. This time, alas, a
series of devastating floods ravaged the region, so his savings went to rebuild
homes. Another fifteen years passed, and as luck would have it, this time
everything was going pretty well—no floods or famines, wars or forest fires
or plagues. When the monk's monastery was completed, a visitor exclaimed at
how beautiful it was. "Yes," said the monk, "it is lovely. But you should have
seen the first two."[21]

To use a phrase that is virtually a cliché in spiritual teachings, it is not the
goal, or the desire, that is the problem; it is our attachment to it. We can want
to "build a monastery"—in whatever form that takes for us—but that wanting
will only be part of a spiritually developed life if we are willing to give up the
goal when something more important comes along. Or if we simply cannot
get what we want. Only this attitude faces life as it really is—rife with disappointments and frequently out of our control—and enables a relationship with
God based in devotion rather than bargaining to make sure that we get what
we want. The essential task is not to get what we want, but to make the most of
what we end up with. If we can do that, the result will be a kind of equanimity
that provides a basis for all the other spiritual virtues and also a kind of unique
personal freedom: From a Hindu source: "Equal in pain and in pleasure, equal
in hope and in disappointment, equal in life and in death, and complete as you
are, you can find peace."[22] And from a Taoist one:

> The True Man of ancient times did not rebel against want, did not grow
> proud in plenty, and did not plan his affairs. Being like this, he could com-
> mit an error and not regret it, could meet with success and not make a
> show. He could climb the high places and not be frightened, could enter
> the water and not get wet, could enter the fire and not get burned.
>
> He ate without savoring and his breath came from deep inside.
>
> The True Man of ancient times knew nothing of loving life, knew nothing
> of hating death. He emerged without delight; he went back in without a
> fuss. He received something and took pleasure in it; he forgot about it and
> handed it back again.[23]

Until we accept that we have only limited ability to make the world give us
what we want—even if what we want is a good thing—we will face the endless
suffering to which spiritual values are the alternative. In this way, spirituality

is about letting go at the same time that we hold on, being able to give oneself completely to a task—the monk, after all, spent forty-five years building his monastery—and also detach from it. Detaching spiritually means without desperation, a haunting sense of personal failure, or a bitter rejection of a universe that did not give you what you wanted. In a discussion of the relation between desire and conflict, Krishnamurti assures us that the absence of attachment, of society's commonplace "psychological structure," can be a life of "complete inward and therefore outward tranquility. Which does not mean that we shall vegetate or stagnate. On the contrary, we shall become dynamic, vital, full of energy."[24]

Second question: aren't some desires better than others? A ruthless drive for success is one thing, but isn't hoping that my sick child will recover from cancer something else? What could possibly be wrong with wanting my child to be healthy? Yet from a spiritual perspective, while love and care are positive, a driven attachment to their results is not. As a father, I can want health and happiness for my child, but I cannot compel the universe to provide them, nor force my child to make the right choices in life. If my desire for a good life for my daughter takes a compulsive form—imposing her choice of colleges or clothes or religion, demanding that she believe what I think is right—I will in all probability alienate her from me or limit her capacity to develop a mature identity. If things go badly for her, I am likely to descend into a near-hysterical and almost certainly fruitless insistence that she be what I want her to be. If she becomes terribly sick or emotionally lost, will my despair make her better? We can give love to other people; we cannot guarantee what happens to them. As natural a response as it may seem, desperation in response to things going badly for those we love helps nothing.

"Do your best," it is often said, "and leave the rest to God." This attitude is not fatalism, passivity, or an impossible mysticism, but a hard-nosed, ultrarealistic assessment of life's most basic truth. Even the richest man in the world will grow old and die; even the most powerful governments find themselves frustrated by terrorists, the global economy, or offshore wells that won't stop gushing oil into the ocean; even the most loving of parents can have children who die in car crashes or become alcoholics. Recognition of these truths is found across the wide span of spiritual literature, from the more than two-millennia-old Hindu *Bagavad Gita*'s "The man who is devoted and not attached to the fruit of his actions obtains tranquility; whilst he who through desire has attachment for the fruit of action is bound down thereby"[25] to nineteenth-century Christian philosopher Søren Kierkegaard's "The true ethical [or spiritual] enthusiasm consists in willing to the utmost limits of one's powers, but at the same time being so uplifted...as never to think about the accomplishment"[26] and to countless contemporary spiritual voices.

Third question: how can I accept, let alone feel grateful for, the evils of the world? It is one thing to say that even if I just got fired or my wife is having an affair with my best friend, I can be thankful for my health or the beauties of nature. But what is a spiritual response to the Holocaust or the polluting factory poisoning my village's water supply?[27]

The relation of spirituality to social suffering is the focus of chapter 10, and there I will describe how some have combined spiritual insights and political activism to lessen injustice. Here is the beginning of an answer.

From a spiritual perspective, some of the usual responses to oppression—for example, a desperate desire to change a horrifying reality or a hatred of the perpetrators—have very undesirable consequences. They often lead to activist exhaustion, a relentless self-righteousness that blinds us to our own faults, and an endless transfer of anger from one set of enemies to another: first against those we view as oppressors and subsequently against anyone with a different perspective or strategy. Only a response to suffering that combines compassion—even for the oppressors—with honest self-awareness and nonviolence promises a fundamental change in the social order and provides a basis for a long-lasting, emotionally healthy life for the social activist.

Yet when people are suffering unjustly, it is as natural to be angry as it is to be in physical pain if you are struck. That is why spiritual teachers do not advocate a life in which painful emotions never arise. "Impatience," said the Dalai Lama, "isn't always bad... it can help you take action to get things done... impatience to gain world peace—that certainly can be positive."[28] If we feel sad that people's lives are ruined by the collateral damage of uranium mining or mountaintop removal, Buddhist environmental activist Joanna Macy reminds us, our grief is a sign of our connection to what has been lost.[29]

Spiritually, however, when we weep, we weep, and then we put away our tears and do what needs to be done. When we are angry, we are angry. But the anger does not shift over to hatred and bitterness, get internalized as useless guilt, or cause us to rage at everyone who disagrees with us on what we should do next. Even in the face of the world's many monstrous injustices, we can take in the fact that no one comes into the world as an oppressor. Somewhere along the line, the most ruthless dictator or lying bureaucrat was changed from an innocent child to an immoral adult. Perhaps the person was traumatized in his youth. Almost certainly he was conditioned by a social order that sanctioned this form of behavior. Such reflections do not excuse immoral acts, but they render those who commit them less alien to us.

Perhaps most difficult, the spiritual response to injustice includes the necessity to reflect on our own moral failings. Have we ourselves never been dishonest, selfish, and thoughtless? Have we not acquiesced with systems of oppression? If we have, can't we muster at least some understanding for agents of injustice we oppose—and see at least something of ourselves in them?

Discipline, Authenticity, and Criticisms of Spirituality

Even if we are willing to sacrifice, the benefits of spirituality do not come simply because we want them. The habits of the conventional ego are so entrenched, the untrained mind so skittish and disorganized (like a monkey with epilepsy on a hot tin roof being stung by bees, a Buddhist teacher once suggested to me), that a day-to-day discipline of self-transformation is needed. Even after being catapulted to the heights of spiritual inspiration by tragedy, insight, or charismatic teacher, the vast majority of us will soon return to our ordinary minds. Whatever lessons we learn in those special moments will need continual reinforcement to last.

By analogy, we might say that every person not born with serious disability is capable of good health. Yet to realize that natural promise, we have to get over our attachments to alcohol, sugar, the excitement of stress or the clutch of anxiety, and too much sitting around watching TV. We need to exercise, break the chains of bad habits, and keep the goals of good health at the forefront of our minds. As natural as good health is, it can be sustained only by healthy practices. The same is true of an enriching, fulfilling spiritual life.

Consider the runner, injured the third time from overtraining. From time to time, she may see that her athletic compulsion makes no sense and that she needs to be in touch with how her body feels, not what her watch says. But when for years she has lived the other self-defeating way, how will she keep that insight in mind?

Imagine Ivan Ilych, illuminated by a realization of the importance of love, miraculously recovered from his illness. After a lifetime of conformity, selfishness, and avoidance of reality, how will he remember what he learned on the sickbed? Without the help of spiritual teachers more familiar with this insight than he, how will he know what "he wanted them not to suffer" even means in the complicated realms of family dynamics? And how will he learn to live that resolve in each moment?

The emphasis on demanding discipline is part of what distinguishes authentic spirituality from its cheapened imitations. And it is what defends spirituality from many of its critics. Indeed, a number of people disparage the very idea of spirituality as an "inconsequential dabbling that is doomed to disappear almost as quickly as it appeared,"[30] "a new cultural addiction and a claimed panacea for the angst of modern living" that displaces essential ideas of social justice,[31] a form of "junk capitalism" that decorates the interior self while the world burns,[32] a kind of lazy egotism avoiding the demands of God and serious religion,[33] or an orientation to "inner truth" and "personal experience" that attempts to replace revealed truth with the worship of the self.[34]

There is some truth in these criticisms. A fair amount of what is called "spiritual teaching" today is glitzy, highly oversimplified, and riddled with false promises.

A quick survey of ads for workshops reveals numerous examples of shameless self-promoting by self-proclaimed gurus who for a few hundred dollars will enable you to completely transform your life in a weekend.

Yet criticisms of spirituality often disregard how every organized faith, political movement, scientific practice, industry, and political institution has its failures, distortions, and cheap imitations. How much of traditional religion, which is the cultural background of some of spirituality's sharpest critics, has been involved in violence (Crusades, Holy Wars, fundamentalist violence), institutional self-protection at the expense of the faithful (the church's handling of sex abuse), service to governments (endorsement of wars), or just plain moral blindness (treatment of women, failure to perceive the environmental crisis)? How many times are traditional religions used to keep us from facing the fear of death or to support a comfortable priesthood at the expense of a starving peasantry? Given how much of their own houses are made of glass, members of traditional faiths might ask themselves if they are really the ones to be casting the first stone at spiritual perspectives.

For secular critics, the problem is at least as bad. Social activists who see spirituality as just another narcissistic escape for the privileged might remember how often progressive political movements have failed to live up to their own ideals. From the moral collapse of European socialism in 1914 to the totalitarian nightmare of the Soviet empire, from the self-destructive infighting of the world Green parties to the opportunistic self-promotion of many leaders of minority or women's movements, activists have their own failures.[35] Similar practical and moral failures of government, industry, technology, and science are perhaps too obvious to require discussion.

"But," it will be protested, "the Inquisition (or Stalinism, or Mullah-sanctioned terrorism, or the role of science in the Holocaust) is not 'really' Christianity (Marxism, Islam, science)." And surely there are better or worse, healthy and sick versions of all belief systems and social movements. And the very same thing can be said of spirituality. Consumerist, trendy, "take all you can get without giving up anything" spirituality is not "really" spirituality.

Alternatively, some might argue that renunciation of control and power is simply a defense mechanism to mask helplessness. Christian ideals of forgiveness and peacefulness, said Nietzsche, were designed for weak people too powerless to resist their oppressors. Their feebleness was glorified as a virtue. Buddhists, he added, were just people who could not withstand suffering, so they tried to detach from the richness of life. Similarly, Ayn Rand tells us that ideals of compassion and acceptance contradict the self-directed creativity and monetary exchange that embody humanity's greatest accomplishments. There is nothing wrong with selfishness, and nothing wrong with an ego seeking to conquer nature through reason. To renounce either of these is to devolve into a self-effacing irrationality that will nevertheless depend on the powerful, intelligent, and self-willed for physical survival.[36]

In a way, both Nietzsche and Rand are at least partly right. Certainly, many people are attracted to spiritual values because they feel bereft, in pain, and overwhelmed by life—and spiritual insights encourage them to give up trying to control what is beyond their power and to accept how much of life is difficult. It is a general and obvious rule that people will adopt perspectives that fit their needs and interests—whether to rationalize their weakness or justify their aggressive personalities.

But what both Nietzsche's[37] and (even more) Rand's criticisms miss is how often spiritual life can generate great strength. Such strength is manifest in the lives of spiritual social activists who demonstrate personal courage, discipline, and strategic intelligence[38] and in adepts of yoga and meditation who can exercise enormous control over their bodies and minds. In contexts of service, spiritual ideals help people sit with the dying and tend the sick, initiate complicated projects of social betterment, and overcome enormous obstacles. Indeed, it is an intriguing paradox that while spirituality may begin with a sense of despair and helplessness, serious spiritual discipline often makes people more resilient, active, and brave.

To see in greater detail how spirituality involves self-discipline rather than ease or weakness, let us look at two cardinal spiritual virtues: mindfulness and gratitude.

Mindfulness

A coworker looks over your recent work and dismisses it as pathetically incompetent. Instead of thoughtlessly responding with hostility of your own, a more spiritual reaction might include the composure not to react defensively, an ability to comfort your hurt feelings, a recognition of the vulnerabilities beneath the other person's outer obnoxiousness, and a willingness to see if there is even a little truth in what he said.

In a reflective moment, it might be easy to see that this more spiritual response is a lot better for everyone. This insight is not a minor realization, for to accept it, you have to give up the widely held view that the best way to react to an insult is to respond in kind. But once you intellectually accept the value of the spiritually oriented response, how are you to embody that truth in the heat of the moment?

The practice of mindfulness offers one answer. This ability to see clearly what is going on in our own minds can be developed by extended and regular practice of meditation—a practice central to traditional Buddhism that in recent years has been widely taught in the west.[39] It is simply observing the mind's activities. Seated in a comfortable position, we place our initial attention on our breath—the rise and fall of the chest or the spot at the base of the nose where breath enters the body—and for the next ten, twenty, or sixty minutes, we witness what the mind does. There will be memories, fantasies, obsessions, lingering resentments, doubts about our worth, anxieties about taxes or mammogram results, and a maddening itch between the shoulder blades. We will wonder why we are sitting here when we could be doing something fun or important, remember some unpleasant chore we neglected, and become acutely conscious of a stiff muscle in our lower back.

Yet if we stick with the practice long enough, we will begin to see certain patterns: combinations of sensation, emotion, and belief that make up our sense of who we are. In seeing these patterns unfold, shift in form, and repeat, we may begin to see them less as immutable, rocklike features of an essential reality and more like mental constructions that may at times be quite useful and at other times quite destructive: self-doubt that drives us to overperform until we are drained and empty, anxiety that prevents us from enjoying the simplest of life's pleasures, the fires of anger that make us will the suffering of others, the way we live in a past that is long gone or an imagined future we dread or covet. When we are not aware of the degree to which our own minds make our lives what they are, we are at the mercy of our illusions, compulsions, and confusions. The *Dammapada*, an early and central Buddhist text, begins:

1. All that we are is the result of what we have thought: it is founded on our thoughts, it is made up of our thoughts. If a man speaks or acts with an evil thought, pain follows him, as the wheel follows the foot of the ox that draws the carriage.
2. All that we are is the result of what we have thought: it is founded on our thoughts, it is made up of our thoughts. If a man speaks or acts with a pure thought, happiness follows him, like a shadow that never leaves him.

The basic premise of mindfulness is that our thoughts are not an inevitable, necessary response to reality, but a form of action that can be evaluated as helpful or unhelpful. If we are "willing to be attentive to the whole range of our experience,"[40] we can see how much of it is a product of distorted, unreflective, and unhelpful beliefs. Ultimately, Buddhism teaches, this awareness can give rise to detachment from both unhappiness and happiness, joy and misery, and allow us to rest in a "purity of mindfulness which is equanimity."[41]

Consider the encounter with the nasty coworker. The spontaneously angry response may include a raised heartbeat, a tightening in the stomach, and clenched fists; we may feel a psychic shock that is the emotional equivalent of a slap in the face; and there is the absolutely intolerable way the combination of all these things feels. A tension is created that we are compelled to dissipate, and it seems obvious that the only way we can dissipate it is by striking back.

Mindfulness practice may teach us some different ways to react. First, we can learn how to simply observe beliefs, emotions, and physical sensations without immediately responding to them. What used to feel like something we had to dissipate is now something we can endure, investigate, and learn from. What is that sensation in my stomach? What beliefs arise ("I hate him," "I don't deserve this")? Second, as we develop the patience to study the structures of anger, we discover its essentially transitory nature. Often the destructive power of an emotion resides precisely in the way it seems like an inexorable totality rather than a particular combination of elements, the removal of any one of which will change the overall reality. If you break up anger into its constituents (sensations, emotions, beliefs), it may start to dissipate of its own accord. "I hate him" may turn into "I see how much I am like him" or "I wish he respected me" or "he scares me." Tightness in the chest, after a few minutes of calming breaths, may lessen. "I have to do something about this, NOW!" may slowly shift to "So he acted like a jerk, I've done that myself a few times" or "He certainly is unpleasant, but underneath he's scared about getting fired in this bad economy."

Clearly, there is nothing weak about a sustained mindfulness practice. It can increase our tolerance of emotional discomfort and our ability to act intelligently and reasonably. Also, it is not about sacrificing one's interests on the altar of some externally imposed imperative—something we need because we are sinful and need to be whipped into shape. Rather, it renders us freer, more flexible in thought and action, and less needlessly anxious. The change it supports is quintessentially spiritual: through discipline to develop virtues that make you a person who is both more content and a lot easier to be around. As later verses in the *Dammapada* promise, "The virtuous man delights in this world, and he delights in the next; he delights in both. He delights and rejoices."[42]

Gratitude

Gratitude plays a vital role in spiritual life—as much in traditional religion as in the more eclectic spirituality of the present. Contemporary Catholic spiritual teacher David Steindl-Rast suggests: "Gratitude is the heart of prayer." German medieval Christian mystic Meister Eckhart (1260–1327) advises: "If the only prayer you said in your whole life was 'thank you,' that would suffice."[43]

In gratitude, we find an experience, a day-by-day practice, and a way of life. It is a feeling that arises spontaneously within us, something we can consciously cultivate, and a habitual response that shapes our actions.

A traditional example: the Jewish prayer book is filled with long and complicated verbal formulas to organize the adult Jewish man's relation to God, but the day's prayers begin with a simple appreciation for being alive: "Thank you God, for returning my soul to my body." Whatever else the day holds—a midterm we haven't prepared for, a medical procedure, seeing our parked car slammed into by a drunk driver—at least for these few moments, we will have cultivated appreciation for what we have.

Gratitude attunes us to the immense value of what actually exists now: having our lives, our senses, a family, a bed to sleep in. Given how much there always is to be disappointed by, afraid of, or mad at, this focus requires a deliberate act of mind. I will have to remember that I have a wife who has loved me for forty years, not her nasty comment at dinner last night or the way she forgot our anniversary. I will have to focus on my ability to walk, even though I've hurt my foot and can't play in the weekly basketball game I enjoy so much. I must appreciate the birch tree outside my window, rather than bitterly envying the folks who get to hike in Colorado. In these mental movements, I grasp what the Talmud had in mind when it defined wealth not as a particular quantity of money, but as being satisfied with what one has.[44]

The second element of gratitude is the sense that the precious things we have are a kind of gift. Do we earn the existence of music in the world? The flowers in spring? The mysterious intelligence of our eyes? In the realm of gratitude, we do not. That is why theistic religion often teaches us that "everything is a gift from God" and why Rabbi Abraham Joshua Heschel (1907–1972), who combined traditional Jewish observance with a compellingly poetic spirituality, teaches: "Only one response can maintain us: gratefulness for witnessing the wonder, for the gift of our unearned right to serve, to adore, and to fulfill. It is gratefulness which makes the soul great."[45]

Oddly, no matter how much more satisfying it is to focus on the good than the bad, gratitude requires a great deal of conscious effort. And this is true whether we believe we are thanking our Creator or are simply enjoying the miracle that we are alive. The tendency to focus on the negative is every bit as natural, or at least as widespread, as any capacity for joyful appreciation. Aldous Huxley laments, "Most human beings have an almost infinite capacity for taking things for granted."[46] Fear, regret, a burning resentment that we were cheated out of our just deserts, desperate longing for something that is out of reach—all these possess a powerful emotional magnetism. The spirituality of gratitude requires the hard, recurring choice to focus on this rather than that, to feel better rather than worse.

Just because it requires shifting attention from one kind of thing to another, gratitude is as much an act of will as a moment of grace. As a discipline it is enormously difficult, yet it offers profound benefits. Internally, grateful people are contented, cheerful, and able to find pleasure in the midst of difficulty. Externally, gratitude is likely to produce a person of generosity and unselfishness, significantly less susceptible to consumerist enticements or to being dishonest in business. And it is far easier to be compassionate and take joy in the happiness of others when you treasure what you have. A five-century-old Persian Zoroastrian text makes the links between gratitude and kindness clear:

> The Sage asked the Spirit of Wisdom thus: "Which is that good work which is greater and better than all good works, and no trouble whatever is necessary for its performance?"

> The Spirit of Wisdom answered: "To be grateful in the work and to wish happiness for everyone. This is greater and better than every good work, and no commotion whatever is necessary for its performance."[47]

Like all aspects of authentic spirituality, gratitude is a task for a lifetime. There will always be something for which we can express thanks and, in all likelihood, always some pain or loss on which to dwell. Each day, each moment, gives us the opportunity to choose how we will respond.

2

The Spiritual Path

*Every single thing that a person sees or hears is an instruction to
him in his conduct in the service of God.*

BAAL SHEM TOV[1]

*The virtues of the righteous seem to be sins for those
closest to God.*

SHARAFUDDIN MANERI[2]

SPIRITUALITY IS A movement away from suffering and toward a way of life that liberates us from the self-defeating patterns of the conventional social ego. To further this movement, we need a new understanding of ourselves and practices to transform that understanding from a momentary flash of insight to deeply engrained habits.

The sequence of pain, new understanding, practices, and developing virtues is often called the "spiritual path." Here spirituality is not a static philosophical belief or a blinding mystical illumination, but a long, difficult, uneven, and unpredictable process. In this chapter, I describe some of the characteristic features of this journey: the contextual nature of spiritual virtues, the dangers of "spiritual materialism," some paradoxes that arise, how the comparatively unimportant role of verbal creeds combines with the absolutely important place of spiritual discipline, spirituality's connections to and separations from mysticism and morality, how spirituality manifests itself in a wide variety of styles, and the inevitability of suffering.

Spiritual Context and Spiritual Materialism

Despite how they are conventionally understood, meditating, praying, serving others, feeling at one with the universe, and the like are spiritual only if they are actually furthering the development of spiritual virtues. What is crucial is how they are affecting us and how we are using them. It is the overall context, not the practice, feeling, or belief considered in isolation, that matters.

Imagine, for example, a once devoted Catholic whose participation in the Mass has devolved into habitual repetition of prayers and superficial confessions. When he goes on a five-day retreat to think about the meaning of his faith, this can be a spiritual shift if he uses the time to seriously examine his relation to Christian values such as charity and forgiveness. Similarly, quiet reflection—asking yourself what you are really doing with your life, or even your week—is spiritual relative to a daily grind of nonstop action, distraction, and exhaustion. Doing your work in the world and enjoying it for what it is can be spiritual relative to always striving for advancement and payoff. Even ten minutes of mindfulness meditation in which you develop a little understanding of your patterns of thought is more spiritual than not meditating.

Yet today's challenging, immensely rewarding pursuit can easily become tomorrow's boring, deadening *un*spiritual background. Retreats can become occasions for self-congratulation, in which case the spiritual task is not just to do them, but to do them with humility. The quiet moment may still be dominated by self-preoccupation, and then what is necessary is to learn how to focus attention on someone else's needs. If the work I do even without attachment to "success" has immoral consequences, then I need to widen my awareness of the effects of my actions. Meditation has little spiritual value if I wall it off from the rest of my life. Or if it furthers my arrogance: "Look at me, meditating, while those other folks are just being ordinary, unspiritual."[3]

The Tibetan Buddhist teacher Chogyam Trungpa (1939–1987), who was educated in England and subsequently achieved a substantial following in the United States, coined the term *spiritual materialism* to describe the context-bound nature of spiritual development. For Trungpa, the key issue was the ego's tendency to treat spiritual teachings or practices as possessions and accomplishments.

> The problem is that ego can convert anything to its own use, even spirituality. Ego is constantly attempting to acquire and apply the teaching of spirituality for its own benefit. The teachings are treated as an external thing, external to "me," a philosophy which we try to imitate. We do not actually want to identify with or become the teachings....It does not matter what we use to achieve self-justification: the wisdom of sacred books, diagrams or charts,...esoteric formulae, fundamentalist religion, depth psychology....Whenever we have a dualistic notion such as, "I am doing this because I want to achieve a particular state of consciousness, a particular state of being," then automatically we separate ourselves from the reality of what we are.[4]

A similar point is made by Augustinian priest Martin Laird. The development of a serious Christian contemplative practice requires, Laird says, that we "realize that we do not search for God in the way we search for fame, fortune, and fulfillment."[5] That is, we cannot own, achieve, or possess spirituality. We can only live it. This insight is common to virtually every spiritual tradition.

These reflections reveal one of the central challenges of spiritual life. On the one hand, to bring the truths of the teachings into our own lives, we will have to do things: pray, meditate, study, serve. On the other hand, any time prayer, meditation, study, or service is taken as a method to turn us into somebody else, sources of pride, or mere habits that we do without attention or intention, it will be of little value. It is better to meditate than not meditate. A life without some form of inner silence and reflection is liable to great sufferings. Yet, when meditation is treated as an addition to the ego's collection of trinkets (I went to an elite university, I have a great job, my kids get straight As—*and* I meditate), it will be of little value.

Thomas Merton, who spent much of his adult life as a Trappist monk, described this difficulty similarly. Speaking of the meaning of a contemplative, cloistered life:

> I am by my whole life committed to a certain protest and nonacquiescence [to the demands of conventional society] and that is why I am a monk. . . . Yet . . . protest and nonacquiescence must extend to certain conceptions of monasticism which seem to me to be simply a fancy-dress adaptation of what we are claiming to have renounced. As if . . . "leaving the world" were adequately summed up by those pictures of "the Trappist" with his cowl over his head and his back to the camera, looking at a lake.[6]

From Jewish tradition, there is a well-known tale of how a rebbe—in Hasidic Judaism, a rabbi who is a model of religious virtue and wisdom—had not arrived when services were about to start on the evening of Yom Kippur, perhaps the holiest and most solemn religious service of the year. The rebbe was found in a small hut, serenely rocking an infant to sleep. He had heard the baby crying, realized that the mother had gone to synagogue, and stayed to watch over the child.[7]

The point of this last story is not that the prayers of Yom Kippur, with their emphasis on moral self-examination and repentance, are spiritually unimportant—any more than Trungpa wants us to forgo spiritual practices. The point is, rather, that for this particular rebbe, at this particular time, something else was required for his particular spiritual path. Having prayed these prayers for decades, having attended to the state of his own soul, it was time for him to care for the infant. Would it be right for me or you to do that? That would depend on so many different facts about our particular emotional, intellectual, and spiritual condition that there simply are no universal rules. Sometimes it is critical that we meditate or pray; sometimes something else is called for. There is no objective measure, no formula (no "cowl over the head") for spiritual development, except, that is, that we are becoming more mindful, compassionate, and grateful.

The same considerations arise when we talk of spiritual teachers, guides, or gurus. Many people find a student-teacher relationship on the path very valuable. In some traditions, such as Zen Buddhism or Hasidic Judaism, it is often seen as essential. For one thing, a true spiritual teacher supports the student's faith that it is actually possible to live by spiritual virtues. We perceive the teacher as mindful, compassionate, and loving—able to take joy in everyday life and transcend the nagging resentments and petty attachments that mark our experience. She is closer to God or to spiritual truth, and being in her presence renews our faith. Also, since the teacher has been on the spiritual path far longer than the student, she can instruct us on how to deal with its challenges. She can prescribe the right practices at the right time, offer the needed insight when it is needed, and reassure us that difficulties and setbacks are to be expected. Overall, the teacher seems to make the whole enterprise of spirituality real in a way that, for many people, books or practices alone do not.

Yet as with any practice, text, or object, one can also relate to a teacher in a spiritually materialistic way, for example, using the teacher's judgment and insight as an excuse not to develop one's own, believing that the teacher can magically enhance one's own spiritual strengths without any effort except one's own subservience, trusting that the teacher has transcended human limitations—that everything he says is perfectly true and every action he takes is completely moral. Out of such an abandonment of spiritual responsibility comes a vulnerability to abuse by mesmerizing individuals who possess sizable moral weaknesses alongside their charisma. There are numerous accounts of renowned spiritual authorities who committed sexual or financial abuses. That is why, as with any other tool of spiritual development, a teacher must be viewed with respect but also great care, a source of knowledge and comfort but not something that can replace our own efforts and awareness.

The fact that yesterday's resource can be today's impediment, or that an insightful teacher can also possess deep flaws, confirms the widely held idea that the spiritual path has no end point, no finish line. Any practice may be immensely important for a time and then a distraction. But even as the resources we bring to them shift, the essential tasks of spirituality do not change. A person will always face the intense demands of her ego, need to discern what love for others means in a particular situation, and confront pain and loss. The spiritual social activist will have to be aware of the perils of self-righteousness or burnout. Even after decades of prayer or meditation, a person will have to be alert to the dangers of complacency. To see spiritual development as something to be accomplished and completed, like getting a PhD or climbing Mount Everest, is to fundamentally misunderstand it. Kierkegaard advises: "Suppose a man were assigned the task of entertaining himself for an entire day, and he finishes this task of self-entertainment as early as noon: then his rapidity would not be meritorious. So also when life constitutes the task. To be finished with life before life has finished with one, is precisely not to have finished the task."[8]

Paradoxes on the Path

A college friend of mine spent a week at a Buddhist center, meditating several hours each day. At first, my friend, who had the usual (and maybe a little more than the usual) amount of middle-class American neurosis, self-absorption, and mental jumpiness, found the sessions severely uncomfortable. His mind raced around, his body fidgeted, and he would alternate between nearly falling asleep and nearly running out of the meditation hall screaming. Yet by the sixth day, something fell into place, and his mood changed. He had never felt so calm, accepting, and at one with everything in the world. He eagerly shared his experience of overwhelming peace with his teacher. "Do not cling to this peace," his clearly unimpressed teacher cautioned; "it will hinder your progress."

This story reveals a critical paradox of spiritual teachings, which a brief examination of Buddhism will illuminate. Beginning with the idea that desires create unhappiness, Buddhism asserts that desires only seem to be about the objects desired, when in fact they are really about the condition of feeling lacking, in some sense incomplete or wrong. Thus attachment to desire is about a separation between oneself and contentment. "Only after I get... (better grades, a lover, approval from my parents, a great job) will I be happy." This "only after," says Buddhism, is the critical, destructive illusion that makes our lives a waking nightmare, the compulsion that leads to painful personal relationships, addiction, obsessions, and even war.[9] Buddhism aims to have us realize the futility of attachment to desire and to learn to discern the patterns of desire in our own minds. Only then will we discover a long-lasting state of peaceful acceptance of life and spontaneous joy and compassion. Although this description of what is wrong with attachment is characteristically Buddhist, similar views can be found throughout spiritual literature, from traditional Christianity to 12-step programs.[10]

Those of us distressed by unfulfilled desires might yearn for a state of mind where we no longer focus on what we do not have. The idea that we could be really, really happy regardless of whether we get what we want, while outlandish, might have an unexpected and exotic appeal. It would be the reverse of the fairy tale in which, after rubbing the magic lamp, we get three wishes, the fulfillment of which typically leaves us worse off than when we began. Here we rub the lamp, make a wish, and nothing happens—except we feel much better. We might then see the point of one description of spiritual development in the *Bagavad Gita*: "Neither agitated by grief nor hankering after pleasure, they live free from lust and fear and anger. Fettered no more by selfish attachments, they are neither elated by good fortune nor depressed by bad."[11]

Despite its attraction, this line of thought raises a very important conceptual difficulty. Let us, following Buddhism, call the experience of either having no desires or not being attached to them a state of enlightenment—a reasonable English translation of the Sanskrit word *Nirvana:* a state of being beyond desire, attachment, and suffering.

Isn't the desire to be enlightened just another desire? Isn't the attempt to eradicate attachment simply...another attachment? In a Christian or Jewish setting, we might ask: Isn't a "selfless" love of God just another a calculated attempt to please an authority figure and get something good for ourselves?

The first answer is "of course." The ego will interpret the teachings of Buddha, Jesus, and every other form of spirituality from its own standpoint, which looks at virtually every encounter as an opportunity to get what it wants. Therefore, spiritual virtues will appear as just more things to be desired. But if a person interprets everything he is taught about spirituality through the lens of his existing, nonspiritual self, spiritual progress would seem to be impossible. Aren't we stuck in a kind of psychological lockdown?

Spiritual teachers offer a variety of answers to this very real dilemma. One is that although most of a person's energy and mental space is given over to the frustrating pattern of desire–action to fulfill desire–eventual frustration, not all of it is. There are fleeting moments when we taste something else: watching the full moon reflected in a lake, seeing a child take her first steps, serving a higher ideal without thought of personal accomplishment. Such experiences and attitudes confirm that another form of life is possible. Even the most constricted and limited of egos can glimpse the possibility that we can live, work, and love in a different way.

Also, the ongoing discipline of spiritual practices gives us experience of a different kind of consciousness (the peace my friend felt on his meditation retreat) and may literally transform us into a different kind of person. Extended periods of meditation may dramatically lessen our attachment to our thoughts.[12] Spiritual exercises under the guidance of a highly developed teacher can lead us toward a new sense of how we might live. Immersing ourselves in service to others can alter our sense of what action in the world is for. When this happens, we see that enlightenment or devotion to God is not the same old self getting something new, it is a transformed self that is no longer (so) concerned with getting. The field of desire is changed not by a pleasing reshuffling of the wanted objects, but by a fundamental reform of the wanting subject.

A second paradox arises when we hear the frequent claim that the spiritual path is not about becoming someone new but (finally, truly) becoming ourselves and that this transformation is available to everyone. Reaching your true self does not depend on wealth, power, intellectual accomplishment, or special talents. If we can focus the mind; curb our bad habits; live a life of modesty and discipline; put our complete energy into prayer, meditation, and good works; and (for those in theistic traditions) turn to God with humility and gratitude, it will happen. We do not have to become something radically different, we need only systematically cultivate what was there all along—even though right now it feels about a million miles away. In the analogy of one teacher: the true self is like a lightbulb that is always on, yet it is in a large tub filled with muddy water constantly being churned by a spinning paddle. As the paddle (the mind with its desires and illusions) slows down, the mud (distracting thoughts, attachments) begins to settle to the bottom, and the light becomes clearer. It was there and shining brightly all the time.[13] A Christian spiritual writer describing the path of contemplations tells us that the "spacious, silent land [of] a depthless depth of awareness ... is and always has been closer to us than we are to ourselves."[14]

Another Buddhist teacher who had an important American presence, the Japanese Zen master Shunryu Suzuki (1904–1971), expresses the idea this way:

> One day, while he was studying under Nangaku, Baso was sitting, practicing zazen [meditation]. He was a man of large physical build; when he talked his tongue reached to his nose; his voice was loud; and his zazen must have been very good. Nangaku saw him sitting like a great mountain or like a frog. Nangaku asked, "What are you doing?" "I am practicing zazen," Baso replied. "Why are you practicing zazen?" "I want to attain enlightenment; I want to be a Buddha," the disciple said. Do you know what the teacher did? He picked up a tile, and he started to polish it. In Japan, after taking a tile from the kiln, we polish it to give it a beautiful finish. So Nangaku picked up a tile and started to polish it. Baso, his disciple, asked, "What are you doing?" "I want to make this tile into a jewel," Nangaku said. "How is it possible to make a tile a jewel?" Baso asked. "How is it possible to become a Buddha by practicing zazen?" Nangaku replied. "Do you want to attain Buddhahood? There is no Buddhahood besides your ordinary mind"[15]

Our final paradox: Not only do we not have to become someone essentially different but also enlightenment itself, far from taking us to a fundamentally new and magical realm of endless light, simply brings us fully into *this* world. "Before I was enlightened," goes an old Zen story, "a mountain was a mountain and a river was a river. Then I studied Zen, and the mountain and river became illusion, distraction, temptation, a product of the five 'heaps' (*skandas*, technical Buddhist way of understanding the temporary and dependent nature of reality). Then I became enlightened, and once again a mountain was a mountain and a river was a river."[16] When we pray, Rabbi Heschel reminds us, "We do not step out of the world...we merely see the world in a different setting...we shift the center of living from self-consciousness to self-surrender...[enabling] us to see the world in the mirror of the holy." And to realize: "Just to be is a blessing. Just to live is holy."[17] Dietrich Bonhoffer, German Protestant theologian executed for taking part in a plot to assassinate Adolf Hitler, cautions Christians not to look for the supernatural outside the world, but to face the tasks history set for them in it, taking a "suffering God" as the model for how to live.[18] Over and over, contemporary spiritual writers teach us to find "spirituality in everyday life."[19] And in doing so, they echo Kabir (1440–1518), beloved Indian mystical poet, who beseeches us to focus on what is all around us:

> *Friend, hope for the Guest [God, spiritual*
> *illumination] while you are alive.*
> *Jump into experience while you are alive!*
> *Think...and think...while you are alive....*
> *If you don't break your ropes while you're alive,*
> *Do you think*
> *Ghosts will do it after?*[20]

Ultimately, from a spiritual perspective, everything embodies the miracle of existence. "The world," in Christian poet Gerard Manley Hopkins's telling phrase, "is charged with the grandeur of God."[21] As attachment to "me" and "mine" diminish, as we relinquish the compulsion to control life to our benefit, a kind of gentle, nonpossessive love—for all other people and perhaps for nature—naturally emerges. There arises a kind of boundless care for all the beings we encounter. "In the end," said a prolific Jesuit theologian, "God is the person you're talking to, the one right in front of you."[22] Transformed by meditative self-awareness, two American Buddhists suggest, we find that "compassion is the spontaneous response of an open heart."[23]

The universality of the sacred in everyday life is reflected in the Qur'an's counsel: "Wherever you turn, there is the face of God" (2:115). Interpreted spiritually, this is a reasonable equivalent of Jesus' statement (Luke 17:21) that "the Kingdom of God is within you"—because no matter what you are looking at, there must be a spiritual spark within *you* to see it as God's face. Manifesting this insight is frequently described as a critical element in spiritual awakening. In the words of Meister Eckhart, "To grasp God in all things, this is the sign of your new birth."[24] Therefore, every encounter with another person can be an opportunity to develop ourselves, and even the most pedestrian of objects—a coffee cup, your shoes, a park bench—can be treated with attention and respect.

Because a spiritual perspective sees God or spiritual meaning everywhere, there is no place where the tasks of spirituality, and their fruits, cannot be found. And this is true even in the midst of enormous suffering. A Catholic priest who spent 23 years in Stalin's prisons, five of them in solitary confinement, tells us that "salvation means no more and no less than taking up daily the same cross of Christ, accepting each day what it brings as the will of God, offering back to God each morning all the joy, work, and suffering of that day." He discovered that it was possible to be happy even in a prison cell or a Siberian labor camp. "If it all seems too simple, you have only to try it to find how difficult it is. But you have only to try it to find out also the joy and the peace and the happiness it can bring."[25]

Finding the sacred in everyday life is not easy. This point was made with austere clarity by Mother Teresa, when she was asked how she was able to physically interact with people grossly deformed by leprosy. "I try to remind myself," she answered, "that they are simply Christ in one of His more distressing disguises."[26] This statement contains a stark spiritual honesty. She admits that the disfigured faces and missing limbs distress her. And Teresa does not say that she always remembers she is looking at God, but only that she tries to.

Pointing at the Moon

It is not learning that makes a man holy and just, but a virtuous life.... I would rather feel contrition than know how to define it.

THOMAS À KEMPIS[27]

Just as meditation may be absolutely necessary one day and a distraction from learning how to respond compassionately to other people the next, so any particular belief about spiritual life can be helpful, even necessary, for one person at one time and irrelevant or worse for someone else.[28] Verbal teachings are at best tools whose usefulness depends greatly on the particular needs of the particular spiritual seeker. Like everything else in spiritual life, their value is context bound.

Some analogies: Talk about spiritual life is like a menu listing available dishes. To satisfy our hunger we must eat the food, not the menu, and if nothing on the menu attracts us, we can always go into the kitchen and poke around until we find what we need. Or religious doctrines are like the reports of several blind men touching different parts of an elephant and each thinking they know the full reality of what they are touching.[29] Or the verbal teachings are like the glass that held the wine: once we have taken in the wine, the empty glass is unimportant. From a traditional Christian source: "The mind is...most perfectly in possession of knowledge of God when it is recognized that God's essence is above everything that the mind is capable of apprehending in this life."[30] And from Taoism: "Words exist because of meaning; once you've gotten the meaning, you can forget the words."[31]

Of course, since humans are talking beings, we use words. We cannot do without them. But there is no orthodox spiritual creed, no walls between the true believers and the infidels. People rooted in different traditions can explore variations in meditation and prayer practice, beliefs about God and soul, or contrasting approaches to the role of bodily practices like yoga or the study of sacred texts. But since the ultimate truth cannot be encapsulated in any particular verbal formula, and the goal of that truth is a life of spiritual virtue, our conversations are more like 10 people discussing what they love about their children than like reporting the measurements of the living room rug. If what you believe helps you be compassionate, and what I am saying helps me be mindful, what is there to disagree about? There can be no holy war because there is nothing to fight over. It would be like demanding that you take the medicine that cures my illness.

A traditional Zen story illustrates this point.[32] All his life Hikaru had been looking for the moon, in cities and villages, on the seashore and deserts and mountains. But Hikaru always thought that the moon was down on the ground, and so while he sometimes searched late at night in its light, he never saw it directly. One hot summer evening, after yet more hours of fruitless searching, under a full moon in a clear sky, he stopped by a clear pond to cup some water in his hands to drink. Only then, in the water cupped in his fingers, did he see a reflection of the moon. Instinctively, he opened his fingers and let the water out, raised his eyes to the heavens, and beheld, in all its beauty, the moon. The moral: As a reflection of the moon in water cupped in our hands is to the moon, so teachings about enlightenment are to enlightenment. When we directly see that which we seek, we can let the teachings go. Yet until then, they may be helpful—even necessary—to get us to look in the right place.

Suzuki has another version of this idea. Two friends were having a rather arcane disagreement about the differences between Theravada (original, more individually oriented) and Mahayana (developed later, more keyed to collective rather than individual Nirvana) Buddhism. Virtually in the middle of the intellectual confrontation, one says simply, "We have had enough discussion, so let's have a cup of tea!" Suzuki comments: "It is impossible to give a verbal interpretation of our way... when my talk is over, your listening is over. There is no need to remember what I say; there is no need to understand what I say. You understand; you have full understanding within yourself. There is no problem."[33]

None of this means that spiritual seekers do not have beliefs. When spiritual teachers say that selfishness will make you unhappy, for example, they are saying what they believe about human moral psychology. Spirituality in general is based in the very particular idea that virtues make for a distinct kind of long-lasting inner peace, and other forms of life do not.

Further, many spiritual seekers accept statements about God, reincarnation, heaven, angels, or earth goddesses; the lives of individuals such as Buddha, Jesus, or Muhammad; and the sacred nature of particular texts like the Talmud or the *Bagavad Gita*. In the fourteenth century, Christian mystics prayed to Jesus and took his virtues as models for their own lives because they believed he was the Son of God. In the twenty-first century, expansive spiritual teachers like Rabbi Arthur Waskow or Vietnamese Zen Buddhist Thich Nhat Hanh refer frequently and respectfully to the wisdom of other traditions, yet in their own lives, they clearly privilege Jewish and Buddhist teachings, respectively.[34]

What, then, is the difference? When Rabbi Waskow says the Talmud is a holy book, and when a traditional, ultra-Orthodox rabbi says the same thing, where do they diverge? Why would Waskow be considered an example of "spirituality" and the rabbi more an exemplar of traditional religion?

Waskow is not saying this is the only holy book. He would not assert, as Rabbi Dovid Gottlieb does, that Judaism is literally true, and so when other faiths contradict Judaism, they are not true. In a similar vein, from a spiritual point of view, Pope Benedict's refusal to allow interfaith prayer at a Vatican-sponsored event, out of fear that onlookers might get the "mistaken idea" that all prayers are of equal value, simply makes no sense.[35] Waskow actively looks for shared truths among different traditions and views differences as occasions for mutual instruction rather than hostility. With other figures who are clearly within a tradition of spirituality, he shares the premise that spiritual seekers are all attempting to live by spiritual virtues and that this commonality is more important than differences among our descriptions of God. The point is to see the moon, not to worry about which substance reflects its light.

Here are two expressions of this perspective.

Ram Dass, who went from being Harvard University psychology professor and early LSD experimenter Richard Alpert to a spiritual teacher for many in late-twentieth-century America, was asked whether "Emmanuel," a nonphysical teacher supposedly being channeled by a woman named Pat Rodegast, was real or just an invention of Rodegast's imagination. His answer reveals a great deal about the spiritual perspective on religious truth.

As a psychologist, I allow for the theoretical possibility that Emmanuel is a deeper part of Pat. However, experientially, I know Emmanuel as quite separate in personality, language style and vibration from the way in which I know Pat. *In the final analysis, what difference does it really make?* What I treasure is the wisdom Emmanuel conveys as a spiritual friend. Beyond this his identity doesn't really matter.... Cosmologies [whether Emmanuel is real and comparable religious claims] by the nature of the metaphysics with which they deal, have no scientific or empirical base. *We must seek ultimate validation in our deepest being.*[36]

Some religious traditionalists might complain that without belief in the absolute truth of religious teaching, there will be no motivation for moral behavior. If it all depends on an individual's own "validation," what is to keep the individual from being attracted to theft, murder, or sexual misconduct? My answer: If only belief in the absolute truth of one's religious tradition made one moral, how much more pleasant would human history be, not to mention daily life in Iraq, Israel-Palestine, or Nigeria! The sad truth is that with or without the modern spiritual account of the status of beliefs, people find reasons to be cruel, selfish, or violent if they have not developed the virtues of self-awareness and compassion. It is the requirements of the virtues that discipline us, not beliefs about the nature of the universe.

To explore this idea of the role of beliefs in spiritual life in the context of a particular spiritual journey, consider the life of Stanford Addison, a Northern Arapaho spiritual healer, medicine man, and teacher. In journalist Lisa Jones's captivating account,[37] Addison had been reckless, involved with alcohol and drugs, sexually irresponsible, and promiscuous—about as far away from traditional Native American spirituality as a young Indian could get. Then tragedy struck, and a brutal car accident left him almost completely paralyzed from the neck down. Multiple hospitalizations, near-death experiences, infections, and medical complications later, however, he emerged as a changed and changing man. In the hospital, he began to have visions of spirits who carried messages to him. He saw people no one else could see, heard voices, and received instructions. Initially frightened, then bitter and resistant, Addison eventually took these spirit guides as real, developed into a widely recognized spiritual guide, and with extensive support from family and friends, has been a source of solace and healing to hundreds of people.

Were the spirits he saw real? From the spiritual point of view, we echo Ram Dass, "What difference does it make?" Instead of permanent depression and incapacity, Addison grew into a vital resource for the people around him, a man of humor, gentleness, and wisdom. Is that not real enough?

This same response can be made to *any* traditional religious belief. If the teachings help us toward personal peace, compassion for others, gratitude, self-awareness, and healthy connection to the world, then—and in just that sense—they are real and true. The test will be whether our response to the words of Allah, Adonai, or Krishna leads us in the kind of direction Addison took—or toward some far less loving place.

Compassion: Not as Easy as It Looks

Not only are the right beliefs comparatively unimportant on the spiritual path; so are the rituals defined by traditional authority, giving so much money to the church, or making sure your children follow your ancestors' traditions. Of course, spiritual development is not about *not* doing these things either. They may help develop awareness, gratitude, and compassion, or they may simply reinforce your obsession with your holiness, religious correctness, and license to despise unbelievers.

The fact that there is no clear orthodoxy, no objective list of demands, does not mean that spirituality is a walk in the park designed for the lazy. Consider, for example, compassion, which may be understood as both an emotional openness to the suffering of others and an active response that seeks to lessen that suffering. Compassion is praised in all forms of spirituality. The Mahayana Buddhist ideal, the Bodhisattva, seeks to end the suffering of all sentient beings. In Jainism, all of life is considered sacred, and therefore causing suffering is always a grave spiritual fault. God in the Hebrew Bible (Deuteronomy 4:31) and Jesus in the Christian Bible (Matthew 14:14) are described as compassionate. Further examples from a wide variety of sources are easy to find.

Sometimes compassion is relatively easy. If we encounter a good person whose suffering is not his fault and can be alleviated by a not too demanding action on our part (take care of him for an afternoon, offer a hug, give a small amount of money), and we ourselves are in relatively good shape, then compassion may flow easily.

But think of Steve, who is always overspending: here he is again, desperately needing cash. And at the same time, I am facing my own serious money troubles (family illness, stolen car). Now compassion may give way to impatience or irritation. "What about me?" I will think, or "For God's sake, stop creating your own troubles."

What if the suffering we encounter is part of the endless round of misery that accosts any reasonably well-informed person in today's information overload society? Famine in Sudan, tornadoes in Missouri, rape in the Congo, pollution-induced lung disease in China—and that could be just a single Web site on any given morning. Here we might develop a case of compassion fatigue, what psychologist Kaethe Weingarten calls "common shock"—physical and emotional distress caused by witnessing the pain of others.[38] We numb out and retreat into an essentially dismissive place, saying to ourselves, "I just don't want to hear about it."

Here is the most difficult setting: can we have compassion for the perpetrators of crimes as well as their victims? After 9/11, could we think of the hijackers as human beings marked by enormous emotional and moral disorientation, lacking the gift of being able to have an empathic connection to the innocent strangers they meant to kill? Can we think of cruel, selfish people as deserving of happiness? Can we, as Dante asked, have compassion for the damned?[39]

Seeing how hard compassion is shows that even without unshakable doctrine and inflexible rules, spirituality is no day at the beach. To be compassionate even when we are needy or suffering requires that we observe our own distress without attaching to it or using it as an excuse to feel disdain for all those who "don't really suffer like I do." Dealing with compassion fatigue requires a vigilant awareness not only of all the terrible things happening in the world but also of the effect of our knowledge of those things on our own minds and bodies. It requires the humility and self-awareness to admit "I simply cannot take in any more information now," the faith that life is worthwhile even with all the suffering in the world, and the farsightedness to see that despite all their pain, human beings are still more than the sum of their woes.

And the ruthless dictators, drug lords who poison children, and Mafia hit men who enforce protection payments? Don't they deserve to be hated? Compassion means that we are able to recognize everyone's suffering—even that of people who act very bad. The spiritual task here includes admitting our own moral weaknesses so that we can see what we have in common with the guilty and developing a moral clarity that allows us to act caringly in the face of pain without needing to be motivated by hatred.

In all these contexts where compassion is exercised, we will have to be open not only to the other's suffering but also to their own understanding of their lives and therefore to what we have to learn as much as what we have to teach. "Compassion," insists a Catholic priest who spent decades intervening in Los Angeles gang violence, "is not a relationship between the healer and the wounded. It's a covenant between equals."[40] Anglican Archbishop Rowan Williams suggests that this covenantal relationship requires a loving attention that allows the other person to develop, choose freely, and come to a better, truer life by his own energies. Such an attunement to the other requires that we, too, be willing to change. The great temptation, Williams tells us, is seeking to have the last word, to control what the other says and how they live.[41] This may be relatively easy if the person is an innocent victim. The more they are complicit in their suffering, or a victimizer rather than a victim, the more difficult it becomes.

Thus true compassion is enormously challenging, something that might well take a whole lifetime to get good at it, let alone master. And this is true of the other spiritual virtues, which always require attention, energy, and a willingness to let go of old habits. Every day, every moment, I am invited to choose love over hate, acceptance over bitterness, confidence in my connection to people and the world over frightened isolation. In this light, then, spirituality is not a relaxed or cheapened version of traditional faith or an escape from social life, but a demanding and in some ways heightened version of both religion and social engagement.

As we have seen, although spiritual life can be described fairly simply—just live out the spiritual virtues—that does not mean it is easy. And even with the best of intentions and rigorous discipline, there is another difficulty, that of knowing *how* to express (for example) love or compassion in a particular situation.

Face-to-face with someone suffering from addiction, do we offer endless sympathy or the demands of tough love? Watching someone make what is to us clearly a serious mistake, do we step in and try to prevent their fall or allow them to learn the precious lessons of experience? If a university, employer, or government agency does something we do not like, is it equanimity and acceptance or nonviolent social activism that is called for? If we are trying to make anything better, what is the best way to do so?

The more we are engaged in the real-life relationships of family, social institutions, politics, and friendship, the more such questions arise. The precise way we respond to them will depend not only on our spiritual views or character but also on our beliefs about human psychology, social justice, and practical or technological issues. As vital and significant as spiritual teachings are, as transformative as are its virtues, they do not stand alone as sufficient for a life. Spiritual practices may help us face difficult questions more calmly and think more clearly about them, a commitment to love and compassion may guide us toward gentler and less harmful actions, and spiritual acceptance may help us face the times when things go badly. But the need to act on very imperfect knowledge, resting only in the hope that you are doing the right thing, remains.

Mysticism

The basic idea of mysticism is that just as we can see a tree, touch a loved one's hand, or hear a musical instrument—that is, just as we can have a direct experience of these things—so we can have a direct experience of God, with that term interpreted any way you like. When medieval mystic Julian of Norwich saw visions, when Moses heard God's voice in the burning bush, when Arjuna saw that his charioteer was actually the Lord Krishna, they had, we are told, an immediate encounter with divinity. They were not reading words that someone else assured them had been written by God or imagining what God might be like. Comparable encounters with an overwhelming sense of belonging, unshakable peace, or universal love for others are part of spiritual traditions not centered on a deity.

Experiences of this kind are sometimes described as the very basis of religious life. Theology, prescribed rituals, or supporting an ongoing church are said to be ways of living out or getting back these original, revelatory encounters. Many add that the dogmatic attachment to creeds or the self-protecting actions of religious bureaucracies actually detract from this quest: far better to keep the spiritual truth contained in our experience of God, or at least try to live so that we might have such an experience, and drop all the arguments, religious wars, and heretic hunting.

Spiritual teachers may appeal to mystical experiences to tell us what a spiritual life can bring. If you follow Buddhism's combination of moral rules and spiritual practices (the eightfold path), you will, it is taught, enter into Nirvana—a condition in which spiritual truth is lived rather than merely hoped for. Alternatively, medieval Christian mystics like Julian of Norwich and Hildegard of Bingen said that just because they had encountered God, they were able to manifest acceptance, gratitude, and compassion. The profound awe some feel in the presence of mountains, oceans, or even particular animals can give rise to a unique serenity, one not available in the context of cities and culture. It is that experience, those who find spirit in nature tell us, that enables them to lead spiritual lives.

A mystical encounter may reassure us of our essential spiritual worth even if we are not succeeding in business or our marriage is falling apart. It may give us some faith in the goodness of life even after a child has died, make us feel loved and worthwhile although our mothers are cold or our fathers abused us, or give us hope when everything around us—in a prison or a concentration camp, on a battlefield or in the face of crushing poverty—pushes us toward despair. It can enable us be generous when we have practically nothing, courageous when we are terrified, or calm in the face of nearly endless chaos. And it does so because it teaches us that we are not our social identity, income level, possessions or needy psychological selves that require constant reassurance. We are actually all children of God, beings of light, immeasurably fortunate participants in the miracle of life. The universe is not a cold, uncaring theater of the absurd, a place of blind or hostile forces.[42] As personified by God, as expressed in nature, or as found in our capacity to move beyond the limitations of the ego, it is welcoming, comforting, and awe-inspiring. It is, in the best sense, home.

Yet for all the positive effects mystical experiences can have, they are not the defining element of spiritual life. They arise as a result of a multitude of factors over which we usually have no control. Mood, health, what has been happening in our lives in the preceding hours or weeks, or even taking a substance like peyote or fasting for a long time may lead to a mystical breakthrough but do not guarantee it. And nothing can ensure that we will ever have such an experience again. Mysterious, magical, potentially life-changing—it comes and it goes.

And after it is gone, then what? Then we return to the long, difficult, often frustrating, and even boring process of practicing the spiritual virtues in as many aspects of our lives as possible. Maybe last week I had a vision of the Virgin Mary, but this morning what I feel is a really bad toothache. Maybe yesterday you saw a heron come to rest in the lake and felt a connection to all of life, but tonight the college kids next door are having a drunken party at two in the morning. Maybe last month the truth of our tradition—Judaism, Islam, Methodism—struck us with a power that seemed could come only from God, but today the prayers seem empty, cold, tediously familiar. If we try to depend on *feeling* something, such gray moments might stop our spiritual movement altogether. As my piano teacher said when I was struggling with a Beethoven sonata, "Roger, you can't rely on being inspired to play well, because a lot of the time you won't feel inspired. You have to play well no matter how you feel."

Spiritual life may get great energy from our mystical moments. Our memory of them may be a kind of anchor, a promise that our daily struggles have purpose and that the spiritual life makes sense. But their power inevitably fades unless they give rise to the continual practice of the virtues. What was given by chance can be taken away just as easily—becoming first a beautiful memory and then merely a lifeless relic.[43]

Morality

The man of highest virtue appears lowly. He who is truly pure
behaves as though he were sullied. He who has virtue in abun-
dance behaves as though it were not enough. He who is firm in
virtue seems like a skulking pretender.

LAO TSU[44]

Just as a mother loves and protects her only child at the risk of
her own life, we should cultivate boundless love to offer to all
living beings in the entire cosmos.

BUDDHIST SCRIPTURE[45]

Like mysticism, morality is an aspect of human life that overlaps with—but is distinct from—spirituality.

On the one hand, spiritual life absolutely requires honesty, integrity, and care for others and forbids selfishness, sexual misconduct, theft, or cruelty. Except in the most extreme situations, violence—physical, certainly, but also emotional and verbal—is unthinkable. Impeccable integrity and exquisite sensitivity to the needs and feelings of fellow beings are hallmarks of people described as spiritually advanced.

The list of well-known ethically exemplary spiritual teachers who devoted themselves to the common good is very long. Dorothy Day (1897–1980) gave herself to the Catholic Worker movement, whose "houses of hospitality" joined ministering to the bodily needs of the poor with social justice work. Contemporary Buddhist Thich Nhat Hanh worked to rescue the "boat people," exiles from his native Vietnam preyed on by soldiers and sea pirates. A great rabbi may be remembered for chopping wood to warm an old widow. A Martin Luther King Jr. offers his life in defense of the oppressed and the poor. To help, to serve, to be with the pains and needs of the world—and certainly not to make them worse—this is essential to spiritual life.

On the other hand, morality and spirituality are not the same. Spirituality is not, as some might think it is, just a mellow version of morality.

Why?

For one thing, secular morality tends to take the standard social ego for granted and try to do right by it. The "greatest happiness for the greatest number," which defines utilitarian morality, accepts a fairly conventional understanding of happiness. The rights and freedoms on which other moral theories center generally understand people as separate individuals with interests, property, and social position or as members of oppressed groups suffering from racism, sexism, homophobia, or the like. Even the morality of care favored by many feminist theorists, which stresses empathy and relationality rather than abstract ethical principles and interpersonal separation, often accepts conventional emotional needs for recognition and reassurance as given.[46]

A spiritual approach challenges all these presuppositions, viewing our ultimate human identity as encompassing far more than conventionally understood material welfare, political rights, society, or psychological comfort. Our spiritual task, if we choose to accept it, is to realize a different identity than the one presupposed by typical social assessments of what we need or deserve. Seeking a spiritual life will lead us away from ordinary ideas of happiness, away from attachments to many of the things protected by legal rights, and toward a kind of inner contentment that makes familiar forms of emotional support considerably less necessary.

Clearly, however, this is not where most of us begin. That is why spiritual teachings offer two views of morality. Initially, ethical codes of honesty, kindness, charity, righteousness, and (in some cases) celibacy train the mind away from attachment, self-concern, and violence. Later, as the true self begins to emerge more clearly, moral behavior is a free expression of virtue that is part of a fulfilling life, one marked both by the service it provides for others and the lasting personal contentment it promises.[47] Moral behavior is then not a limitation on one's self but a spontaneous manifestation of who one is.

Indeed, many ethical frameworks take for granted an essential split between morality and self-interest. There is "what you want," and there is "what is right or good." There is lying on your income tax or telling the truth, cutting corners at work or being straight about everything you do, taking that long-awaited and well-deserved vacation or going to help your aging parents because they can't manage anymore. In the typical ethical system, a moral person acts out of universal rules, concern for the general happiness, or interpersonal needs for empathy and compassion—not self-interest.

As a form of virtue, spirituality does not accept an essential split between self-interest and goodness. Its view is that in the short run, the selfish act may produce a burst of pleasure, but the degree to which we attach to that spasm of feelings is precisely the degree to which we guarantee that before too long, we will suffer longing, frustration, boredom with what we have, or jealousy because someone has more. It may require spiritual discipline to learn to discount the immediate in favor of the long term or even to experience the less ego-based, less possessive, less self-oriented contentment of spiritual existence. That is what practice and the faith that real personal change is possible are all about.

For example, I often teach sitting on a desk in front of the classroom, and I often take my wallet out of my back pocket and toss it on the desk next to my backpack. Imagine yourself one of my students, finishing up her notes after class or taking a quick phone call from a roommate. As you gather your things to leave the room, you notice that the professor has left his wallet. You are completely alone. You can take the whole wallet or just remove the $120 in cash from Gottlieb's early morning ATM withdrawal. No one will ever know.

Why not do it? You might agree that it is morally wrong to steal, but why should you care about being morally wrong? You could not justify taking the wallet, but why should you feel the need to justify yourself? "What if everyone did it?" doesn't have much hold, since one unseen act is hardly about to change all of social life, and a tremendous number of people are doing this sort of thing already. I've set up the example so there is no danger that you will get punished. And if you say, "My conscience will bother me," I'll make the case more pointed by offering you an imaginary pill that—like Dramamine does for seasickness—will take away your queasiness. So unless you have simply decided to be a moral person, your self-interest will win out. And even if it doesn't, the difference between doing the right thing and getting what you want is clear.

From the standpoint of virtue, however, the situation is different. Here we ask not "What is the right thing to do?" but "What kind of life will you have, what kind of person will you be, if you steal?" And the answer is "Not a very happy one." As a thief, you will relate to other people as potential victims of your thievery, and thus your chances of having emotionally close friendships will be radically diminished. (If a pickpocket sees a saint, we might say, all he sees are pockets.) As well, the thief's sense of his own lot in life is always one of "lack"—he is always thinking of what he doesn't have and always wanting more. Thus because he never feels he has enough, no matter how much money a thief may steal, he is always unsuccessful.

For reasons such as these, the virtuous person can say, "I don't steal because I do not want that kind of life. I would rather be content with what I have and have friends that I can trust." Of course, one still has to choose friendship and contentment over the adrenaline rush of grabbing what is not yours and all the pleasures money can buy. And one might abstractly believe that stealing will have negative effects but—like the guy at the bar who asks for just one more when he knows he has had enough—go ahead anyway. But at least one is then choosing between two different kinds of self-interest tied to two different senses of self, not between self-interest and something categorically different.

Finally, there is what we might call a contrast of tone or style between spirituality and at least some forms of morality. People who are highly moral with no touch of spiritual grace can sometimes be stiffly self-righteous, rigidly self-denying, and arrogant. There may be a frequent reminder to others that "this is what moral behavior looks like—and you'd better do it, too." Some may be so busy being right and noticing the faults of others—often in areas of sexual or political correctness— that their own failings and inconsistencies simply go unnoticed.

By contrast, spiritual teachings usually depict the moral person as humble, self-confident without arrogance, and remarkably relaxed. Because compassion is the natural response of a non-ego-driven mind, there is no struggle to do the right thing.[48] Because the sense of self-identity—"I am this, I am that"—has been eroded by spiritual practice, the morally developed spiritual person is not sitting around telling himself or others how morally developed he is. The tendency to self-aggrandizement so often present in the ethically upright (and uptight) is just not there, and the joy that one gets from helping others arises more clearly because of a diminished attachment to one's own pleasures.

All this is wonderfully expressed in Lao Tsu's (sixth–fifth century B.C.E, approximately) Taoist response to the duty-oriented Confucius, in which we may note how moral behavior is understood as being as spontaneous and effortless as the behavior of nature:

> All this talk of goodness and duty. These perpetual pin-pricks unnerve and irritate the hearer—You had best study how it is that Heaven and Earth maintain their eternal course, that the sun and the moon maintain their light,... the birds and beasts their flocks, the trees and shrubs their station. This you too should learn to guide your steps toward Inward Power, to follow the course that the Way of Nature sets, and soon you will no longer need to go round laboriously advertising goodness, and duty.... The swan does not need a daily bath in order to remain white.[49]

These reflections apply not only in comparatively mundane encounters but also in the face of large-scale violations of our collective well-being. While the spiritually developed moral person is perfectly willing to name immorality for what it is and to oppose it, she also attempts to do so without hatred or self-righteousness and with a full consciousness of her own moral failings.

As I write these lines, we are now in the 104th day of the British Petroleum oil spill in the Gulf of Mexico, which is pouring untold millions of gallons of oil into the ocean, damaging wildlife and humans, destroying livelihoods and habitats. What is a spiritual response to this biological and moral catastrophe?

There is no single answer to this question, but a variety of answers indicate how to respond *more* spiritually. If it is too upsetting even to think about, perhaps the first thing that is needed is to calm down, bring the mind into the present moment, and engage in an awareness practice of reading only a few sentences about it each day. If it is depressing, you might need to do something to help, even if only sending a contribution to the cleanup efforts. And if you are looking for a spiritual way to think about the gross injustice and irrationality of the entire system of oil extraction and fossil fuel use (oil companies, corrupt federal regulators, irresponsible legislators, Gottlieb's daily commute), consider the following prayer:

I am the ocean, mighty, wild, and free
and I am being poisoned with oil.
From a hole humans drilled into the earth's skin flows a stream I cannot stop,
threatening all I shelter.
Breath to breath, body to body, we are One.
So be it.
I am a worker injured in the Deep Horizon explosion and I worry about the
safety of the oil industry.
I want to know why the regulations and procedures that were supposed to protect
us failed.
Breath to breath, body to body, we are One.
I am a fisherman and I worry about my livelihood.
Vast areas of the ocean have been closed to fishing, and now oil is creeping into
the estuaries and marshlands that serve as fish and shrimp nurseries.
Breath to breath, body to body, we are One.
I am an executive from British Petroleum (or Transocean or Halliburton) called
to explain to Congress how this disaster could have happened, and I want to
blame it on someone else.
Breath to breath, body to body, we are One.
I am the CEO of BP and I am willing to publicly take responsibility for the oil
spill but I also want to protect my company from liability and the huge costs
of the cleanup.
Breath to breath, body to body, we are One.
I am a wildlife rescue person and I want to save the lives of as many innocent
creatures as I can.
I am heartbroken at what I am seeing in the Gulf and hope the affected popula-
tions can recover.
Breath to breath, body to body, we are One.
I am a fish (or a crab or a shrimp).
My environment has turned into a toxic soup of oil and chemical dispersants. I
am having trouble breathing in the waters I call home.

Breath to breath, body to body, we are One.
I am a user of oil and petroleum products.
I know I should reduce my consumption
and live more lightly upon the Earth, but I resist owning up to my responsibility
   for the oil spill.
Breath to breath, body to body, we are One.
So be it.[50]

This astute and compassionate perspective combines factual knowledge with a deep sense of the moral connections between all the beings affected by the oil, including the speaker's own moral responsibility. There is no avoidance of reality, but neither is there a self-righteous condemnation of an evil that is always elsewhere. There is empathy as well as serious criticism, a wide view of the full scope of the damages and causes, but also a mirror held up to the vastly imperfect self.[51]

Something for Everyone

A story I heard from a friend, many years ago: Yogananda, author of the widely read *Autobiography of a Yogi*, which helped spread some of the basic ideas of eastern spirituality in the west during the cultural upheavals of the 1960s, was being interviewed on a TV talk show. The interviewer, responding to the fact that Yogananda was more than a little overweight, asked: "You're kind of fat, how can you be a yoga teacher?" Unfazed, Yogananda smiled back: "There are some people who need a roly-poly guru, and I am for them."

This engaging anecdote leads us to another interesting characteristic of spiritual teachings: how they combine deep similarities in content with a remarkable variety of styles. A high value is put on mindfulness, appreciation-gratitude, compassion, and loving connection by traditionally observant Jewish Hasidic rabbis in the late eighteenth century and contemporary, most definitely *not* traditional "Jewish Renewal" rabbis today, by Buddhists from Tibet and Burma and China, by people who pursue Tai Chi as a spiritual discipline or have lived their adult lives as Catholic nuns or who find God—or spiritual truth—in the forest.

Despite these commonalities, however, what a variety of tone and manner these different sages may have![52] Consider these contrasting examples.

Saint Francis of Assisi (1181–1226) has for seven centuries been an inspirational figure for many both within and outside the Catholic Church that defined his life. His faith rested on a mystical encounter with the divine and took the shape of extreme humility, loving-kindness, compassion for the suffering of animals along with that of people, the pursuit of peace, and an intense personal identification with the poor and oppressed.[53] Throughout all of this, there was a passionate self-emptying toward Francis's image of God; an attempt to fill himself up with what he thought of as divine virtues revealed in the scriptures rather than with his own conventional selfhood of attachment and self-interest. Francis believed he was literally erasing his own personality and weaknesses and replacing them with God's goodness. His pursuit of spiritual virtues depended on the passions of faith and the experience of a transcendent deity.

This understanding of spiritual life as a transmission from a source outside the self is echoed by twentieth-century Thomas Merton:

> Our discovery of God is, in a way, God's discovery of us. We cannot go to heaven to find Him because we have no way of knowing where heaven is or what it is. He comes down from heaven and finds us. He looks at us from the depths of His own infinite actuality which is everywhere, and His seeing us gives us a new being and a new mind in which we also discover Him. We only know Him in so far as we are known by Him, and our contemplation of Him is a participation of His contemplation of Himself.[54]

The approach of a contemporary, freelance spiritual teacher Byron Katie, by contrast concentrates on a reflective, self-transformative method emphasizing individual and definitely nonmystical self-awareness and acceptance.

> Katie became severely depressed in her early thirties. For almost a decade she spiraled down into rage, self-loathing, and constant thoughts of suicide; for the last two years she was often unable to leave her bedroom.

> Then one morning in February 1986, she experienced a life-changing realization.

> I discovered that when I believed my thoughts, I suffered, but that when I didn't believe them, I didn't suffer, and that this is true for every human being. Freedom is as simple as that. I found that suffering is optional. I found a joy within me that has never disappeared, not for a single moment. That joy is in everyone, always.

> She realized that what had been causing her depression was not the world around her, but the beliefs she'd had about the world. Instead of hopelessly trying to change the world to match her thoughts about how it should be, she could question these thoughts and, by meeting reality as it is, experience unimaginable freedom and joy.[55]

This method, keyed to the careful dissection and reorganization of one's thoughts, is light years away in style from the devotion to God of Francis or Merton. Yet both may lead toward a less self-concerned and negative form of life.

As an alternative to both St. Francis and Katie, there is the highly relational and earthy tone of feminist-oriented Goddess spirituality described by Starhawk:

> The law of the Goddess is love: passionate sexual love, the warm affection of friends, the fierce protective love of a mother for child, the deep comradeship of the coven...the love of the Goddess is unconditional. She does not ask for sacrifice—whether human or animal—nor does She want us to sacrifice our normal human needs and desires. Witchcraft is a religion of self-celebration, not self-abnegation....Pleasure...is not superficial but becomes a profound expression of the life force; a connecting power linking us to others, not the mere sensation of satisfying our own isolated needs.[56]

Interestingly, Starhawk brings into spiritual life an element—sexuality—that other traditions often reject as too compulsive and self-oriented. But she reorients our understanding of sexuality—now a "connecting power linking us to others" rather than simply a search for personal pleasure.

These and myriad other examples teach us that spirituality exists with or without God, as serious or playful, as relational or intensely isolated. Traditional Hinduism captures a form of this idea with its suggestion that "Yoga" ("union" of the different facets of our essential being, to make possible a union with God) in its broadest sense takes different forms to match the variety of temperaments or talents a person might have. There is the yoga of the philosophical attunement of intellect, of meditative discipline (of which physical postures, Hatha Yoga, are a preliminary aspect), of love for a particular spiritual master or God, and of devoted, moral work in the world. Christianity offers images of the desert fathers who retreat from the world, and the Mother Teresas who serve it. There are roly-poly gurus, rail-thin vipassana teachers, mysterious Sufis, jovial rabbis, goddess worshippers in love with the earth, dreamy-eyed mystics in love with eternity, and Native Americans who purify themselves in sweat lodges. There is, as the saying goes, something for everyone.

Suffering on the Path

Even as spiritual perspectives promise equanimity, appreciation of what one has, and compassion for others, they also warn us of the inevitable suffering that will be found along the way. All the excitement of having, controlling, and achieving dissipates, as does the illusory safety or pride of an essentially isolated self. For a time, we may be left with a deep sense of our own emptiness. If we are fully open to other people, Chogyam Trungpa warns, we will develop a "genuine heart of sadness."[57]

A more extreme version can be found in an old Zen story in which Bodhidharma, who (as legend tells us) brought Buddhism from India to China, refused to teach the aspiring monk Huike. Day after day, year after year, the hopeful student waited in vain. In desperation, he cut off one of his arms and held it up to show the master, who finally relented.[58] We do not have to take this rather gruesome story (which can be found illustrated in old Zen manuscripts) literally to understand its essential point: that one must want spiritual truth with all one's being and be ready to sacrifice all one's attachments to get it. Jesus' spiritual demands included the renunciation of both wealth and family. The image of death as metaphor for spiritual growth is common.

Along the path, it is not only our conventional attachments that are lost but also a sense of God or spiritual truth. There can be a "dark night of the soul" as described by sixteenth-century Catholic Spanish Carmelite monk St. John of the Cross: a kind of overwhelming despair in which both everyday social identity and customary religious practice lose all meaning. The powerful presence of God, which may have been the initial motivation for spiritual life, fades away.[59] Mother Teresa, popularly known as the very model of spiritual engagement and absolute faith, actually spent much of her life riddled with spiritual hopelessness. She wrote to a friend: "Jesus has a very special love for you. As for me, the silence and the emptiness are so great that I look and do not see, listen and do not hear."[60]

It is not surprising that people feel real anguish on the spiritual path. We are being asked to create ourselves anew—to be, as some Christians say, born again. Birth is almost always difficult and painful, and there is always the chance that we will not survive it. Even if we all carry a spiritually true self within us, it is usually buried so deep that a lot of psychological and moral excavation is needed before it will see the light. And there is so much to cast off, so many dreams to be abandoned, that suffering is inevitable. Our attachments to success, power, wealth, pleasure, being responsible for something wonderful in the world, even—if this is our fate—the hope that we will be married, or have children, or live a long life. Our addictions to tobacco or alcohol or chocolate, the secret delights of self-righteousness or contempt for those less intelligent or virtuous than ourselves. The sloth that reassures us "You can relax your discipline today, you were good yesterday" or the self-deception that counsels us to cut a few corners morally; it won't hurt anyone. The anger that says revenge is justified because we—or others—have been hurt. A sense of confidence that prayer or meditation will always relax or comfort us or that we will feel God's presence just because we want to. In the renunciation of all these things, there will be real pain.

We may imagine that the caterpillar is asleep as it changes into a butterfly and does not realize what it is losing. But we can only learn to fly if we are awake and willing to give up everything that allowed us to live as we were before—all the while hoping that some blessed day we, too, will become brilliantly colored and lighter than air.

3

Spirituality in Religious Tradition

SOME PEOPLE BELIEVE that spirituality is both historically new and fundamentally opposed to organized religion. Yet neither is the case. Scriptures advise us to live by spiritual virtues, saints and beloved teachers embody them, hundreds of stories show how they connect us to God, and many classics of religious literature—even ones from centuries ago—have the word *spiritual* in their titles.[1]

Since much of contemporary spirituality results from adopting traditional religions' spiritual teachings and taking an agnostic or metaphorical attitude toward their metaphysical claims, this is not surprising.[2] Still, it is instructive to see in some detail exactly how much of what we consider an eclectic or nondenominational spirituality can be found within tradition itself. The following four examples, taken from very different contexts, demonstrate the close kinship between contemporary spirituality and past facets of organized religion.[3]

Compassion and Paradox in Mahayana Buddhism

Buddhism begins with the four noble truths: life is suffering, suffering is caused by attachment to desires and to a fixed sense of self, this attachment can be overcome, and the way to overcome it is through the eightfold path, a combination of understanding, intention, moral discipline, and meditation. Thus defined, Buddhism is perhaps the archetypical spiritually oriented religion. It calls for no metaphysical commitment to gods or heaven, takes as its proof only the way it eases our suffering, and is centered on virtues rather than beliefs. The Buddha frequently makes it clear that arguing about theology is quite beside the point, which is to find a way to end our misery and not to get correct doctrine. Holy wars and inquisitions have never been part of Buddhist history, and when the third-century B.C.E. Indian emperor Ashoka converted to the faith, he abandoned his policy of military conquest, embracing humanitarian care for his subjects.[4] In recent years, Buddhist teachers the Dalai Lama and Thich Nhat Hanh have become respected worldwide for their humane and universally oriented messages of inner peace and outer compassion.

Yet Buddhism is also a traditional religion like any other. Where it flourished, a class of monks and priests lived off the generosity of laypeople; ordinary folk embraced a vast mythology of miracles, lesser gods, terrifying demons, and legends of Buddha's earlier lives; and complicated rituals, offerings, and prayers were practiced. Whatever distance one might note between, say, the Sermon on the Mount and the later Catholic Church, a comparable gap developed between the philosophically oriented discourses of the Buddha and the lived Buddhism of India, Southeast Asia, Tibet, China, and Japan.

At the same time, what I am calling the spiritual elements of Buddhism remained extremely significant. For an example, let us look at the role of compassion and paradox in Mahayana Buddhism.

Three centuries after Buddhism began, Mahayana grew up in response to central contradictions of the early teachings. Originally, *Theravada* (the "wisdom of the elders") Buddhism took as its model the arhat—the person who has laid down *his own* defilements that cause suffering; who has overcome *his own* delusion, greed, and attachment; and who has found *his own* insight, detachment, and serenity. But, challenged the Mahayana thinkers, how can this stress on "his own" result in anything but a continuation of the sense of selfhood that is the cause of the suffering to begin with?[5] If we concentrate on making ourselves feel better, won't we simply be reinforcing our sense of self—the actual root of the suffering? How can we reach Nirvana—an end to suffering based in an end to our sense of self—if we are constantly thinking "*I* want to escape *my* suffering"? Mahayana thinkers also asked: how does a Buddhist avoid rigid attachment to the beliefs that motivated their participation in religious life in the first place? Defining oneself by a doctrine—"I think this about that"—is just another way of emphasizing one's separate, distinct personhood.

Mahayana thinkers responded to these dilemmas in a variety of ways, most important, through their emphasis on the Bodhisattva's universal compassion and their use of paradox to undermine attachment to doctrine.

The Bodhisattva is the Mahayana ideal. Her goal is not her own liberation, but that of *every* sentient being. Unlike the Aahat, who is like a glowworm whose light can barely be seen, the Bodhisattva is like the sun that illuminates everything.[6] She has "taken all beings under [her] protection."[7] The hallmark of the Bodhisattva is not isolated serenity, but an engaged compassion that feels with and for everyone else. In an ability to empathize that helps define her, she feels experiences other people's sadness and joys as her own.[8] Bodhisattvas want "to become capable of pulling others out of this great flood of suffering...find pleasure in doing good for others, without any egoistic preoccupation."[9] It is through limitless compassion that the Bodhisattva trains her mind away from a concentration on her own problems and pains. This spiritual aspiration is emphasized in two of the Bodhisattva's defining oaths: "However innumerable sentient beings are, I vow to save them."[10] "I will take upon myself the burden of all suffering, I am resolved to do so. I will endure it. I do not turn or run away, do not tremble, am not terrified, nor afraid."[11]

The Bodhisattva model has considerable psychological force. If your main pre-occupation is your own situation, it is very hard not to remain stuck in a kind of psychological and spiritual dead end. You try to get further along the path of selfless-ness, but you always end up thinking about...yourself! "Am I realizing the truth of the teaching? Are my thoughts pure?" And so on. So the transfer of concern from *my*self to *all* selves, so that everyone else's pain and joy are equally as important as my own, can serve as a kind of disciplined refocus. And it makes sense that if other people's happiness means as much to us as our own, just to that extent we have actually already overcome our sense of self and conquered our conventional ego. Isn't a good deal of what it means to have a conventional ego just to feel that my pains and pleasures are so much more important than anyone else's?[12]

This Buddhist ideal of selfless, universal compassion can be celebrated by peo-ple with other religions or none at all. From Mother Teresa to Martin Luther King Jr., from Gandhi to a "secular saint" like Paul Farmer, who has established medical clinics in some of the most impoverished and dangerous places on earth, the spiri-tual value of compassion is celebrated. One need not be a Buddhist to embrace it, one can reject the entire Buddhist mythology and still respond to the moral beauty of the idea, and any serious Buddhist can see echoes of the Buddhist version in the ideals of other religions and secular moral or political movements.

Then there is the question of the role of religious doctrines. Whatever else the great Mahayana texts tell us to believe, they also assure us that having cor-rect beliefs is really a comparatively unimportant aspect of Bodhisattvahood. That is why thousands of pages of detailed and often long-winded Mahayana descrip-tions of psychological states, morality, meditation styles, and legends of the Buddha include paradoxical, nearly nonsensical statements that put all the other pages into question. This undermining process can be found in Mahayana Indian Buddhist philosophy and the often absurd riddles and poems of Chinese and Japanese Zen.

From India, we have what seems to be a veritable rejection of some of the essential principles of Buddhism, frequently voiced immediately after the prin-ciples themselves.

First example: The goal of Buddhism is Nirvana, the extinction of craving and selfhood. Nirvana is often defined as escape from samsara—the round of birth and death in which we are a slave to our desires, aversions, and ego. Buddhism thus directs us toward Nirvana and away from samsara. Yet the extremely influential second- to third-century Mahayana Indian philosopher Nagarjuna taught: "There is no difference at all between Nirvana and Samsara."[13] Similarly, the Buddha—founder of the religion, he who achieved Nirvana—is said to be no different from all the people caught in samsara: "The one who understands that Buddha and sentient beings are not different can liberate all sentient beings from disease and calamity, end the cycle of birth and death and attain perfect, complete enlightenment and Nirvana."[14]

Second example: As we have seen, the Bodhisattva is distinguished from earlier images of Buddhist sages by his concern for others, his commitment to lead all beings to enlightenment. And yet, Mahayana texts repeatedly tell us, "There are no beings." Everything is "empty," and all separate identities, including that of the speaker and the hearer, the Buddha and the original disciples, arhats, Bodhisattvas, and philosophy professors writing books on spirituality are simply illusions.

People have interpreted the first of these enigmatic statements as a way of asserting that enlightenment is not some overwhelming experience but simply being able to go about our most ordinary activities carefully, lovingly, and compassionately. The claim that all beings are an illusion may be just a rather overstated way of getting us over our attachment to a separate identity or a rather flamboyant version of the truth that nothing exists without an entire universe of relationships that create, sustain, and reflect it.

However they were intended, the practical result is that fundamental Mahayana doctrine remains fluid, indeterminate, and certainly not the kind of thing on which one could hang an orthodox hat. Since the doctrine is so intellectually opaque, a developed Buddhist will show extreme intellectual reticence about theology and certainly not be aggressive in its promotion. As one commentator says, "What is expected of a Buddhist is that he should do no violence to others by imposing his view upon them."[15]

This is as modern an attitude toward religious difference as that of any spiritual teacher giving workshops today. It is fully compatible with the idea of lifelong spiritual seeking through different traditions, taking whatever beliefs make for progress on the spiritual path and rejecting any claims to special privilege on the part of a particular faith. Could there be a better basis for what we in the modern world call interfaith cooperation, one that encourages members of different faiths to learn from and appreciate each other's spiritual insights?

In China and Japan, the philosophical paradoxes of India give way to the downright loony koans of Zen Buddhism.[16] Zen students were instructed to meditate for weeks, months, and even years on these often bizarre questions or stories, with the degree of their development measured by the spontaneity and authenticity of their responses. Since for the most part the koans were literally absurd, lacking any rational solution, something other than a rationally correct answer was called for. Classic questions like "What is the sound of one hand clapping?" or "What did your face look like before your mother was born?" do not move in the realm of conventional meaningful assertion.

Sometimes the questions come with "answers":

> A monk asked Ummon: "What is Buddha?" Ummon answered him:
> "Dried dung."
> "Why did Bodhidharma (the monk who brought Buddhism from India to
> China) come to the West?" Answer: "The Cypress tree in the yard."
> Two monks were arguing about a flag. One said: "The flag is moving."
> The other said: "The wind is moving." The sixth patriarch happened to be
> passing by. He told them: "Not the wind, not the flag; mind is moving."[7]

Of the stories that are a little more accessible, many emphasize privileging practice over theory and direct experience over reflection, thereby supporting a perspective for which verbal accounts of religious truth are at best servants to be used rather than articles of faith to cling to.[8]

> Yamaoka Tesshu, as a young student of Zen, visited one master after another.
> He called upon Dokuon of Shokoku.
> Desiring to show his attainment, he said: "The mind, Buddha, and sentient
> beings, after all, do not exist. The true nature of phenomena is emptiness.
> There is no realization, no delusion, no sage, no mediocrity. There is no
> giving and nothing to be received."
> Dokuon, who was smoking quietly, said nothing. Suddenly he whacked
> Yamaoka with his bamboo pipe. This made the youth quite angry.
> "If nothing exists," inquired Dokuon, "where did this anger come from?"

Could these stories, or the meditations based on them, ever be the basis for dogmatic attachment? Could they be the subject of violent differences and the creation of warring sects and subsects? Could they, in short, be treated religiously, with all the negative connotations often meant by people who say they are "spiritual but not religious"?

Probably, yes, for there is no limit to the ways in which we people will attach ourselves to things and puff up our egos by telling ourselves how (religiously, spiritually, morally) correct we are and how incorrect other people are. But insofar as formal religious teaching, growing up in a premodern, traditional cultural setting, can work to guard against such a response, Mahayana writings do so. They offer a way to understand spiritual virtues that is fully compatible with some of the defining trends of contemporary spirituality. If a detailed history of that spirituality were to be written, they would be found to be part of what shaped its history in the first place.

Some might argue that because Buddhism has no single, all-powerful deity, it just is less likely to give rise to attachments to doctrinal orthodoxy keyed to God's commands.[19] Further, many suppose that eastern religions just are "more spiritual" than those of the west. Buddhism, Taoism, and Yoga have often been the destination of seekers who find their childhood western religions too constrained, formalistic, or experientially empty.

In reality, the world's dominant monotheistic religions possess rich spiritual resources in some of the most traditionally oriented and highly respected figures of Judaism, Christianity, and Islam. When they arose, most of these teachings were inseparable from a particular context of religious belief, ritual, and community. Yet the particularly spiritual quality of their insights makes their wisdom accessible to anyone.

The Passions of Sufism

Sufism refers to the mystical form of Islam, which goes back almost to the religion's origins in the seventh century.[20] Islamic mysticism has a long and complex history, its wide range of manifestations affected by historical change, interactions with neighboring religious traditions and cultures, and the distinct personalities of its charismatic leaders.[21] The Sufi insights I draw on here, while authentic to the movement, represent only a minuscule portion of the whole.[22]

At times, Sufis have been persecuted by more orthodox Muslim groups, both Sunni and Shi'a, and accused of heterodox beliefs and practices, excessive attachment to individual charismatic teachers, and insufficient attention to Shari'a law in favor of meditational practices and mystical experiences. Since at least the eighth century, tensions have existed between Sufi groups and the class of legal scholars, the ulema whose authority was often challenged or undermined by Sufi masters, at times leading to violent suppression of Sufis. In a description that could probably apply to many faiths, one commentator argues that there has been a fracture in Islamic history between the "legalists who are hunters of heresy and haters, and the mystics who are pluralists and lovers."[23]

Although some early western scholars sought in Sufism a less threatening, even extra-Islamic origin to Islamic mystical movements, for the most part Sufism emerged from and remains firmly rooted in an undeniably Islamic context. The overwhelming majority of Sufis have considered themselves Muslims and were devoted to the Qur'an, the prophetic identity of Muhammad, Islamic tradition and scholarship, pilgrimage to Mecca, almsgiving, and daily prayers.[24] If some Islamic literalists found the Sufis insufficiently orthodox, one sees little difference with the sometimes violent schisms that have marked the history of other religions: Protestant and Catholic, Hasidic Jews and the *mitnagdim* who rejected them, evangelical and liberal Protestants.

Sufism teaches all of the virtues I have described so far: self-knowledge, acceptance of and gratitude for life, compassion for others, and connection to other people and the divine. It stresses the importance of spiritual practices to help us remember God,[25] the need for a kind of total break with our normal social identity, and the difficult truth that only with great devotion will spiritual insight arise. Service to others as a source of knowledge of God and the use of paradox and humor to dislodge the conventional ego are also found.

But of all these, I believe one stands out: love. Within Sufi tradition, there is an eloquent, heartfelt, desperate yearning for a connection with God, an ecstasy of self-realization and dissolution of self when the divine embrace is felt, and a heart-breaking loneliness when it is not. The evocative spiritual poetry with which Sufi masters have expressed this love can resonate with anyone who has ever longed for God as an alternative to the pains and disappointments of ordinary life and who seeks to be the compassionate and joyful person that arises in the presence of the divine.

Here is an early voice taken to be one of the classic inspirations of Sufism, the Iraqi female mystic and teacher Rabiya Al-Adawiyya, who died in 801 c.e. To original Islam's emphasis on morality, worship, and obedience, Rabiya added the element of passionate devotion. "I have never worshipped God so that I would be rewarded; nor have I prayed to be saved....I pray only because I love God with all my soul. To weep and cry out for God's mercy would be for nothing; for all I want is to approach God and dissolve my inner self in Him."[26] This sincerity and devotion echoes voices from other traditions. Certainly the Hebrew author of the biblical Song of Songs and the early Christian desert saints would understand Rabiya's lament: "The source of my grief and loneliness is deep in my breast. This is a disease no doctor can cure. Only Union with the Friend [God] can cure it."[27]

Rabiya's passion for God is heard again in later Sufi teachers, including two of its most famous and currently widely read authors, Hafiz and Rumi.

Hafiz (1326–1390), the beloved Persian poet, was a self-educated student of languages, politics, law, mathematics, and science. He held a variety of jobs and moved in and out of favor with the political and religious establishment of his time. Overcoming a series of personal struggles, and during a long-standing attempt to reach spiritual heights, his poetry became famous in Persia in his lifetime, and after his death, his tomb was a place of pilgrimage. To this day, his poems remain popular both in Iran and globally, and his spiritual insights and poetic mastery drew the admiration of western readers such as Goethe and Emerson.

The major theme of Hafiz's poems is love of God. Symbolized by wine, an intimate relationship with the divine becomes a kind of exalted drunkenness—as the limitations and constraints, fears and compulsions of the ordinary mind give way to a euphoric connection to the creator:

> *O Winebringer, if You really love us*
> *Then bring us all the wine you have!*
> *This Winehouse is full of salesmen who sell crystals and healing charms,*

But I want only the juice from Your vine.
O friends, you that are alive and still have hearts,
Hear what this drunkard has to say.
You who are crying, give up your wail,
For compared with the world of Love, everything else is pale.
In the path of Love, a poor honest beggar
Is worth more than all the rich man's gold....
O Master how many more tears will Hafiz have to cry?
Won't you call for him now that his heart has been broken in two.[28]

For Hafiz, this love of God takes precedence over all other forms of religious observance and concern and can make up for any other lack or insufficiency in one's life or character: "In the School of Truth, one sits at the feet of the Master of Love.... If God should shine His lovelight on your heart, I promise you'll shine brighter than a dozen suns...don't sit there thinking: go out and immerse yourself in God's sea."[29]

Rumi (1207–1273), who was born in Balkh in what is now northern Afghanistan and who traveled throughout much of the Middle East, is another enormously popular Persian poet whose influence continues to the present.[30] Rumi's teachings inspired the foundation of the Mevlevi (Turkish for "our master") Sufi order, which gave us the world-famous whirling dervishes. Despite persecution from the Turkish government in the 1920s, the order today has branches throughout the world, including Turkey, Europe, and the United States.[31]

Rumi, too, had an interesting life, in his case marked by a spiritual (and perhaps physical) love of a mysterious Sufi teacher named Shams-e Tabrizi, who periodically appeared and disappeared, finally driven away (it is said) by the jealousy of Rumi's son, friends, and pupils.

Like Hafiz, Rumi invokes the power of single-minded love of God. But in an added twist, he at times suggests that God is as much within us as outside of us, that what we seek is present in ourselves already, and that God and the seeking self are identical. "I used to think that lover and beloved are different. I know now they are the same. I was seeing two in one."[32] This insight was foreshadowed by Hallaj, a ninth-century Sufi who taught—and was put to death for teaching—that "I am both the lover and the beloved...I am truth as a manifestation of God."[33]

For Rumi, love of God and the insight that God is an internal as well as an external reality lead naturally to love of other people, whatever their explicit belief system. Since all are manifestations of God, all are worthy of respect. "Whoever you may be, come, Even though you may be an unbeliever, a pagan, or fire-worshippers, come, our brotherhood is not one of despair, Even though you may have broken Your vows of repentance a hundred times, come."[34] Carrying into the present, as recently as 2007, a speaker at a Sarajevo conference on Rumi asserted that the poet "calls for friendship, collaboration, peace and fraternal relations between people, invoking love towards all human beings as the supreme Divine creation, regardless of religious, cultural, civilizational or spiritual garments in which each of us...is clad."[35] Because God and self are fused, or can be if we take away the blinders that lead us to a false sense of separation, our capacity to connect with other people is far greater than we have realized. Love ends the sense of ego: "I've heard it said there's a window that opens between heart and heart. But if there are no walls, there's no need even for a window."[36]

As all people contain a divine spark, so all sincere forms of devotion can fan that spark into a spiritual blaze. Hierarchies of religious expertise or doctrinaire attachment to one version of the ultimate truth become irrelevant. There is only the heart's longing for God. Consider this Rumi parable:

> Moses heard a shepherd praying to God, offering to comb God's hair, wash God's robe, and kiss his hand. Moses scolded the shepherd for his blasphemy. That night God appeared to Moses and admonished him: "You have driven away a worshipper from his worship. In his sincere simple way, that shepherd was much closer to me than most scholars and ascetics."[37]

Ibn Arabi, a twelfth-century Sufi philosopher and mystic, made a similar point about what we today would call religious tolerance. Echoing the Islamic teaching that God spoke through the Torah, the psalms, and the New Testament, along with the Qur'an, Arabi wrote: "My heart is a pasture for gazelles and a convent of Christian monks, a Temple for idols and the Ka'bah of pilgrims, the tables of the Law of Torah and the Book of Qur'an. I follow the religion of Love; wherever Love takes me, there is my religion and my faith."[38]

Once a deep realization of the soul's connection to God arises, Sufis teach, spiritual virtues become natural, spontaneous responses rather than a tortured discipline or an anguished self-sacrifice. Compassion for others, simple joy in daily life, an ability to give based in a sense that one's own reality is an expression of God's infinite resources—all these are the stock in trade of the advanced mystic. These virtues express *marifah*—defined by a contemporary Sufi as an "ongoing state of attunement with God and with Truth."[39] In this state, the fetters of ordinary consciousness are broken, and love of God, celebration of life, and selfless kindness toward others fuse. As Rumi put it, "Unlike someone who begs on the street for bread, a dervish [practicing Sufi] begs to give his life away."[40] And this endless generosity, Hafiz tells us, is ultimately rooted in our awareness of and participation in God's generosity: "The Beloved does not mind repeating, 'Everything I have is also yours.'"[41]

If people who live like this are, to say the least, not something we encounter very often, the Sufi image of a love can nevertheless resonate with virtually anyone who seeks a spiritual life. If for traditional Sufis this image is rooted in Islam, the virtues it proclaims are accessible to people of other religions or none. Their rejection of religious formalism and narrow dogmatism echoes the openheartedness of people who seek spiritual truth in virtue rather than doctrine.[42] What they celebrate will be at home anywhere people seek to replace fears, greed, and compulsions with selfless contentment, generosity, and delight. "The goal of the Sufi," one scholar puts it simply, "is to become so at one with God, that 'me' is no longer even heard."[43]

Spiritual Humility and Christianity

In contemporary America, many "spiritual" people believe that Christianity is inherently doctrinaire, intellectually repressive, and intolerant. To many serious Christians, "spirituality" is a simply a self-indulgent, unserious, perhaps even heretical fad.

I believe that both these positions are seriously mistaken.

And yet they both have some truth in them. From the Inquisition to the religious wars of Europe to historical anti-Semitism to the Florida Protestant pastor who gained publicity by threatening to burn a copy of the Qur'an, public manifestations of Christianity have many times been marked by claims to possess absolute, literal truth and a willingness to use verbal or physical violence in support of that claim. Yet, similarly, as I have suggested already, there are countless contexts in which contemporary spirituality is narcissistic and disconnected from personal or social transformation. Both Christianity *and* spirituality contain individuals and groups who sometimes treat their own beliefs and institutions ("the church") as idols or use their beliefs as an excuse to turn their backs on the world.

This is not, by any means, the end of the story. A Qur'an-burning pastor gets endless publicity; the healing work of Catholic hospitals, Mennonite peacemakers, or a local parish minister who provides emotional support after the death of a child does not. Every hate-filled statement of a fundamentalist is taken seriously, but the quiet work of Catholic relief workers or Protestant environmentalists is taken for granted. On the other side, there are millions of people for whom spirituality means the slow, difficult work of becoming more compassionate, loving, and self-aware.

Is there a place for Christianity and a contemporary understanding of spirituality to meet, a place actually rooted deep in Christian tradition, rather than shaped by contemporary Christian voices who might already be seen as tainted by political or religious liberalism?[44] Actually, such a place is not at all difficult to find. Spirituality, as I have described it, has a rich presence in Christian tradition. Compassion and love, generosity of spirit and gratitude, humility and service to others have been a constant theme in Christian teaching. If they have not always been at the center, they have always been part of the circle. Of the literally countless places where such meeting can occur, I will discuss but two that reveal a completely orthodox, traditional Christianity in which doctrine is less important than virtue, in which being a Christian depends far less on judging the beliefs of others than on judging oneself. In this version of Christianity:

> God wants people to be humble, merciful and peaceful. The best way to live is to accept people who hurt you and mistreat you rather than to struggle with them or seek revenge. In fact, you should even be kind to and pray for people who are nasty to you. Do good deeds, pray to God, be generous, but keep this part of your life private rather than seeking praise for it. Learn from animals and children how to live—simply, accepting your lot in life, delighting in each day, trusting in God to provide. Remember, the pursuit of money and power will lead you away from God. Try to give your heart and soul to God, but do not judge those who don't.

If meditative mindfulness is not stressed here, almost everything else is: compassion, humility, delight in life, detachment from conventional social goals, trust in the benign nature of the universe rather than in calculating and manipulative power. Clearly, the emphasis is on action and attitude, not doctrine. And everything in that paragraph is an exact paraphrase, in language just a little more casual than most English translations of the Gospels, of what Christians believe Jesus said. You can find all of this in Matthew 5–7, repeated with a slightly different emphasis in Luke. Whatever else he was, in this sense Jesus was a spiritual teacher. He instructed his disciples to abandon conventional social roles and demonstrate their love of God by love and care for other people.

Surely, there is a good deal more in the Gospels: claims about God, heaven, and Jesus' special relation to God; dire threats against those who would mistreat his followers; and miracles in which people get what they want (bread, wine, cures of illness or disability) through extraordinary intervention in the physical realm. And of course, there is the resurrection: a man killed, a God reborn, death defeated.

Are Christian spiritual virtues detachable from these specific metaphysical claims? I believe they are. Whatever Jesus' special relation to God, and even given the scriptural demand to have faith in Jesus, we would still need to ask: what does it *mean* to have faith in him? to believe as a Christian? Does it simply mean to repeat "I believe that Jesus is the son of God and that he is my personal savior (or that he will save me through the mediation of the church)"? No matter how many times that sentence is repeated, we still can ask whether I *really* believe it. After all, many people claim to believe in honesty, yet lie, or in marital fidelity, yet cheat on their marriage partners. Some people tell us they are generous or brave and really think they are but are sadly mistaken. Ultimately, we know that someone believes in the God of Christianity not by what they say, no matter how often or how loudly they say it, but how they live. Are they kind to their enemies? Do they help the poor? Do they refrain from telling everyone how holy they are? If the answer to these questions is yes or at least "to some extent and I'm trying hard to get better," that will be the proof of faith. And if they are living that kind of life, they will surely reap spiritual rewards now, whatever happens after they die. As generous people, they will feel blessed that they have enough; as kind people, they will get the benefits of feeling good about others; as forgiving people, they will not be tortured by the furies of rage or bitterness. But openhearted love, even for one's enemies, and a focus on goals other than wealth are quintessential spiritual values. From a spiritual point of view, we can develop them with or without a belief that (for example) Christ is the Son of God, and in any case a person will be able to authentically claim to believe in Jesus only if he lives out these values.

Nevertheless, it might still be argued, Christianity is surely not just the Gospels. Particularly in Catholicism but in other denominations as well, there is an encompassing apparatus of authority, theology, and doctrine. We may opportunistically grasp at a few biblical verses, but beyond the Gospels, Christian spirituality evaporates.

There are dozens (at least) of spiritual voices[45] in Christian history I could cite to refute this view, but I will offer simply one: the German Catholic priest and author Thomas à Kempis (1380–1471). Kempis was a cloistered monk for some 70 years, and from his early teens to his death, his entire life was shaped by Catholicism and monastic discipline. Out of his spiritual aspirations and experiences came many writings, the most important of which is *The Imitation of Christ*. This slender book, divided into brief chapters of spiritual advice, admonishment, and encouragement, is among the most popular books ever written.[46]

The Imitation of Christ deals with many issues: from how to read scripture to obedience, from how to think about death to personal peacefulness. Out of this wide range, I will focus on Kempis's repeated insistence on personal humility and self-examination. Against a widely held spiritual criticism that Christianity is all about judging others, condemning unbelievers, and rejecting those who disagree, Kempis offers—from an unquestioned position of Christian orthodoxy—a very different tone. "If you should see another openly sin, or commit grave faults, you ought not to esteem yourself better: because you know not how long you may remain in a good state. We are all frail: but think no one more frail than yourself."[47]

For Kempis, the natural state of a human being is a tendency to weakness, error, and morally mistaken choices. Being a Christian does not remove this tendency, and thus being a Christian does not confer the right to harsh judgment of others. Such judgments are unjustified—since the person making them is almost certainly as prone to error as the person they judge—and a distraction from the essential spiritual task, which is always to transform oneself toward the virtues taught by Christ. "Who has a stronger conflict than he who strives to overcome himself? And this ought to be our business: To strive to overcome ourselves: and daily to gain mastery over ourselves: and to grow better and better."[48]

This business is not easy, among other reasons because our moral judgments are unjustly favorable to ourselves.

> You know well how to excuse and gloss over your own deeds, but you will not accept the excuses of others. It were more just for you to accuse yourself, and to excuse your brothers. If you wish to be borne with bear also with others. See how far you still are from true charity and humility, which knows not how to feel anger or indignation against anyone but oneself.[49]

The personal need for humility, based in unflinching awareness of one's own moral faults, can then lead to a kind of vital spiritual camaraderie with other people. Far from advocating a harshly judgmental attitude, this particular Christian writer asks us to engage in sincere moral fellowship:

> But now God has so disposed things that we may learn "to bear one another's burdens" (Gal 6:2); for there is no man without defect; no man without his burden; no man sufficient for himself; no man wise enough for himself; but we must bear with one another; comfort one another, assist, instruct and admonish one another.[50]

Insofar as spirituality implies loving human relations across the boundaries of faith, race, class, nation, gender, or politics, could there be a more spiritual understanding of human relationships? It supports the compassion of the Bodhisattva and the everyday love of a generous neighbor, values that can be found in both world religions and secular moral traditions. It is universal because it roots our emotional and moral fellowship in our shared need for help in dealing with our moral weaknesses and personal sorrows. Surely one need not agree with the finer points of Catholic theology to appreciate the value of this idea, nor accept Jesus as one's personal savior to have a more loving life if one tries to practice it.

Hasidic Joy

Somewhere in high school, I came across a book of short stories by the late-nineteenth- to early-twentieth-century Yiddish writer I. L. Peretz. *Prince of the Ghetto* introduced me to a Jewish spirituality that my comfortable, 1950s suburban, success- and comfort-oriented, science, academic success, and sports-respecting, watered-down Reform Jewish setting did not encompass in the least. Peretz himself was not particularly observant, but he was ethnically, culturally, and politically identified with the Jewish community. And he had a love-hate, attraction-repulsion relation with the most fervent, devout, and orthodox of eastern Europe's Jewish communities, the Hasidim.

Peretz's stories told of rabbinical students who responded to crushing poverty with God-dedicated fasting, joy in God's service that transformed shabby synagogues and threadbare clothing into palaces and robes fit for a king, and a great rebbe who changed into a peasant's clothing to bring firewood to an infirm widow. And *this*, the tale said, not his Talmudic learning or ritual observance, put the rebbe "higher than heaven."

And there was the tale of an ordinary Jew, not a wonder-working rebbe, a scholar, or even a hidden righteous man on whom the fate of the world depends.[51] No, just an ordinary Jew who comes home from Friday evening services to find the dinner table in his tiny living room set for the Sabbath meal—candles burning, special Sabbath foods prepared, the house as clean and neat as a poor family's can be—and finds that his heart is simply overflowing with a joy he must share with his creator:

> "Almighty Father! Do you think I am frightened of You and Your power, Your laws and commandments and prohibitions? Not a bit of it! Here!" And bending down, he blew out the Sabbath candles! Desecration of desecrations!...The little Chassid, his face irradiated, straightened up, lifted his arms to heaven again, and exclaimed jubilantly: "But, Lord of the world, I'm just crazy about You!"[52]

(Surely Rabiya and Hafiz would have understood!)

Because it so intensely contains elements of both, Hasidism offers us a remarkably clear example of the tensions between religiosity and spirituality. As a movement, Hasidism was a response by the eastern European Jewish community to particular disastrous events and to a generalized condition of poverty and oppression. In the mid-seventeenth century, hundreds of thousands of Jews were killed by nationalist pogroms, illness, and captivity in the Ottoman Empire. A series of messianic movements, in which particular individuals claimed to be sent by God to end Jewish suffering and usher in an age of perfection, culminated in bitter disillusion. (The final and largest concluded when the self-proclaimed Jewish messiah, faced with a choice of converting to Islam or being executed, abandoned Judaism altogether.) Internally, the Jewish community was dominated by a highly developed, specialized caste of scholar rabbis, and religious learning, defined by knowledge of a vast body of religious literature, was seen as the most important Jewish value.[53]

In short, ordinary Jews tended to be poor, to think of themselves as not having much religious value, and to be persecuted by their gentile neighbors. Everyday life was difficult, fearful, and filled with despair.

There then came a spiritual change of such magnitude that its effects are being felt to this day. The Baal Shem Tov (1698–1760)—literally, "master of the good name"—developed a new understanding of how to relate to God and how to bring that relation into one's daily life. Many legends surround the life of the Baal Shem Tov, but what seems fairly certain is that he was orphaned at an early age and therefore did not have a standard Jewish education or upbringing, lived in a variety of settings and worked at a variety of menial or semiskilled jobs, married and had children, and somewhere in his thirties began to teach.

To be clear, there is nothing in the Baal Shem Tov or in his followers that disputes the essential tenets of traditional Judaism: that the Torah and the Mishnah (the core of the Talmud) were dictated by God to Moses, that the commandments of the Torah (all 613 of them) as interpreted by the Talmud are binding on all Jews, that Jewish learning from the Talmud to Maimonides and beyond are of great value, and that living a Jewish life ritually and ethically is what God wants of the Jewish people.

Yet alongside a belief that Judaism is different from any other religion and that the Torah and the Talmud are true in the most straightforward sense, there is something else. Like a single flute heard over a large orchestra, we are told that the humblest person can be the most spiritually exalted, the most ordinary setting can be a place of spiritual riches, devotion counts for more than learning, and God wants not only obedience, but joy. In the face of the deprivations and losses of the Jewish community, Hasidism rouses us to believe that no matter how downtrodden, we have the power to respond to life with delight. If we can love God enough, we can live in the ecstasy of God's love for us.

The Baal Shem Tov, comments Elie Wiesel, told the Jews:

> that every one of them existed in God's memory, that every one of them played a part in his people's destiny... that a simple but sincere prayer has as much merit as a mystical incantation, that the fervor born in a pure heart is greater than the one born of a complex and unfathomable thought. He said "The coachman who kisses the holy scrolls of the Torah pleases God more than the angels who praise Him and do nothing else."... that pride derived from knowledge is worse than ignorance... that man requires little to elevate and fulfill himself, as long as that is what he longs for, he longs for with all his heart.[54]

It is an emotional and spiritual truth that can we celebrate our lives only if we feel they are valuable. And only if that value is tied to something essential in *all* people, can that celebration be accessible to everyone: to the rebbe's coachman as well as the rebbe. It is on this basis of the essential spiritual worth of the individual Jew, no matter how poor, ignorant, or oppressed, that the particularly Hasidic sense of joy in life can be cultivated. This celebration of the value of ordinary people undermines normal society's stress on hierarchy and privilege. From a spiritual perspective, the learned are not better than the simpletons, the rich than the poor, the successful than the beggar on the corner. It is hard to imagine a more radical, antisocial in the best sense, *spiritually* based understanding of the human condition, one no more Hasidic than it is Sufi, Buddhist, or part of secular political radicalism.

Another story:

> A villager used to pray on Yom Kippur in the synagogue of the Baal Shem Tov. He had a very slow-witted child who did not know how to read. On his 13th birthday, his father brought him to the synagogue to prevent him from eating. During the prayer he said to his father: "Daddy, I want to blow my flute!" "No! for Heaven's sake! Don't do it!" and he firmly held the boy's pocket to prevent him from taking it out—because it is forbidden to play instruments on Yom Kippur. In the last prayer of the day the boy pulled his pocket forcefully from his father's hand, took the flute and gave a "big sound" with the flute. The worshipers were horrified. As the Baal Shem Tov heard the flute sound, he made his prayer short. After the prayer he said: "This young boy, with the sound of his flute, has brought our prayers up to heaven."[55]

On the basis of a profound sense of spiritual equality, Hasidism builds a limitless sense of joy in life. There are tales of Hasidim dancing in desperate circumstances, delighting in the midst of tragedy, even—strange as it may seem—singing as they were moved toward the gas chambers during the Holocaust.[56]

From Jewish philosopher Martin Buber:

> The Hasidic movement...kindled both its simple and intellectual followers to joy in the world as it is, in life as it is, in every hour of life in this world, as that hour is.... Hasidism shows men the way to a God who dwells with them "in the midst of their uncleannesses," a way which issues forth from every temptation, even from every sin. Without lessening the strong obligation imposed by the Torah, the movement suffused all the traditional commandments with joy-bringing significance, and even set aside the wall

separating the sacred and the profane, by teaching that every profane act can be rendered sacred by the manner in which it is performed.[57]

That we are all equal in the sight of God is a profound lesson. But to learn that lesson, how much has to be unlearned! I must turn my back on all the messages that proclaim the superior value of the rich, powerful, smart, good-looking, and lucky and the thought that I am too ordinary to merit anyone's love, let alone God's. I will have to find within myself the strength to accept the idea that even with my countless weaknesses and hidden flaws, God can love me—*but only if I love him back*. And how do I show that love? By taking delight in what God has given me. Service to God does not mean just following the rules but finding goodness in everything I touch. No matter how sad I am, I can still thank God for my life. No matter how poor, I can still sing. As long as I can move, I can dance to welcome the Sabbath or celebrate a wedding, the New Year, a new life.

If for the Hasid, such a life of spiritual virtue makes sense only when it is embedded in a religiously conservative attachment to Talmudic Judaism, surely someone else could find it another way. This illuminating frame of mind and heart might arise in the consciousness of a Christian saint, a Muslim student, or a Hindu householder.[58] And it need not even be the God of the Bible, the Vedas, or the Qur'an that is the source. We can find our equality and worth because we are all products of evolution, all living beings, all centers of thought and feeling. The promise of these spiritual insights, the virtues that flow from them, and the difficult demands they make are essentially the same whatever the tradition or lack of tradition.

Toward the Present: How Spirituality Became Modern

FOR NAGARJUNA, THOMAS à Kempis, Hafiz, or the Baal Shem Tov, compassion, humility, and the sacredness of ordinary life simply *are* Buddhism, Christianity, Islam, or Judaism and are therefore closely tied to those religions' claims about ultimate reality and revealed texts.

Today, however, it is possible to cultivate compassion, seek joy in daily life, be moved by stories from rebbes or Sufi masters, and nevertheless say one is not religious or, as is the case with contemporary spiritual teachers like Rabbi Zalmon Schachter-Shalomi or the Catholic David Steindl-Rast, define oneself by a specific religious identity and also emphasize the insights and values shared with other religions or with people who have no religious identity at all. We have Buddhist-Jewish dialogues, "Holy Yoga" with a "foundation in Christ,"[1] rabbis quoting Sufi stories, and Catholic nuns practicing vipassana meditation. There are devoted members of traditional faiths, like Catholic Father Gregory Boyle, who can define their spiritual life's work of service to an oppressed and distressed community in language taken from Sufi poets and Buddhist monks, as well as Christianity.[2] We have people (such as myself) who have no attachment to the literal idea of God yet treasure religious wisdom.

In the vast majority of earlier cultural settings, this sort of thing would have been virtually impossible. If one occasionally finds a Sufi mystic celebrating the mutual value of all religions and Yoga and Buddhism shaping each other's development, spiritual teachings have generally unfolded within, rather than across, uniform bodies of belief and practice. Even if elements from neighboring traditions were assimilated, they were quickly defined as part of "our faith," not something joyfully adopted from outside. Now, however, there is a spiritual world in which ideas, narratives, and practices from all religious contexts coexist. In this world, the question is less "How can I be the best X?" (Buddhist, Jew, Lutheran, etc.) than "How can I, with the help of any or all of these traditions, become more peaceful, find more joy in life, and have more compassion for others?" The spiritual self is not a resource for some tradition, charged with continuing the faith of our fathers. The traditions themselves are a resource for the spiritual self.

How did it become possible to detach spiritual insights from the rest of religious doctrine?

Peaceful Coexistence

To begin, there is the interesting story of the growth of religious tolerance, itself partly a direct response to more than two centuries of violent conflict in Europe, the experience of religious pluralism, and the emergence of modern science.

Centuries of religious wars left Christianity no closer to settling disagreements between Catholics and Protestants, or among Protestants, than when the conflicts began. During the same period, the rise of modern science provided a counterexample of a comprehensive worldview that did advance and was capable of reaching consensus after disagreement. The enormous scope of scientific knowledge and the striking power of the new technologies contrasted starkly with endless arguments that never moved toward resolution. It seemed that since none of the many faiths that asked for our belief offered convincing evidence, attempts to impose one true faith could only lead to pointless bloodshed. In time, Europe and the Americas gradually became a heterogeneous society in which many religions (no matter how uneasily at times) coexisted.

The pluralism of Christian Europe was dramatically increased as colonialism, imperialism, and globalization brought the world's faiths into ever greater contact. Despite whatever divided Catholics and Protestants, after all, they still agreed on many things. Even with Jews, they shared a powerful attachment to the Hebrew Bible and, with Islam, monotheism. In Hinduism, Buddhism, Taoism, and Confucianism, however, they faced ancient, complex traditions whose metaphysical postures were radically different. The result was an ever wider range of equally defensible (or indefensible) religious ideas.

This striking increase in religious diversity led some to cling to their beliefs even more ferociously than before. But for others it, like the rise of science, made possible the critical realization that what was crucial about religion was not the truth of its metaphysics, for example, its descriptions of God or the afterlife. Religions could not be expected to compete with physics or chemistry in their literal description of the physical world or hope that their untestable claims of revelation would be accepted in the same way testable ones are. For some people, this exhausted the potential utility of religion, which they sought to condemn to the dustheap of history. Others, however, saw that there was more to religion than literal truth or faith in the unseen. There was an accumulated wealth of hard-won wisdom, profound psychological and ethical insight, and an immeasurably valuable vision of a life infused with moral values and equanimity. That vision and the teachings and practices it inspires are a major part of what we mean when we talk about spirituality.[3]

Locke's Toleration

English philosopher John Locke (1632–1704), best known for his theoretical justification of political democracy, also wrote some extremely interesting and influential essays on religious tolerance. Perhaps the most important argument he made was that religion, by its very nature, is not something that can be compelled. God wants faith freely given, wrote Locke, and if we force people into a particular faith, freedom is absent, and we actually end up with no faith whatsoever. Therefore, personal understanding and assent are religiously essential in ways they are not for, say, scientifically based rules of hygiene or car maintenance. We can follow rules set by doctors or car mechanics without understanding or agreeing with them. But we cannot be truly religious unless we actually believe. Even though Locke did not extend his arguments to non-Christian religions, it is not hard to do so. Therefore, even if Locke still believed that Christianity was true and other religions false, his arguments for toleration help create a conceptual space in which the centrality of the individual's relation to the religious doctrine starts to become as important as the doctrine itself.[4]

If Locke is correct about the unique nature of religious belief, then two ideas follow. First, we cannot legitimately expect or demand uniformity in religious belief the way we can in science or everyday perception. Because conclusive evidence to support any particular religious viewpoint does not exist, the focus turns increasingly to the individual's personal attachment to one or another of the many available religious alternatives. We spend less energy proving that our theology is true and much more asking whether our faith in it is actually shaping how we live. This shift is consistent with the Protestant Reformation's stress on the sanctity of the individual's personal relation to God. While emphasizing individual religious conscience might have initially been a weapon against the Catholic Church, it created an opening for the primacy of personal experience and spiritual choice. Seventeenth-century embodiments of this idea can be found in the Quaker emphasis on knowing God "experimentally" (through personal encounter) and in protofeminist attempts by women—claiming their universal right to establish an individual connection to God—to establish themselves as preachers alongside men.[5]

Second, if our personal assent, our preference, is a critical component of religious faith, what is there to prevent us from picking and choosing to fashion our own unique religious perspective? If religious beliefs are not the kind of thing for which we have shared public justification, there arises a virtually endless possibility of religious belief—from age-old traditions to eclectic fusions I cook up in my living room, from spiritual readings of the sacred texts to combinations of different scriptures, from spirituality without religion to spirituality within or alongside it.

This is not yet modern spirituality, but it creates the space for it. And as the globalization of economy and politics has led to the globalization of culture, this space has expanded dramatically. We now have access to written records of the vast majority of the world's spiritual traditions translated into each other's languages. If part of the attachment to one's own tradition as exclusively true was based in honest ignorance of the similarities between one's own and other faiths, that ignorance is now easily dispelled. Consider, for example, how Jewish teachings judge disparaging speech (*lashon hara*, literally "evil tongue") a great sin that, the Talmud tells us, damages "the person who speaks it, the person who hears it, and the person about whom it is told."[6] How close this is to one of the 57 slogans that form part of Tibetan Buddhist Chekewa Yeshe Dorje's eleventh-century *The Root Text of the Seven Points of Training the Mind*: "The instruction 'Don't talk about injured limbs' means," the commentator writes, "not taking delight in somebody else's defect."[7] Similarly, in texts that offer support to spiritual feminists, we have the Christian "there is neither Jew nor Greek, slave nor free, male nor female, for you are all one in Christ Jesus" (Galatians 3:28) and the Buddhist legend of Tara, a female Bodhisattva, telling a patriarchal critic: "Here there is no man; there is no woman, no self, no person, and no consciousness. Labeling 'male' or 'female' is hollow."[8]

As such similarities become increasingly evident, spiritual life becomes increasingly eclectic. Today, yoga books can make free use of terminology derived from Chinese as well as Indian body-mind systems.[9] Four doctors, discussing the psychological benefits of meditation, can talk of equanimity as a mental state "highly valued across contemplative disciplines...described as 'divine apathea' by the Christian Desert Fathers, 'euthymia' by Stoics, 'dispassion' by yogis, and 'serenity' by Hassidic Jews. In Buddhism, equanimity is one of the seven factors of enlightenment."[10] In such instances, we see that the unit of thought is not a particular tradition, but a generalized understanding of how a person can best live, that is, a transcultural understanding of spiritual virtue.

Seeing the essential teachings as shared across traditions, contemporary spiritual seekers do not believe they have to fully identify with a particular religion to get that religion's wisdom. An internationally revered teacher can reveal that he grew up believing that his own religion "was the best" and no other faith "could rival its depth, sophistication, and inspirational power" but that he eventually learned to "accept the full worth of faith traditions other than his own."[11]

Kierkegaard's Spiritual Faith

In my view, Danish philosopher and religious writer Søren Kierkegaard (1813–1855) is the paradigmatic transitional figure in the creation of modern spirituality.

On the one hand, he was a devout Christian who considered it his task to preach the truth of Christianity to others. However, and ironically, he felt that part of what made this task difficult was that all the people he was addressing considered themselves Christians already—and even the same kind of Christian as himself. They all believed the same things about, for example, the Trinity and the New Testament. But Kierkegaard stressed that these kinds of beliefs were not the heart of Christianity. Something else—which he often termed *subjectivity* or *passion*—was the key: an inner state of single-minded devotion and dedication, a choice to commit oneself completely to one's religious identity, and a focus on a personal connection to God in the absence of a conceptual description of that connection.

Kierkegaard saw two main opponents to his vision of Christianity. The first was the comfortable Christian conformist who believed that he could be confident of his Christian identity because he went through the socially acceptable motions of Sunday services or relied on the fact that "since Danes are predominantly Lutheran Christians, and since he was certainly not a Jew, what else could he be but a Christian?"[12] Such an understanding of what it meant to be a Christian made one's eternal relation to God and the fate of his soul a matter of habit and social conformity—for Kierkegaard, a complete contradiction.

Kierkegaard's second opponent was the presumed philosophical objectivity advocated by Europe's dominant philosopher, G. W. F. Hegel (1770–1831). Hegel taught that a kind of impersonal reason manifested itself in human history, leading to a series of historical shifts in the direction of greater knowledge and philosophical sophistication. At its time, for example, Christianity conventionally understood as the worship of a God who had sacrificed his son to redeem humans from sin was the most advanced form of religious understanding. But its hidden truth, argued Hegel, was the deeper message that just as God and Jesus were one, so human beings as an evolving totality were themselves, collectively, divine. As Christianity had been historically predestined to evolve out of the less advanced Judaism, so Hegel's philosophical form of Christianity would necessarily supplant—by embodying the hidden truth of—the Christianity of the nineteenth century.

On the surface, the comfortable religious conformity of middle-class Copenhagen and Hegel's rarefied philosophy would seem to have little in common. Yet Kierkegaard saw both as leaving no place for the individual's passionate commitment to faith. For the conformist, simply being part of the crowd of other Lutherans was enough. For Hegel, simply being swept along by the dictates of impersonal, transhistorical reason and getting the benefits of an impersonal, rational progress was sufficient. In neither case did what Kierkegaard often called the "existing individual" have to actively choose to devote himself to God, give up any kind of comfort, stand out from the crowd, or take a chance on something not supported by reason. For both the conformist and the philosopher, religious life is easy, safe, and comfortable.

In a series of complex, brilliant, at times bitterly funny, and at others endlessly repetitive works, Kierkegaard constructed an elaborate philosophical refutation of both these positions. A detailed examination of that refutation would take us very far afield, but we can gain insight into Kierkegaard's enormous contribution to the idea of spirituality if we look at one of his writings, indeed, a small part of it.

Kierkegaard called *Fear and Trembling* his "most beautiful book," and it is certainly his best known—if for nothing else than introducing the phrase "leap of faith." (As we will see, this phrase is pretty much entirely misunderstood!) *Fear and Trembling* focuses on Abraham's response to God's command to sacrifice Isaac. This command, Genesis says, was a test,[13] and because of Abraham's willingness to face it, God confirms him as the founder of Judaism and, in Kierkegaard's words, the "father of faith" for Christians, too. But exactly where, Kierkegaard asks, does Abraham's greatness lie? In answering that question, Kierkegaard develops his own demanding concept of faith, one defined by passionate subjectivity, and along the way provides a model for many of the dimensions of modern spirituality.[14]

How, asks Kierkegaard, could Abraham not only do what he did but also do it *the way* he did it? As he raised the knife, Abraham showed no bitterness that he was being commanded to sacrifice the son for whom he had waited so long and did not try to protect Isaac's faith by saying that it was Abraham, rather than God, who had ordered the act; and he moved with calm grace rather than despair as he led his son to the altar. Abraham showed complete confidence in what he was doing and complete willingness to give up the most precious thing he possessed.[15] He neither delayed nor came early. If it had been me, Kierkegaard adds, I would have come early just to get it over with.[16]

How is such confidence and equanimity possible? asks Kierkegaard, and answers—because Abraham had faith. And it is in Kierkegaard's peculiar use of this term that we find an enormously rich spiritual resource. Abraham did not obey because he had no feelings for Isaac, for if he had not loved his son completely, there would have been no greatness in the act. Abraham did not trust in the future because he expected to be rewarded in heaven. God had promised him a reward on earth, in history, by being the father of a great people. Were Isaac to die, that promise would have been nullified. Abraham had not surrendered all hope by entering into what Kierkegaard calls "infinite resignation"—a religious position in which we believe that we cannot have both the world and God, and we renounce the former. In resignation, he would have been withdrawn, depressed, or at least emotionally cut off from Isaac, and he was not. Finally, he was not depending on reason—as if he had made a survey of past times when God commanded a patriarch to kill his heir and found that in all but two of nine earlier instances God had relented at the last minute. ("Aha," thinks Abraham, "I've got a 78 percent chance of making out all right.") No, says Kierkegaard, Abraham proceeds with perfect confidence that everything will be all right, even though he has absolutely no reason to believe so.

All this, says Kierkegaard, is maddeningly hard to fathom. Although he has never met such a "knight of faith" who could do such a thing, he can imagine him; and in this long description (in which I will emphasize key phrases), we will find the heart of his idea of faith.

> Good Lord, is this the man? Why, he *looks like a tax-collector!* I draw closer to him, watching his least movements to see whether there might not be visible a little heterogeneous fractional telegraphic *message from the infinite,* a glance, a look, a gesture, a note of sadness, a smile.... His tread? It is vigorous, belonging entirely to finiteness...he *belongs entirely to the world....* One can discover nothing of that aloof and superior nature whereby one recognizes the knight of the infinite [i.e., infinite resignation, where everything has been given up in exchange for God]. He *takes delight in everything* with the persistence which is the mark of the earthly man whose soul is absorbed in such things.... He goes to church. No heavenly glance or any other token of the incommensurable betrays him; if one did not know him, it would be *impossible to distinguish him from the rest of the congregation,* for his healthy and vigorous hymn-singing proves at the most that he has a good chest.... Toward evening he walks home.... On his way he reflects that his wife has surely a special little warm dish prepared for him, e.g. a calf's head roasted, garnished with vegetables.... As it happens, he hasn't four pence to his name, and *yet he fully and firmly believes* that his wife has that dainty dish for him. His wife hasn't it—*strangely enough, it is quite the same to him.... With infinite resignation he has drained the cup of life's profound sadness...he senses the pain of renouncing everything,* the dearest things he possesses in the world, and yet *finiteness tastes to him just as good as to one who never knew anything higher....* He resigned everything infinitely, and then he *grasped everything again by virtue of the absurd.* It is supposed to be the most difficult task for a dancer to leap into a definite posture in such a way that there is not a second when he is grasping after the posture, but by the leap itself he stands fixed in that posture...that is what this knight does...to be able to fall down in such a way that the same second it looks as if one were standing and walking, *to transform the leap of life into a walk*...that only the knight of faith can do.... [17]

Although Kierkegaard's brief description does not cover every aspect of spiritual life—most important, there is nothing here about morality—a great many of the themes of a broad, nondenominational spirituality are defined with remarkable clarity.

To begin, the knight's appearance is "nothing special." Externally, "objectively," he is no different from other people in his clothes, manner of speech, facial expression, or mannerisms. There is none of what Trungpa called "spiritual materialism." Further, he is fully rooted in ordinary life, offering us no messages "from the infinite." He has given up his attachments to the world, but he is also able to enjoy the world as completely, perhaps more completely, than people who have never gone through resignation. This is not without some emotional suffering, the "pain of renouncing everything," yet even as he gives everything up, he gets it all back! *This* is the "leap of faith" that allows a dancer to elevate (to the "infinite" of the complete surrender of resignation) and without a moment's hesitation return to being fully at home on earth. The knight of faith leaps off the earth in resignation, giving up attachments to possessions, social status, and physical pleasures. But in having given them up, they are returned "by virtue of the absurd," that is, by virtue of his appreciation for each moment of life, an appreciation infinitely enriched because he no longer has the craving to control, possess, or dominate. He is able to manifest his spiritual virtues in the most ordinary of life's encounters, to look forward to a special dinner, and feel equally content if it doesn't happen.

While clearly Kierkegaard thinks of the knight of faith in a Christian context, there is nothing essentially Christian about him.[18] His faith would resonate with Zen Buddhist tales of monks capable of serenity in the face of turmoil, Catholic David Steindl-Rast's emphasis on gratitude, Rabbi Marcia Praeger's account of Judaism's constant reminder to bless God for virtually everything we encounter in life, and with countless others teachers' descriptions of the spiritual power of living in the moment, taking delight in what you have, and trusting in the essential goodness of life.[19] The virtues he describes, though obviously not his Christian vocabulary, would make perfect sense to Nagarjuna or Lao Tzu or Rumi. Just as the knight of faith is equally happy with or without the calf's head soup, so in the very different context of Hasidism, the Maggid of Meseritch, the Baal Shem Tov's immediate successor, put it simply: "The God-fearing man says 'enough' to whatever God gives him."[20]

The background belief or source of inspiration for detachment, humility, joy in the moment, and confidence based in acceptance rather than control can come from a devotion to Christ, the Talmud, the Qur'an, our connection to nature, 12-step work, empathy based in care for family or strangers, the blend of psychology and spirituality offered by teachers like Byron Katie, or Hafiz's love of God. They can be found in Dostoyevsky's description of the young monk Aloysha in *The Brothers Karamazov*, whose openness, loving temperament, and basic goodness of heart radiate a spiritual connection to others that, while based in his Christian beliefs, is detachable from them. And in Ralph Waldo Emerson, who held that each individual could directly perceive the divine nature of the universe and his own place in it and could through that perception develop a freedom from the constraints and conventions of normal, economically focused social life. Or in a deep ecological sense of an enlarged and grateful self that is connected to the biosphere.[21] Or in a feminist fusion of interpersonal connection and joy in bodily existence.[22] Or in Kabir, who echoes Kierkegaard's rejection of formalistic religious identity and his stress on subjective religious passion:

> *Suppose you scrub your ethical skin until it shines,*
> *But inside there is no music,*
> *Then what?*
> *The yogi comes along in his famous orange.*
> *But if inside he is colorless, then what?*[23]

It is not surprising that Rabbi Abraham Joshua Heschel, European-trained and traditionally oriented Jewish spiritual voice (he was a leading teacher at Conservative Judaism's rabbinical school), could focus an entire book comparing Kierkegaard to the important nineteenth-century Hasidic Rebbe Menachem Mendel of Kotsk (1787–1859). The virtues of the knight of faith belong to a world of spiritual teaching and have never been the sole province of any one faith or philosophy.[24]

That is why for Kierkegaard, as for the leading voices of contemporary spirituality, it is not the formal theology or the religious labels we give ourselves that are important, but the seriousness of our commitment. Belief in God is optional—though a decisive personal commitment to a Godly, or spiritual, life is indispensable. If our focus is on the "objective truth"—somewhere out there is a God, who has such and such characteristics, and we can prove this claim—then we will be forgetting, Kierkegaard tells us, the most important thing, which is that religious life is essentially subjective. And "for a subjective reflection the truth becomes a matter of appropriation, of inwardness, of subjectivity."[25] When truth is objective—as in science—it makes no difference who knows it and what you feel about it. That is what is meant by scientific objectivity—that its claims are true for everyone. But in spiritual life, it is precisely the degree to which I have altered my life in the direction of the spiritual virtues that is crucial, not what I think is true about the objective state of the universe. I can focus on the objective question— whether God exists—or on the subjective one: "whether the individual is related to a something *in such a manner* that his relation is in truth a God-relationship."[26] And for Kierkegaard, this latter focus is the soul of religion. He warns us that the true Christian is not the person who concentrates on believing the right things about the Trinity, but the one who is passionately concerned that he is living his life as God wants, that nothing gets in the way, that anything that might get in the way gets sacrificed, that joy in and gratitude for his life fills as many of his waking hours as is possible. And in this account, we can—though Kierkegaard might not—substitute "true Jew, Muslim, Taoist, nature-lover, Wicca, spiritual-but-not-religious, yogi," or anything else for "true Christian."

> If one who lives in the midst of Christendom goes up to the house of God, the house of the true God, with the *true conception* of God in his knowledge, and prays, but *prays in a false spirit*; and one who lives in an idolatrous community prays with the entire *passion of the infinite*, although his eyes rest upon the image of an idol: where is there most *truth*? the one prays *in truth to God* though he worship an idol; the other prays *falsely to the true God*, and hence worships in fact an idol.[27]

Metaphysics are dispensable. If they help to orient you to a Godly life, to prayer "with the entire passion of the infinite," they have done their job. If you have not reached that level of passion, you will be worshipping an idol no matter what you say you believe.

We have now moved from traditional spirituality unquestioningly embedded in the beliefs of a particular faith to modern spirituality in which attachment to those beliefs takes a very different form, so different that openness to radically different beliefs is no impediment to recognizing an essential spiritual kinship, and the beliefs themselves are only as valid and important as the spiritual life they help a person to lead.

5

Spiritual but Not Religious?

*This is my simple religion. There is no need for temples; no need
for complicated philosophy. Our own brain, our own heart is
our temple; the philosophy is kindness.*

DALAI LAMA[1]

*Survey after survey shows that increasing numbers of people
now prefer to call themselves "spiritual" rather than "religious."*

PAUL HEELAS[2]

SPIRITUAL VIRTUES CAN be practiced without religious belief. For example, the
mindfulness and gratitude described in chapter 1 can serve a spiritual purpose
without acceptance of the formal doctrines of either Buddhism or Judaism.
Whatever our larger framework of beliefs, we can reap self-awareness or the benefits of appreciation. Similarly, Tolstoy wrote *The Death of Ivan Ilych* against the
background of a powerful belief in Christianity, and the light Ivan encounters
when he resolves to renounce his earlier life was for Tolstoy the light of Christian
divinity. Yet readers certainly need not accept Christianity to appreciate the spiritual truth that love is better than selfishness and driven conformity.[3]

Practicing mindfulness without Buddhism, a gratitude prayer without Judaism,
and Christian love without belief in Jesus are ways people can be, as many people
say they are, "spiritual but not religious."[4] At the same time, mindfulness meditation and the particular practice of gratitude I described earlier do come to us from
religious traditions. In fact, contemporary eclectic, nondenominational spirituality is clearly shaped by insights and values that can be found in traditional faiths,
and countless spiritual writers directly quote explicitly religious sources—from
Jesus and Rumi to Buddha, Lao Tzu, and the *Bagavad Gita.*

What *is* the relation between spirituality and religion? Are they fundamentally
opposed? Is spirituality simply a way of being religious? Or is it the part of religion
that is the individual's "personal, experiential relationship with God"?[5] Are archetypical *spiritual* experiences such as oneness with God or gratitude for being alive

the authentic source of *religion*—which then turns these living moments into boring and oppressive institutions? Are some religions—for example, Buddhism—more spiritual than others? And are some forms of a particular religion—for example, Islam's Sufism or Hasidic Judaism—more spiritual than other forms of the same faith?

These questions take us into the heart of both spirituality and religion. In response, I will reflect on the idea of truth, the nature of belief, and the role of individuality and choice, as well as some of the common criticisms spiritual but not religious people make of traditional religion.

There is, I believe, continuity between sacred scriptures and the most eclectic, free-spirited spirituality of today. But there are also important differences. The stress on virtues like awareness, generosity, and compassion is often identical, but modern spirituality does not believe that these virtues require one particular description of God or a single sacred text. What Jesus said about wealth, that it is an enormous impediment to spiritual development; what the Buddha said about anger, that it is like a poison within us; and what the Qur'an teaches about generosity, that it is an essential part of our relation to God, are as contemporary as anything on tomorrow's New Age best-seller list. Yet the idea that a single person can, say, benefit from the teachings of Buddhism *and* Christianity *and* Islam, that the differences between them (and there are many) are spiritually less important than the way they invite us to a life shaped by a shared understanding of spiritual virtues—*this* is new.

Truth

Western monotheism asserts that God revealed himself in particular encounters and in particular texts and has made it clear that he wants human beings to behave in certain very specific ways. Because of the importance of what we know to be true about God, we should support institutions for the preservation and spread of this knowledge to other people and to the next generation. The ideas themselves are so complex and the piety required so rigorous that we need to create religious authorities—priests, imams, theologians—who will be our guides and teachers. Finally, it is these beliefs and the institutions that rest on them that define our religious identity. This one, and no other, is the religion we hold. Any perspective that would lessen the sanctity of revealed truth is a distortion and a temptation. Any suggestion that other forms of religion—Gods with other names, other holy books, other practices—might be just as good or other paths to the divine is heresy. The idea that individuals could decide for themselves whether religion works for them is self-indulgent, sinful nonsense—akin to a passenger telling the pilot how to fly the plane or the patient giving instructions to the surgeon. It is we who must conform to God's truth and to the knowledge of that truth that certain authoritative people have, not the other way around.

To begin with, then, when people say that they are spiritual but not religious, part of what they are saying is that they reject the three closely related ideas just expressed—that any account of revelation is *literally true*, that whatever truth it possesses is the *only truth* of its kind, and that it is not the place of *the individual* to determine whether this truth, of whatever kind it is, works for her. It is not belief in God that is the issue. Many spiritual people, including many spiritual people who do not identify with a particular religion, believe in God. Nor is there necessarily a problem with the sacredness of the scriptures. Many nonreligious spiritual people find inspiration in the Gospels, the Talmud, or the Upanishads (though they also reject many parts of them). In essence, it is not whether the idea of God or the words of the scriptures are true that is at stake, it is the *kind* of truth they have. As Rabbi Rami Shapiro puts it: "The Bible speaks to the imagination in the language of the imagination: parables, poetry, dreams, and myth. It is true without being real, or vice versa. You can speak the truth, without referring to real objects."[6] Another rabbi, this one much more traditionally observant than Shapiro, reassures us we can find "faith without fanaticism" when we realize: "You don't have to be wrong for me to be right."[7]

Let us examine this a little further.

Truth is a common, garden-variety word. If you take an extra cookie and say you didn't, you haven't told the truth. If you admit to the four beers you had before the car accident, you have. If it is true that Abraham Lincoln is dead, the opposite— that he is alive—is false. Most of us believe that politicians and advertisers try to shade, disguise, or hide the truth. If we think only of these kinds of uses of *truth* then either "There is a God who is all-powerful, wise, and good" is true or it is not, and, for example, Jesus is or is not his son, he did or did not dictate the Mishnah to Moses on Mount Sinai, and Muhammad was or was not his messenger. Here we would think of the truth of religious statements as more or less the same as statements about how much a person weighs, the height of the maple tree in the yard, or the price of tomatoes.

But we also use the idea of truth in a very different way.[8] For example, we might say that someone is a "true" friend, that Beethoven was a "truly" great composer, that people have a "true" marriage, or, perhaps most relevant here, that a poem or novel is "true" to its subject. What these uses suggest is that certain ideas— friendship, marriage, music, literature—contain within themselves certain ideals of excellence or quality. A true friend is supportive, responsive, and constant over the years. A true marriage weathers the storms of life, preserves sparks of passion and humor, and supports each partner's best qualities and accepts their limitations. True greatness in a composer is distinct from momentary fame or fashion. Literature is "true" not because it is the opposite of something that is false—what is the opposite of *Crime and Punishment* or *Macbeth?* Rather, literature is "true" to the extent that it has captured something vital and real about the human condition. For example, it has not made its characters unrealistically good or evil, or if they are unrealistic, that tells us something about the way people really are.

In this second sense of truth, while we do think of better and worse, more or less real, *there is no sense of a single, exclusive truth.* If Sally is a really good friend to me, Harry might be a good friend to you, and he might do it very differently than Sally. There are countless ways to mess up a marriage, but there are probably as many to make one work. The fact that Beethoven was truly great does not keep Stravinsky, James Taylor, and Tupac Shakur, with their very different music, from also being great. There are hundreds of great novels, thousands of "true" poems. They are true because they are beautiful, provide insights that help us live better and wiser lives, shape a clearer understanding of our own experiences, and help us learn about the realities of other people's. The true ones are distinct (though we can have arguments about particulars) from ones that are not great, that are "untrue," but nothing keeps us from being instructed by ones with radically different styles written from very different points of view. Loving *The Trial*, or even having your life changed by *Anna Karenina*, says nothing about your relation to other novels.

If you write a poem about a sunset, it might be a good poem or a bad poem. It might capture some of the emotion you felt, connect that emotion to other experiences in your life, and make you look at future sunsets and other parts of the world more closely. But that would not make it the *only* poem you could write about a sunset or make very different poems wrong. Nor would you be betraying something if you said, 10 years later, "That's the way I used to feel about sunsets, but I'm in a different place now."

From a spiritual point of view, the truth of religious teachings is like that of friendships, marriages, music, and poems about sunsets, not like people's height and weight or an accurate list of items in a shopping cart. This sense of truth is not an anything goes, who cares, license to be sloppy. Although there is not just one way to write a really good poem about a sunset, it is still really, really hard to do. However many ways there are to be a good spouse or friend, virtually all of them take some combination of discipline, sensitivity, occasional self-sacrifice, and empathy. Just because there are countless ways to express spiritual truth, that does not mean that just any form of life will do so.

From a spiritual point of view, the test of the truth of religious claims is how well they help us understand and grow into the spiritual virtues, for such claims are only a pale, verbal reflection of a truth that is beyond representation that we must try to represent nevertheless—and that is perfectly fine as long as we realize that the real point is not to *represent* God, holiness, spiritual truth, and the sacred but to *express* the values they embody.[9] If your relationship to the Christian Bible or the Qur'an helps you do that, it is spiritually true for you. But if it does not work in that way for someone else, then the matter is settled. Those scriptures are not for her.

In this sense, a spiritual perspective is far from all-accepting. For example, it denies that any scripture or list of articles of faith could ever be the literal truth and that there could ever be one single accurate description of God. Consequently, using verbal or physical force to promote one's faith is a profound error. How silly would it be to claim that one had found the one true poem about sunsets and how nearly psychotic to compel other people to accept that absurd idea! Any pretension to exclusive truth on the part of a religious tradition betrays a profound misunderstanding of what religious language is for. To be spiritual but not religious is to reject trying to do such a thing.

Spirituality within Tradition

The premium placed on spiritually informed conduct over doctrinal orthodoxy is not just something embraced by people who reject tradition in favor of spirituality but can arise within religious traditions themselves. Some devout members of traditional faiths actually assert that spiritual values are the true essence of their religion and that attachment to verbal creeds and institutional power is a betrayal of, or at least a distraction from, their own faith's true purpose. Here spirituality appears not as an alternative to contemporary religion, but as a current within it. For example, Catholic priest Matthew Fox argued that the church overemphasized original sin and derogated the joy of the original blessing of creation and that it gave men unjust power at women's expense. In doing so, it had diminished its original purpose and therefore was deeply in need of spiritual reform. Traditionally trained Rabbi Zalman Schachter-Shalomi found that the spiritual insights of Orthodox Judaism had significant parallels in Buddhism and was grateful for the way his acquaintance with Buddhism could help make him a better Jew.[10] Neither believed he was renouncing Catholicism or Judaism to become spiritual but not religious but was actually finding way to be a Catholic and a Jew that was more authentic and sacred. They could do so because for them what is crucial is how traditional myths, moral codes, doctrines, and ritual practices lead toward love of God expressed as kindness, humility, gratitude, and so forth, in other words, toward spiritual virtues.[11]

To see how this works in practice, consider spiritually oriented interpretations of fundamental religious narratives—for example, Israel's exodus from Egypt and the crucifixion and resurrection of Jesus. Such interpretations give shape to the spiritually oriented Christianity or Judaism of figures like Schachter and Fox and can easily connect to the Buddhism of Thich Nhat Hanh, the Islam of most Sufis, and the eclectic spirituality of people who are "not religious."

Exodus describes the liberation of oppressed slaves from the most powerful nation on earth, in part through a series of plagues that selectively injure their oppressors and ultimately through a divine intervention to destroy an entire army. In the second example, a beloved, inspiring, and prophetic teacher[12] is brutally put to death only to return to life two days later. Both stories are miraculous events that, if true, reveal the influence of a more than human power.

In response to these narratives, the religious question is: "As contrary to the laws of nature as these events are, did they really occur? And are they the only miraculous events of their kind?"

A spiritual approach is likely to be very different, emphasizing psychological and moral dimensions rather than metaphysical claims about God's power. The Jews' liberation from Egypt might then become a symbol—a metaphor—for our own liberation from internal constraints of greed or fear. The courage the Jews needed to leave the security of Egypt and face the wilderness will be a model for the courage we, too, need to face the inevitable pain and disorientation that comes with spiritual growth. Even if God frees us from slavery, it still takes great courage to embrace that freedom. (One midrash suggests that God's parting of the Red Sea occurred only after the first of the Israelites started to walk into the water. Another commentator tells us that "to make a miracle, it takes courage.")[13]

The resurrection of Jesus provides a model of our own capacity to face great suffering and move to a life that is spiritually richer and more blessed. It tells of the inevitability of despair ("My God, why has thou forsaken me"), the divine value of forgiveness ("Father, forgive them, for they know not what they do"), and the simple embrace of ordinary life that can come with a return to our lives ("Come and have breakfast," said Jesus to his disciples, on his third appearance after his resurrection [John 21:12]). The crucifixion and resurrection teach the value, in popular Catholic spiritual teacher Henri Nouwen's words, of a kind of anticommonsense "downward mobility."

> With great persistence [Jesus] points out the downward way; "Anyone who wants to be great among you must be your servant, just as the Son of Man came not to be served but to serve" (Matt 20: 26–28). The downward way is the way of the cross: "Anyone who does not take his cross and follow in my footsteps is not worthy of me...anyone who loses his life for my sake will find it" (Matt 10:39).[14]

This pattern of suffering, despair, rebirth, and return to life can be applied to any serious human suffering whatsoever: an illness or a divorce, recovery from trauma or from depression. It is human, not solely Christian. That is, perhaps, why Gandhi reputedly wept when he first read of the crucifixion and the resurrection.

Finally, occurring in the spring,[15] accompanied with celebratory symbols of new life (eggs, herbs, etc.), both Passover and Easter connect the human passage toward rebirth and freedom with that of nature.

"But did it *really* happen?" the traditional religious believer demands. "Is there *really* a God, did He free the Israelites with miracles, did he sacrifice His son?"[16]

Here the spiritual response is once again to shift away from the question of objective truth and back to that of whether our lives reflect the essential messages of the stories. If I really believe that God indeed did "so love the world that He gave his only begotten son" to suffer human existence, am I living a life that reflects an awareness of that love and a sincere effort to manifest it in the way I think and act? If God liberated my people from slavery to live in freedom, am I still a slave to my unthinking habits, my conformity to social pressures, my fear of discomfort? Whether these stories are myths or eyewitness reports by reliable observers, whatever the videotape reveals, the task of altering our lives to embody the spiritual meanings of these events remains. This process of sifting through the evidence is so endless, cautions Kierkegaard, that we would be much better off simply forgetting the objective question and concentrating on the spiritual one:[17] not "What is true?" but "How am I living?" And if the spirit of religion tells me that there is no reason to live religiously unless God is real, then the spiritual reply is that virtues are their own reward. Compassion, mindfulness, and equanimity will sooth our spirits and bring us contentment, with or without a God.[18]

Because from a spiritual point of view religious assertions are metaphors, there can be no demands for doctrinal purity or hatred of people who use different ones. Because the purpose of the metaphors is to inspire and guide each of us on the spiritual path, there is no telling which tradition or combination of traditions will have the desired effect on any particular person. Because ritual practices like keeping kosher or taking communion have the same purpose as religious beliefs—to help us develop spiritual virtues—they are necessary only to the extent that they further that purpose.

One implication of this perspective is that although there can be spiritual expertise—and, indeed, the world of spirituality is filled with beloved teachers, guides, and gurus—there can be no spiritual authority. The kind of power generally granted to the priests of any faith is foreign to a spiritual understanding. I very well may seek advice and guidance, especially when I am not sure how to make progress, but only I can decide when I am being helped or hindered by experts and, therefore, which guidance to accept and when to change guides.

"But," the voice of tradition responds impatiently, "you are making your relation to God all about *you*: what you understand, what makes you feel good, what you think is right. This is not faith but self-indulgence. You'll shop around, see what 'feels good,' and then move on to something else—just another version of the mall. *What makes you think you know what is good for you?* It is God who is the center, not your ego. It is God's revealed truth that is the cornerstone, and religious authorities and scripture who will tell you what to believe." Christian writer G. K. Chesterton lamented: "Of all conceivable forms of enlightenment the worst is what...people call the Inner Light. Of all horrible religions the most horrible is the worship of the god within.... That Jones shall worship the god within him turns out ultimately to mean that Jones shall worship Jones."[19] A contemporary Christian scholar and theologian states: "True spirituality, Christian spirituality, takes attention off of ourselves and focuses it on another, on Jesus.... Spirituality is always in danger of self-absorption, of becoming so intrigued with matters of soul that God is treated as a mere accessory to my experience."[20]

As we have seen, spiritual teachers share some of these concerns. Many are aware of the dangers of spirituality as consumption or as pleasure, with its self-defeating attachment to the enjoyable, interesting, or narcissistic. Elisabeth Lesser, who is as eclectic and nontraditional a spiritual writer as one can imagine, warns against a "narcissism" in which "self-discovery eventually leads to plain old self-indulgence."[21]

But the simple fact is that spiritual virtues are strict taskmasters who almost never give you anything easily. To achieve even a modicum of what they offer, we have to renounce the illusion that we can control life, self-concern to the exclusion of care for others, attachment to powerful but ultimately transitory emotions like fear and anger, and the cultivation of a sense of separation from other people and the earth. Such renunciation is enormously difficult. Even though spiritual teachers are sometimes described as content, cheerful in the face of adversity, or joyful, there are numerous accounts of what they had to undergo, endure, and give up to get there. For these reasons, criticisms of authentic spirituality as ego-bound or self-indulgent are simply misplaced.

Once again, it all depends on the context of a particular person's life. Perhaps the idea of Jesus being sacrificed to save me from sin will inspire me to humble gratitude for God's gifts and an eagerness to help others. If I am a feminist, however, it might strike me as a glorification of patriarchal violence that, as in God's command for the sacrifice of Isaac, shows male-dominated religion's affinity for cruelty. Perhaps, like the university professors who transcribed it from immaterial voices, I will be inspired to selflessness by *A Course in Miracles*, with its repeated insistence that "only love is real, all suffering is illusion."[22] Or that idea might seem to be New Age treacle that will evaporate in the face of real human suffering. Perhaps I can learn the importance of charity from the Qur'an's (3:92) caution that "you cannot attain righteousness until you give to charity from the possessions you love," but maybe I will get the point by seeing how every organism in an ecosystem gives to the whole.

With or without a belief in the literal truth of any religious teaching, what defines my spiritual life as authentic, real, or true is not the source—which even most religious figures says demands a certain amount of faith in any case—but my response *to* the source. Whether I am prompted by love for Jesus, obedience to the Qur'an, or simple thankfulness for the existence of nature, I still have to subdue my normal ego's desire to control life, compete with others, and endlessly desire more. I will face times when it is practically impossible to accept my lot in life or when disappointment threatens to wipe out any ability to give anything to others. The difficult choice of acceptance over bitterness and the need to direct my psychic energies toward what I have rather than what I do not have will remain.

Suppose the most extreme event occurs, and rather than just reading the scriptures or hearing the minister preach the gospel, we actually have a direct encounter with the divine—a voice from the sky, a vision of Jesus or Krishna. How are we to know that the experience was really of God and not of the devil (or our own ego) masquerading as God? A voice saying, "I am God" guarantees nothing—no matter how loud the voice is or what vision it might be attached to. No single experience of joy, bliss, contentment, or holiness can prove that the source of the experience is eternal or perfectly good. None of us will be around long enough or have wide enough experience to be sure. The only way to verify a voice as being truly sacred is to see whether it leads us to gratitude, humility, and love.

Finally, consider the spiritual meaning of the legend of Satan—who started out as an angel and had plenty of proof that God existed. But Satan *still* rejected him. We might say that for Satan God did not exist, *could* not exist, because for Satan there was nothing in the universe that deserved complete devotion; and because however much love God was offering, Satan just wasn't taking any in. This message applies to us all: whatever we experience, whatever we are taught, whatever happens to us, what we do depends on our choice. Commenting on a Talmudic verse, a mid-twentieth-century rabbi writes:

> "All is in the hands of Heaven except for the awe of Heaven" (Talmud, Berachot 33b). Awe is generated from a person's deep awareness of the Creator and can only be instilled in a person *if he chooses to instill* it. We see from this that our awe of Heaven is *dependent solely* on us.

Christian C. S. Lewis says virtually the same thing, describing a kind of complete freedom in deciding to open himself up to God's presence: "I could open the door, or keep it shut."[23]

The Dark Side

Spiritual people often say they reject religion—or spiritual teachers within traditions call for drastic reforms within the faith—because the literal, dogmatic attachment to religious truth seems to give rise to so much hypocrisy and violence.

As for the first, there is something almost instinctively revolting about self-defined pious exemplars caught embezzling church funds or having illicit sexual affairs. Less dramatic, but in some ways more undermining, are the unprincipled and self-serving attempts to protect "the church" (of whatever faith). Here the Catholic Church's disgraceful cover-up of priestly sexual abuse may leap to mind as a particularly distressing example of religious authorities guarding their group's public reputation while allowing deeply destructive behavior to continue. But comparable problems occur whenever religions let an interest in wealth or public power shape their policy: accepting a big giver onto the board of trustees while ignoring the way his factories pollute, publicly supporting the war (whichever war it is) to stay on the good side of the government, or declaring—as Saudi Arabia's highest religious official did during the Arab Spring—that Islam forbids street protest.[24] All such actions seem to directly contradict the faith's fundamental moral claims.

It is not that spiritual people, or anyone else for that matter, cannot be weak-minded, inconsistent, opportunist, or just plain nasty.[25] The problem is not that organized religion is imperfect. It is the tension between the claim to have access to the sole and essential truth and the utterly human reality of sexual abuse or support for an imperialist foreign policy. It is posing as the moral model while failing to measure up to minimal moral standards.[26]

Violence may be the most extreme example of religion's failure: from centuries of venomous anti-Semitism to suicide bombers and the racist actions of ultra-Orthodox Jewish settlers in the West Bank, from the seventeenth-century church's sanction of the most brutal forms of colonialism to the nineteenth-century church's nearly complete silence about—and indeed its support for—the oppression of women, and from people who shoot abortion doctors for religious reasons to religious nationalists in rampaging mobs. Organized religion, at least in many of its forms, appears to many to be inherently violent—to be the source, as two historians of religion put it, of a "trail of blood."[27] As the source of so much misery, many spiritual people feel, it should be avoided like the plague.

It is true, but it may not help to point out, that secular philosophies and movements have probably been responsible for more violence than religious causes. Or that in some struggles, for example, the movement to abolish slavery, religious voices took the lead. Nor will it reassure to describe the countless figures, such as Thomas Merton, Daniel and Philip Berrigan, Gandhi, Rabbi Michael Lerner, Thich Nhat Hanh, Judith Plaskow, and Rosemary Radford Ruether, who publicly condemn violent and oppressive tendencies within their own faiths.

Spiritual people who reject religious tradition may reply: "Exactly. Take what helps you from tradition, and don't take what you don't want—or what you think is wrong. It is precisely that freedom to make up my own mind on this matter that makes me 'spiritual but not religious.'" They might add that just because the spiritual wisdom the great traditions possess is so powerful, it is even more alienating to see supposed representatives of those traditions endorsing or ignoring violence and selfishness.

It should be clear from this discussion that the quarrel between spirituality and traditional religion is not about tolerance. It is, rather, a question of what differences will be tolerated and which will not. Because of their understanding of religious truth, spiritual but not religious people typically have no problem with those who describe God or the sacred differently: one God, three, or none; Earth Goddesses or oneness with nature or the wisdom of the Buddha. But there is less acceptance, less tolerance, for violations of essential moral principles. Dogmatic demands for conformity and obedience, violence in pursuit of a religious agenda, the oppression of women,[28] and complete lack of concern for the environment are frequent grounds for criticism or rejection. The focus moves from the metaphysical to the moral, from accounts of God to accounts of what we owe our neighbors, and from ritual conformity to inner experience. From a spiritual perspective, the problem is not that traditional or fundamentalist religion is intolerant, but that it is intolerant of the wrong things.

Two Questions

Given everything I have presented so far, we can see why the current round of antireligious, prosecular atheist writings of people like Sam Harris and Richard Dawkins are not relevant to spiritual values and perspectives.[29] Harris's and Dawkins's complaints—that religion is tied to nonsensical beliefs in the supernatural; demands irrational, unthinking obedience; and compels people to sectarian violence—simply do not apply to what I have been describing. Belief in unseen reality—God, heaven, angels, Kundalini, Purusha—while an essential part of spirituality for many, is not essential to the practice of spiritual virtues. To be spiritual and not religious or to be spiritually religious is to put the majority of one's energy into the virtues, not the metaphysical beliefs. As well, adherence to spiritual beliefs cannot be unthinking because such adherence absolutely requires detailed, meticulous attention to how one applies the virtues in every aspect of one's life. Even if the beliefs are there, they are not the center. And even if they are there, they are held in a way that cannot lead to aggression toward people who do not hold them.

Alternatively, it might be argued against my entire perspective that a generalized concept of spirituality, applying over a vast range of cultures and periods, is hopelessly ahistorical and abstract. Whatever an American Jew turned Buddhist like Joseph Goldstein means by the spiritual ideals of Buddhism, it cannot be the same as that understood by Indian Buddhists two thousand years ago or Tibetans in the twelfth century. Catholic nun Joan Chittister preaches an open, expansive, and often feminist Catholicism that would never have been recognized by traditional Catholic spiritual exemplars like Julian of Norwich or Saint Francis.[30]

This point has some validity. As I have suggested, detachment from tradition and metaphysical belief is what is new about modern spirituality. For the historical reasons described, this innovative cultural form might very well not be recognized—and might in some ways be considered heresy—by many spiritual teachers of past centuries. (To be fair, given some of the statements about openness to difference we saw from Sufi teachers, this might not be true for all of them.)

But there are at least two reasons not to give up the idea that spirituality describes a human aspiration that has been with us at least since the time of Buddha. The first is that while the Buddha and Saint Francis might not recognize the Buddhism of Goldstein or the Catholicism of Chittister, Goldstein and Chittister recognize Buddha and Saint Francis. These contemporary teachers define themselves very much by their relation to their traditions—albeit these traditions interpreted and practiced in new ways. Indeed, if we think of spirituality as a tradition, one shaped by both internal developments and many forms of external social change, then a generalized concept of spirituality makes sense in exactly the same way as do comparable concepts of science, art, or music. Would Newton have understood the paradoxes of quantum physics? Could Rembrandt make sense of Picasso or Andy Warhol? Or Bach of Webern? Probably not. But these later manifestations of science and art are partly the product of the earlier forms. A history leads from the earlier to the later. And despite the radicalness of the shifts between the far past and the present, we generally have no problem including both in our histories of science, art, or music.

Second, in some ways our lives are not as different from those of the Buddha, Rumi, Jesus, or the Baal Shem Tov as one might think. Their societies, like ours, are dependent on the contrast between comparatively limited family groups and larger social groupings of tribe, village, and nation; are structured by hierarchies of economic class, religious caste, ethnicity, and gender; employ technological means (irrigation, metallurgy, pottery, nuclear power) to control nature; have centralized governments that exercise a significant amount of power over local settings; and have cultures that recognize tensions between individual or limited group self-interest and that of the whole. Because of all these commonalities, contemporary minds can resonate with the Buddha's critique of desire, with the Torah's caution not to abuse the weak (to "curse the deaf or put a stumbling block in front of the blind," Leviticus 19:14), or with Jesus' chasing the moneylenders out of the Temple. The problem posed by Plato in the *Republic* 2,500 years ago—whether it is better to be a good man thought immoral or an immoral one thought good—is as current as any politician caught lying in a sex scandal or any corporation covering up its environmental record.[31]

Differences there are aplenty in family structure, the power of our machines, the size of our governments, the degree to which we threaten the environment, the (partial but real) liberation of women, economic and cultural globalization, widespread literacy, and the still unfolding computer–cell phone–microchip revolution. But many things have not changed or not changed so much that the spiritual virtues and the difficulties in living them do not remain constant over the years. Just like people in the Buddha's time, a contemporary meditator has to rein in a restless mind; a moral agent has to choose virtue over vice; when we confront death, we still have to overcome despair; and when we see injustice, we still need to respond without making things worse. The essential tasks of life—how to be kind, good, and wise; how to control one's mind and order one's emotions and desires; how to connect to other people and other species with compassion—still present an essential difficulty that no app-laden cell phone or social media will take away.

Spiritual teachings from over the centuries and around the globe were created to deal with these realities, and such realities are still with us.

6

Practice, Practice, Practice

It is impossible to attain absolute calmness of our mind without any effort. We must make some effort, but we must forget ourselves in the effort we make.

SHUNRYU SUZUKI[1]

When we pray to God we must be seeking nothing—nothing.

SAINT FRANCIS OF ASSISI[2]

AN OLD JOKE: Violin case under his arm, the aspiring musician comes to New York City, hoping to see some of the sights of one of the world's centers of classical music. But he's never been to the big city before and gets hopelessly lost. "Excuse me," he asks an old man at a street corner, "do you know how I can get to Lincoln Center, where the New York Philharmonic plays?" The old man looked at the youngster, at his violin case, at the eager light in his eyes. "Simple," he answers, "practice, practice, practice."

There is hardly any form of spirituality, traditional or contemporary, that does not emphasize the importance of spiritual discipline expressed in the repetitive performance of prayer, meditation, physical postures, activities of service, intensive study of religious texts, chanting, systematic moral self-examination, trance work, or the like. Without practice, Sufi teacher Idries Shah suggests, all we can get from sacred texts and philosophical abstractions is like someone "sending you a kiss by messenger."[3]

The goal of practice is to train our bodies, emotions, and intellect to help us become more focused, self-aware, accepting of and grateful for life, ethically developed, and connected to the world and God. A great deal of this will, necessarily, be done alone. We will have to face down the demons of laziness, habit, distraction, resentment, or hopelessness by working with and literally re-forming ourselves. Yet some paths do place more emphasis on collective practice: praying with a community of believers, studying texts with a partner, or partaking of the vibrant silence that arises when 50 people meditate in a common space.

In this chapter, I examine how practices further the development of spiritual virtues and point out some of their common dangers. For all the immense good yoga, meditation, and prayer can produce, they also contain some very particular risks. On the one hand, practices can give us freedom to overcome emotional self-indulgence and spiritual inertia. Yet they can make us that much more bound up in our own bodies, thoughts, and sense of self. Practices can liberate or enslave. And often they are doing something of both at the same time.

Yoga

Many years ago, when I had already begun my practice of Hatha Yoga, I had a good friend who was into it as well. Richard had been a champion fencer, possessed a strong and flexible body, and was graced with straight blond hair and a handsome face. Yoga was just taking off in the Cambridge of 1972, and someone had the bright idea of a yoga calendar, with each month illustrated by a different pose or asana. Richard had become adept at many difficult asanas and was asked to model for two of the months.

A day after the photo shoot, I saw Richard moving with uncharacteristic slowness, grimacing at each step. "What happened to you?" I asked with some concern. Laughing a little at the irony, he said, "They were having trouble with the lighting, so I had to hold one of the asanas much too long. Hurt my back pretty bad." This kind of irony—in which we use spiritual practices for "spiritually materialistic" ends—abounds in all forms of spiritual practice but perhaps in none so much as yoga.

In its broadest terms, *yoga* literally means "union," as oxen are yoked together to pull a cart, and also the effort used to achieve that union. The term is employed in a wide variety of ways: as a general term in Asian religious philosophy for any serious spiritual pursuit,[4] as the specific Raja ("kingly") Yoga geared to realizing enlightenment through advanced meditative states, and as Hatha Yoga, the physical element in Raja Yoga, alongside its other "limbs" or aspects of nonviolence, moral purity, breath control, and meditation. Raja Yoga was encompassed by a religious philosophy that saw the goal of the overall system as calming, controlling, and ultimately stilling the individual consciousness in order to realize its true nature as unity with the divine.[5] (As far as I know, posing for yoga calendars wasn't mentioned.) The term *hatha* itself is a combination of sun ("ha") and moon ("tha") and reflects the aim of using both asanas and *pranayama* (complicated breathing exercises, including particularly vigorous breaths, alternate nostril breathing, and rhythmic sequences of inhale-hold-exhale) to integrate contrasting but complementary aspects of our physical and energetic selves. When in breath and out breath, left and right, expansion and contraction, and active and relaxed are perfectly balanced, it is taught, the true (and truly divine) nature of the self can emerge.[6]

Rooted in a particular religious metaphysics and typically taught by a lineage of masters to devoted students, Hatha Yoga asanas had no separate spiritual identity until recently.[7] Of the tens (hundreds?) of millions[8] of people throughout the world who are practicing Hatha Yoga now, probably only a small percentage have more than a vague idea of its historical background or the complicated religious philosophy on which it was originally based. Many in the west turn to yoga to relax, stay in shape, lose weight, avoid injury from running or dance, or heal after being injured running or dancing. Yet for others, yoga—even without an encompassing account of the role of the mind in constituting reality, the essential qualities that combine to make up all manifest entities, the distinction between the true self and the mind, and so on—is something more than a series of physical movements. Practiced with spiritual intention, it supports awareness of the interplay of body, breath, emotions, and thoughts.

In particular, yoga promotes a spiritual response to the body, one generally absent in today's society. For the most part, our society views the body as a center of pleasure and desire, an object of display, and something of which to be proud or ashamed. The body is for performance, as in the impressive feats of professional athletes, and for sexual advertisement and enticement, as in rock videos. Because it almost never measures up, it needs special clothes, makeup, diet, and plastic surgery. Further, until the recent development of mind-body or integral approaches to medicine and psychology, the body was typically thought of as distinct from intellectual and emotional life.

Hatha Yoga offers an alternative: an experiential exploration of the body in movement and stillness, a narrowing of attention to the moment-to-moment sense of what the body is doing and what it feels like, and a conscious use of the breath to support both movement and rest. These aspects of yoga can be practiced with or without an acceptance of yoga philosophy. But they also take us away from the body beautiful version of yoga and our own tendencies to compete with those who are stronger and more flexible or to push ourselves (just like any runner who thinks yoga is for sissies) to injury.[9] Although yoga in and of itself is no guarantee of spiritual progress, it can be a vehicle for that progress. If it sometimes lends itself to overuse and vanity, it can also cultivate inner calm, awareness of the relation between physical and emotional states, and genuine appreciation for our physical existence.

Since almost everything we do, we do with our bodies, the balance and bodily awareness stressed by Hatha Yoga can play a key role in spiritual development. Even speech is a form of bodily action; even an e-mail requires us to move our fingers across the keyboard. Every emotion is felt in the body, and every expression of emotion is a bodily response: the clenched fists of anger, the twisted lips of grief, the too rapid speech of anxiety. If I can learn to move into a forward bend slowly and gracefully, finding the precise point at which I am sufficiently stretching my back and hamstrings, I can extend that awareness to how I drive my car, sit at my computer, or chew my food. If I can be aware of the ego-oriented self-congratulation that arises when I can—"at my age"—still do the crow (supporting my entire body on my hands as I lean forward from a squat), I can extend that same awareness to how much ego is invested in my writing and teaching. If I can do a series of poses deliberately and calmly, I can go through a day of errands and meetings the same way.

Relating to our bodies in an aware, disciplined, and uncompetitive way is no small spiritual accomplishment. Desperate attempts to accomplish physical feats or achieve some ideal body image are in and of themselves the antithesis of spiritual development. A mindful yoga practice can lead away from those distortions.

In addition, yoga (like Chinese-based tai chi and chi kung) is rooted in a theory of the relation among body, physical health, and consciousness. This theory describes energy pathways (the *nadis*) and centers (*chakras*), the relation of physical and emotional health to the balanced flow of energy through these pathways and centers, and how particular exercises help create such a flow. Insofar as spiritual life is not simply a matter of ideas, morality, and meditative states, insofar as the human reality is always grounded in our physical existence, Hatha Yoga can sustain the practitioner in the spiritual quest in a very significant way. Just as it is unlikely that one can manifest spiritual virtues when one is drunk or extremely sleep deprived, so it is much more likely, or at least supportive of, the spiritual virtues to have body, breath, and mind that are strong, balanced, and relaxed. The actual practice requires, as one of the most influential of modern teachers puts it, that you "become completely and totally absorbed, with devotion, dedication and attention, while performing the pose....The asana has to enshrine the entire being of the doer with splendor and beauty. *This is spiritual practice in physical form.*"[10]

And so...here I am on my yoga mat at 6:32 A.M., beginning my daily practice. At my age, I generally do not wake up feeling fabulous, and given the range and severity of health problems in my family, not to mention my own neuroses, morning often sees me mildly depressed, anxious, and burdened by responsibilities. I move onto my hands and knees and start to flex my spine—arched, rounded, arched, rounded—breathing deeply through my nose in time with the movements, with a slight constriction in the back of my throat. This is the *Ujjayi*, or "victorious," breath that, according to one teacher, "aerates the lungs, gives endurance, soothes the nerves and tones the entire system."[11] Gradually, I move into a series of postures called the sun salute: standing tall, bending forward, into a push-up position, arching my back up, then lifting my hips up while my hands and feet remain on the floor. By now my breathing is deeper, my movements more energetic, and I can feel the fog slowly lifting from my brain. My body's essential energy—called *prana* or *chi* in Indian or Chinese traditions, measured by brain waves, respiration, heart rate, circulation, and blood pressure in the west—is more vigorous and focused. I feel more grounded—less compelled to produce and less fearful of not having enough resources to do what I have to do.

As the practice continues—standing asanas to stretch my shoulders, thighs and groin; balance poses; later a headstand to bring blood to the brain and twists to freshen the blood in the spine—my awareness takes a number of different forms. *Here* I move habitually, without much concentration, my mind back to focusing on the day's demands. *Here* I am evaluating the practice: how far can I stretch toward my toes? how long have I held the headstand?—comparing myself to some mythical ideal of "better" and feeling alternately pleased or dissatisfied, depending on how well I have performed. And *here,* my mind from time to time simply melts into the practice: moving through and holding the poses, adapting my breath to each shape the body takes, fully aware of the interplay of strength, flexibility, and limits—where I can push my boundaries and where I need to recognize that I've gone as far as I can. I also usually do two *pranayama* exercises: bellows breath is a series of forced, sharp inhales and exhales; *nadi shodanah* (literally "channel cleansing") involves alternating nostrils and a precise ratio between inhalation, holding the breath, and exhalation. An awareness of breath and a variety of ways of organizing it is one of the critical ways in which Hatha Yoga is different from other forms of exercise. This emphasis expresses the basic idea of many forms of meditative practice that the breath is intimately related to consciousness.[12] Calm, even breathing signals a calm, even mind, and the reverse is true as well. To the extent that a person can shape and alter her breath at will, she will have developed some of the corresponding control over her thoughts.

And so it goes, until the day's practice ends with the corpse posture—on my back, arms and legs fully extended, eyes closed, and breath slowing to a crawl, as the energy I have raised circulates through my body, and my mind, blessedly, simply shuts off for a few minutes.

As with every spiritual practice, some days are better—or at least easier—than others. Sometimes the embodied concentration is practically impossible to maintain, as my mind jumps from doing the poses well to whether I can finish the chapter in my new book to concerns over my daughter's upcoming medical appointment. Other days, I am more fully at home in my body and fully present to the moment-to-moment experience. No matter what kind of a day it is, however, I can always learn something: what is on my mind, how far or near I am to being at peace with whatever is going on in my life.

There are other dimensions to the practice. Reminding us of the spiritual interpretations of scripture discussed previously, some teachers read asanas as expressions of emotional states and spiritual challenges. In their version of the practice, doing the postures with awareness can contribute to psychological integration and spiritual development. Consider, for example, Swami Sivananda Radha's account of *salamba shirshasana*—the headstand, in which the body is inverted and supported on the forearms and the top of the head:

> In this posture, familiar surroundings are seen upside down. This may cause some unpleasantness, different emotions—even fear...comfort and security are challenged....You may find yourself thinking—What would happen if my life were turned upside down?...Raising the feet in the air, surrendering the security of the earth....It is such an unaccustomed posture...that it demands full attention to maintain....When you take a normal position once more, having explored the reverse position fully, you will have discovered that basic nourishment comes from higher sources.[13]

John Friend, originator of Anusara Yoga, which combines a spiritual attunement to emotions with a distinctive understanding of proper alignment, shows a similar orientation when he instructs budding teachers on how to lead a class in the standing pose Warrior I (one foot three feet or so in front of the other, back foot turned slightly out, front knee bent, back leg strong, arms raised overhead):

> First present instructions that inspire a particular attitude or heart quality (e.g., courage...resolution, acceptance). Then give postural instructions that connect the attitude to the alignment and action of the inner and outer body.... "To do Warrior I, standing with one leg in front of the other, arms raised over the head, with a slight arch to the back: 'Relax and open up to a bigger power that surrounds you and is inside you. Exhale and release any feelings of weakness or powerlessness. This greater power completely supports you....Take a deep inhalation, lift your chest, knowing that you are able to tap this source of limitless power.'...With every inhalation, lift up from inside with a warrior's courage. With every exhalation, soften inside with humility."[14]

Even further afield, teacher Michael Stone suggests that the animal names of many asanas (e.g., cobra, scorpion) indicate a shamanic dimension. As shamans encourage aspirants to go into various forms of trance (prompted by fasting, drumming, or drugs) to connect to other life forms, so yoga students were seeking to relate with the animal aspect of their psychic reality. In each case, an experience that is radically different from the normal ego can teach us the limited and relative nature of our conventional sense of self and serve as an "exploration of the internal workings of mind and body in order to become free of the personal patterns that obscure free and easy awareness." In addition, yoga scholar Christopher Chapple argues that identifying with animals in asana can promote a sense of empathic connection that may further the fundamental yogic value of nonviolence in our treatment of them.[15]

It is true that any physical discipline, from biking to karate, can be done mindfully and with attention to the symbolic emotional dimensions of the activity. The now classic book *The Zen of Running* suggests: "This experience [of running] is a newly discovered form of meditation—or one more way for you to discover you" and that one can run "in a state that is just as meditative, perhaps more so, than when sitting Buddha-like."[16]

Yet as a single-motion, repetitive exercise, running does not balance the body and therefore does not provide the grounding and centeredness of a comprehensive system of physical health like Hatha Yoga. Nor does it define itself by the kind of mental awareness that is essential to asana practice. In the words of an Indian yoga teacher: "In yoga we try in every action to be attentive as possible to everything we do.... As we perform the various asanas we observe what we are doing and how we are doing it.... If we do not pay attention to ourselves in our practice, *then we cannot call it yoga*."[17] Unlike manuals for running or weight lifting, most books on yoga and virtually all of the modern classics that have helped shape the dramatic growth in interest in the west over the last 40 years stress the spiritual aspects of the practice. While most of their pages may describe and picture asanas, there are always significant sections on morality, meditation, and enlightenment.[18] Your average everyday yoga class in your average everyday yoga studio tends to begin and end with some meditative focus and some prayerlike acknowledgment of peacefulness, compassion, or acceptance. *Yoga Journal*,[19] for all its consumerist ads and lovely models, has regular articles on spiritual virtues like awareness, gratitude, and service. Comparable expressions are simply not found in cultural contexts like bike races or the leading jogging publication, *Runners World*. Further, engaging with the moral dimension of spirituality, efforts now exist to connect yoga practice to social involvement. The Green Yoga Association, oriented in particular to environmental issues, offers the goal of "spiritual activism for the planet." In a response to poverty, AIDS, and women's rights, "Off the mat and into the world" seeks to "use the power of yoga to inspire conscious, sustainable activism and to ignite grass roots social change." A new film chronicles the feminist dimensions of contemporary yoga practice.[20]

Of course, it is only if a person wishes to understand her yoga practice as Friend and Radha do or intends asana practice as part of spiritual development that it can have spiritual effects. One can usefully do asanas just for health. But any and all religious activities can be done for nonreligious reasons. We can say the daily prayers of Judaism simply to please our parents, give alms only because we want others to think us generous, and study holy texts to prove that we are smarter than other students.

At the same time, if my yoga practice makes me healthier and calms me down a bit, I still need to ask: what are my health and equanimity for? Does this spiritual practice make me a calmer, more rested, and more focused drug dealer? crooked lawyer? narcissistic housewife? What is the larger context of my life in which my practice arises?

This is the central question not only of yoga but also for any form of spiritual practice. The fact that I can do a serene and single-minded headstand for three minutes means little in and of itself, any more than that I can sit on a meditation cushion for thirty minutes thinking only about my breath. It is not an accident, after all, that these activities are called *practices*. When we do them, we are only *practicing*, in artificial and isolated settings, mindfulness, acceptance, compassion, or love. The crucial task is to bring the qualities these practices have taught us to being stuck in traffic, sitting with our parents as they die, dealing with our wayward children, or responding to social injustice.

Prayer

"I say a little prayer for you," goes the old pop song. "He who has learned to pray has learned the greatest secret of a holy and happy life," writes eighteenth-century English theologian William Law. "God speaks in the silence of the heart. Listening is the beginning of prayer," counsels Mother Teresa. And our old friend Kierkegaard cautions us: "Prayer does not change God, but it changes him who prays." Prayers may be voiced in anguish or wrapped in silence, mumbled dutifully or constructed with care, put to melody or tears. They can be wordless, as Rabbi Abraham Joshua Heschel said that when he marched for justice with Martin Luther King Jr., "my feet were praying." Or as the Hasidic Rebbe Pinchas of Koretz reportedly counsels, "When things are so bad you cannot even recite psalms just sit and hold whatever it is up to God in silence."[21]

There are set prayers that children learn by heart: the Lord's Prayer, the 23rd Psalm, the five-times-a-day prayers of Islam. There are Native American chants, Buddhist meditative formulas asking that "all beings be happy and free from suffering," and the Serenity Prayer of Protestant theologian Reinhold Niebuhr that gets many an alcoholic through the night ("God grant me the serenity to accept the things I cannot change, the courage to change the things I can, and the wisdom to know the difference"). There are prayer services in which dozens or even thousands say the same words at the same time. And there are intensely private times when out of desperation or joy some words come unbidden to our lips. Indeed, virtually all forms of spirituality involve some form of verbal plea, promise, or focus.

What is the spiritual meaning of prayer? It is, we might say, the yoga of the heart. In less poetic terms, it is a way to express and shape our *emotional* lives to a *spiritual* form. Think for a moment of all the occasions on which we pray, what we are doing with our prayers, and what they do for us.

- To express devotion and gratitude
- In the hope that we will have health, material well-being, contentment, and peace
- That those we love be safe and happy
- To celebrate the coming of spring or the birth of a child or to mark the death of a beloved parent
- That we ourselves will be more honest, brave, kind, and grateful
- Amid the chaos of war, a hopeless illness, the devastations of addictions or natural disaster

In these times, what we want or feel or hope for are paramount: burning desires for peace or healing, an indescribable anguish of the soul, fear or joy. And at these times, the act of prayer helps harness the unruly energies of desire and emotion into a direction that can serve us spiritually, that is, can help channel our heart's longings into a spiritual direction.

How is this possible?

A spiritual understanding of and response to emotions walks a complex and often difficult path between two contrasting dangers.[22] On the one hand, there is the risk of repression. We so want to live spiritually, and we understand this to mean always being accepting, kind, and generous. We seek to maintain a God-oriented stiff upper lip, the imperturbable meditative calm of a Buddha statue, the rebbe's ability to find God in everything. As a consequence, we either deny our actual emotions and cravings or treat them like enemies.

However, unless we are fully enlightened beings (and chances are we aren't),[23] we will have plenty of petty resentments, self-centered desires, and nagging fears. Our spiritual progress will be impeded if we deny these parts of ourselves, for then the unacknowledged or repressed emotional energies of anger, lust, or anxiety will express themselves in other ways: physical symptoms, substance abuse, irritability, aggression, or a numbness that can result, Kierkegaard suggests, in a "derangement of feelings" that consists in "not having any."[24]

Acceptance (not indulgence!) of our emotions is therefore spiritually essential. Yet this is not the same as uncontrollably acting them out, which is the second great danger spiritual teachers counsel us to avoid. Our desires do not have to force us to act or, when frustrated, lead to resentment and bitterness. Anger can be experienced without resulting in verbal or physical violence. Despair need not drive us to suicide or depression. Instead of mindlessly reacting to our emotions, we can mindfully observe them.

Our task, in spiritual psychologist Miriam Greenspan's words, is to "befriend" our emotions, to accept them as an ineluctable part of our lives, rather than either exiling them as sinful and weak or mindlessly obeying them. As natural beings, we want things—and when we do not get what we want, we are frustrated or disappointed. We are vulnerable to loss, which causes us grief. We need other people and the earth, and isolation from them or their illness and death will inevitably cause us pain.

And here is where prayer comes in, for prayer is a way of focusing our emotional energy, of giving verbal form to the rush of feelings that is coursing through our bodies and leading to compulsive patterns of thought, and of organizing our desires into positive spiritual energies. Untreated grief can lead to bitterness over what's been lost, a lonely sense that no one has suffered as I have, a persistent sense of meaninglessness. Our yearning to be kinder or more accepting can be no more than a fleeting wish. Even joy, awe, or deep peace sometimes seems so overwhelming we do not know what to do with it.

When our desires and emotions are translated into prayer, however, something else can happen. Those who believe in God can share their misery with the very source of life and goodness. They can feel that someone is listening, even if she makes no reply—someone who cares about us but is so full of power and goodness that our suffering is no threat. Unlike all those who cannot bear our distress, God has endless resources of compassion with which to hear us. Weeping and wailing, we can let it all hang out.

In prayer, the joy we feel can be shared not as an ego-centered experience of "I got mine," but with a sense of deep appreciation for the wonder of life. Instead of simply relating our pleasures to our own desires or ability to manipulate the world, we acknowledge with gratitude a source of existence—the God of religion or the miracle that life exists at all—that is larger than our own selves. Joy then can become a gift that encourages us to generosity.

If it is our wish to be morally stronger, prayer offers a focused expression of that wish. It can help mold the typically muddled, inconsistent wish to be a better person into a focused, disciplined intention to become one. Having prayed to God to be more accepting or less wasteful, we are more likely to take the next steps to accomplish the psychological or practical work we need to do to get there. It is one thing, after all, to have the passing thought that "I ought to be less angry or more grateful." It is another to say this directly to God.

None of this means that prayer can ever guarantee any particular outcome. The vast amount of suffering that has been inflicted on innumerable prayerful victims of war, neglect, and injustice indicates that whatever God is, he is not a vending machine where prayers go in and answered wishes come out. And in any case, whether "God answers prayers" (with the answers we've asked for!) is not a spiritual question. Prayer is spiritual not because it gets us what we want, unless what we want is to develop our spiritual virtues. Prayer is spiritual because it helps us become more accepting of our suffering, more loving to others, and more faithful to the tasks we have been given (incurable illness, a painful divorce, poverty) without succumbing to bitterness.

Here's an example from my own life. The Hebrew *sh'ma*—"Hear O Israel, the Lord our God, the Lord is One"—is a prayer I say every morning and at services at the Reform Jewish temple I frequently attend. As a person whose belief in the traditional concept of an all-powerful personal God is, to say the least, minimal, what am I doing when I say these words?

For me, religious or spiritual faith means faith that *this* life, with its pains and losses, its oppression and desecrations, is worth living; that despite everything, the good outweighs the bad; or, if such a measurement is impossible, that I choose to value what is beautiful even if there is so much that is vile and deadening. But to value existence in this way, I need first to see it in its totality—as the "one" that is sacred and that may be called "God." To see *that*, I need be as aware of death camps as I am of beautiful sunsets, of children starving in the Sudan as much as new babies on my block, of all the species humans have wiped out as much as all the wondrous life-forms that remain. To affirm the holiness of life in the face of what we might call "evil" (for how else to describe pelicans suffocating in spilled oil, women raped and then hacked to death?)—that is the challenge of the *sh'ma*. And so when I chant the words of the prayer, I try to bring into my mind at the same time both evil and the wonders of life: children dying in refugee camps, the song of the robin, my wife's beautiful eyes, the latest statistics on pollution-induced cancer. And as these contrary images and the feelings to which they give rise pulse through my soul, I affirm, have faith in, the whole— the One.[25]

This may be easily described, but I find it very difficult to do. How much easier it is to focus on one or the other—on the good to feel unmixed joy and gratitude or on the bad to sink into anger or despair. But to separate them out is to deny the oneness of God and of this life that I have been given.

This kind of reflection can be extended to any serious prayer. If a devoted Catholic implores "Holy Mary, Mother of God, pray for us sinners," he will have to feel the truth of what he has done wrong and his need for forgiveness—without excuses, minimizing, or denial. If a devout Muslim repeats five times a day "I bear witness that there is none worthy of worship except God," the task is to make sure that he is not worshipping money, power, sexual pleasure, or even the satisfaction of being especially holy. A Hindu may ask of the God-head: "From the unreal, lead us to the Real; from darkness, lead us unto Light; from death, lead us to Immortality." And then in every situation, her spiritual task will be to choose the real and the light, rather than the illusory goals or dark pleasures so available to us.

If this is what prayer requires, then learning how to pray is, as Kierkegaard counsels, "a task for a lifetime":[26] to mean the words as we say them, go through the mental activity the prayers call for, and then choose honesty over self-deception, faith over despair, God and spiritual truth over pleasure or social status when our prayers are done.

Finally, truly spiritual prayer is never a zero-sum game. We cannot pray to win the lottery, the football game, or the promotion at work, because if we win any of these, someone else will lose. We can pray for what we want only if what we want are spiritual virtues: to be kinder, calmer, more compassionate. We can pray for health, for peace, or that all beings (including ourselves) be happy. These gifts take nothing away from anyone else.[27]

Prayer can be addressed to a supreme being or to our better selves, the vast energies of life, images of loved ones, or spirits of inspiring teachers. What makes the words into prayers is not to whom they are addressed, but the seriousness with which we take them. I can vow to stop drinking so that my rages against my family go away, promise myself I will be a kinder man, or sing out my gratitude that trees grow, birds fly, and my eyes still work. If I attempt to put my whole soul into these utterances, they are prayers.

I realize that in its lack of emphasis on the need to address prayer to God I am contradicting some theistic accounts. Adin Steinzaltz, one of the world's leading Orthodox Jewish teachers, states: "Prayer is a direct and unequivocal act of relating to God…direct speech, in which man [sic] confronts and addresses his Creator."[28] Similarly, Seyyed Hossein Nasr, widely respected scholar and exponent of Islamic philosophy and Sufism, claims that the higher levels of spiritual development are not possible without a relationship with God:

> One has to live according to one of the traditions, one of the religions which God has revealed. I do not believe that wholeness, in the higher levels of the meaning of this word, and as it gradually becomes synonymous with holiness, is possible without the door having opened from the heavenly side towards humanity.[29]

In their emphasis on the metaphysical connection rather than the spiritual one, these two wise and learned men reveal a flashpoint of difference between a traditional religious approach, no matter how sophisticated and broadminded, and a spiritual focus on self-transformation that may invoke God for oneself but would not dream of legislating his necessity for others. These statements also, to say the least, shut the door on nontheistic traditions like Buddhism, Taoism, Wicca, or a spiritual connection to nature. All of these can embrace the mystery of prayer, for the purposes I have described, without invoking a single, divine creator.

Meditation

For years, it was a standing joke between my wife and me. As the normal insanity of marriage, work, and child raising combined with the somewhat abnormal insanity of raising a child with multiple special needs, we would periodically become overwhelmed. She would get increasingly obsessive, anxious, and controlling; I would become emotionally distant, irritable, argumentative, and physically clumsy. As we became aware of the pattern unfolding yet again, we would laugh and say ruefully, "We ought to meditate more." Both of us were knowledgeable about different types of meditation, both of us had reaped its benefits many times over, and both of us too often let the practice slip away.

Those benefits are ways of channeling unruly energies and self-destructive mental patterns in a spiritual direction. As Hatha Yoga is to the body and prayer is to the heart, meditation is to the mind. Our thoughts, many spiritual teachers assert, are instrumental in creating our reality. Angry thoughts create an angry reality; jumpy thoughts create a disconnected, often fretful reality; selfish thoughts create a reality of endless, usually unsatisfying, self-concern. Systematic meditation is a way of forging a personal psychic reality that reflects spiritual values rather than conventional structures of greed, fear, or isolation, a way of training our thoughts to support, rather than undermine, our spiritual health.

The value of meditation is rooted in the fact that although our thoughts shape our lives, they themselves are malleable—capable of being ordered, focused, put on hold for extended periods, or simply witnessed with detachment. If a part of our selves believes and wants and fears, there is another part that can learn to observe ourselves believing, wanting, and being afraid. If we often obsess on trivia, or worse, we can teach ourselves to focus on other things: God, gratitude, love.

The two main dimensions of meditation are awareness and focus. In practices like Buddhist vipassana,[30] there is really no immediate goal except awareness. Concentrating on the breath and on the range of physical and mental sensations that arise when we no longer try to think about anything in particular, we develop a detailed knowledge of how our minds work. What thoughts keep appearing, no matter what else is going on? What patterns are we using to define the world for ourselves? How many of any of these really make sense—and how many are simply unthinking, irrational, even destructive habits?

I first learned to meditate in my mid-20s, when I studied Kundalini Yoga. After an hour of intense physical postures with even more intense breathing exercises, the class would sit in a traditional half-lotus meditation posture (cross-legged, with the right foot on top of the left thigh) for 15 minutes, mentally repeating a mantra ("Sat Nam"—roughly "truth name") on the inhalation and exhalation. I have never been particularly flexible, and even after 40 years of yoga, I'm on the tight rather than loose end. So after about six minutes of one of these meditation sessions, my left hip started to feel first stiff, than painfully tight, and then almost unbear-ably strained. Being the goal-oriented "good student" (not to mention competitive) person that I am, I wasn't going to move until the teacher ended the session. My muscles and joints screaming in agony, I was going to do what I had set out to do, no matter what.

When the teacher ended the class and I gratefully unfolded my tortured legs, a (no doubt obvious to anyone else) thought struck me like a thunderbolt: this was simply how I lived much of my life. Set a goal, define my self-worth in terms of meeting it, and damn the consequences. Surely the teacher wouldn't have minded if I had shifted position or even if I told him I needed to sit in a chair. No one cared but me, and I cared because that is the way my mind works—and that way of working, while it had its benefits in terms of self-discipline and getting things done, could also be unnecessarily painful and, in the long run, at times very self-destructive. It would often lead to pushing myself far beyond my capacity, with all the negative consequences of injury, depression, or too much vodka that would inevitably follow.

I did not magically overcome this basic feature of my character that afternoon. In fact, I've wrestled with it ever since. But my experience of that day clearly showed me what I was doing with my mind—how a reality that presented itself to me as inescapable and rock-solid was simply a fabric of my own making.

"A mind," went an old advertisement for the United Negro College Fund, "is a terrible thing to waste." The slogan would work well as an ad for meditation. A mind without the ability to reflect on itself, to monitor its own activity, is likely to end up wasted. Most of the foibles the spiritual virtues are meant to allay can be traced at least partly to a lack of understanding of what we are doing with our minds.

The other major dimension of meditation is focus—concentrating the mind on a thought or image, a desired virtue (kindness or humility), or a sacred figure (God or some beloved and inspiring teacher). Here "what kind of person do I want to be?" becomes for a time the question "what do I want to think about?" And so a Christian might meditate on an image of Jesus—perhaps a face of love and perfect forgiveness or as he was preaching a parable or blessing a repentant sinner. A Jew might take one line, or even one word, from a familiar prayer. Rabbi Marcia Praeger has written an entire book exploring the meanings of each of the words that introduce Jewish prayers of blessing—"Blessed are you O lord our God, master of the universe."[31] A Muslim could concentrate on Allah's infinite compas-sion—or on the fundamental Islamic idea that Allah is greater than any human conception of the divine.

Or consider this exercise, from a less familiar source.[32] Taoist meditation, as taught by Thai teacher Mantak Chia, is a series of exercises that begins with simple affirmations of one's worth by visualizing a smiling face directed at all parts of the body and moves into more complicated forms in which emotions, organs, energy pathways (as defined by Chinese medicine and used in acupuncture), senses (sight, hearing), sounds ("shhh," "whooooo"), and evocative imagery (a child, a dragon, etc.) all work together to invoke physical, psychological, and spiritual balance.

In this particular fusion practice, we begin with some slow, calming breaths and then visualize a Pa Kua (a circular yin-yang sign surrounded by a nested set of octagons composed of trigrams, a series of three lines either whole or broken, each having particular meaning); next imagine Pa Kuas placed below the navel, opposite that on the back, and above each hip. Then we begin a series of mental exercises in which a sound is used to activate a particular organ, a particular sense is directed toward that organ, the particular negative or troublesome emotional energy associated with that organ is collected at a particular spot and then funneled to a Pa Kua, and the corresponding positive energy, and its associated color, are brought into the organ.

For example, in Chinese medicine, anger is rooted in the liver, the liver is associated with vision and the color green, and the positive alternative to anger is kindness. So we begin by subvocally making the liver sound, "shhhhh"; then we direct the eyes internally toward the liver; focusing on any anger we are carrying, we let the angry energy drain to a point above the right hip; last, we bring a rich green color and the energy of kindness into the liver. After performing similar exercises for the kidneys (fear replaced by gentleness), lungs (grief by courage), heart (hastiness, impatience, and cruelty by love), and spleen (nervousness by openness and fairness), we mix ("fuse") the various negative energies through the Pa Kuas and circulate the resulting fused energy in the "microcosmic orbit"—a pathway that begins just below the navel and continues down past the groin to the perineum, up the spine, over the skull, and down through the face, neck, chest, and abdomen.

I am describing fusion at length because it so different from what most of us think of as the essential form of meditation. It is not one thing—an image, the breath, a single-worded mantra—held with as little mental motion as possible. Rather, it is a long, detailed process involving sensory images, emotions, thoughts, and the mental movement of energy throughout the body. If it is, as someone once jokingly said to me, meditation for obsessives, that just illustrates the point that spirituality has something for everyone. Even more, it indicates the essential truth that meditation is not tied to any particular form, but by a resolute commitment to align the contents of one's mind with the spiritual virtues.

Indeed, while vipassana meditation is the best known and most widely taught form of Buddhist meditation in the west, there are actually dozens of other Buddhist forms. For instance, if a student is obsessed with sexual desire for a particular person, he might be told to concentrate on an image of the desired person's body—but of the inside rather than the outside, or of what that body will look like in a hundred years. To make sure the lesson of my own mortality is before my mind, I might be instructed to meditate in a graveyard; if someone has trouble staying awake during practice, she might be placed on the edge of a deep well. There are Buddhist meditations on complicated visual patterns known as mandalas, on chanted sounds, or on *metta* ("loving-kindness"): a simple repetition of "May (all beings, I, my wife, an enemy, etc.) be happy, be at peace, be free from suffering." And although they may not be so central to religious practice, Judaism, Christianity, and Islam have large meditative resources as well.[33]

Like yoga with the body, like prayer with emotion and desire, meditation expresses a spiritual alternative to conventional values and goals. In opposition to the hyperactive and overly reactive consciousness of contemporary culture, the meditation teacher advises: "Don't just do something, sit there! Do you have angry thoughts, physical pains, or burning anxieties? There is no need to respond; simply watch them come and go."

Perhaps even more striking, Tibetan Buddhism offers two practices that completely overturn our usual response to things we do not like. In Tonglen ("giving and taking") meditation:

> You give away your happiness, your pleasure. Anything that feels good. All of that goes out with the outbreath. As you breathe in, you breathe in any resentments and problems, anything that feels bad.... Usually you would like to hold on to your goodness. You would like to make a fence around yourself and put everything bad outside.... *The main point is to develop the psychological attitude of exchanging oneself for others.*[34]

The visualizations of Chod ("cutting off"), a twelfth-century practice aimed at dissolving a sense of the reality of both evil and the ego itself, are even more dramatic. Originally practiced in graveyards to the accompaniment of trumpets and drums made from human bones, Chod asks practitioners to imagine their own bodies cut apart and offered as food to threatening and desperately hungry demons. Initially seen as independent beings, the demons are later understood as manifestations of the meditator's own mind.[35] In all these cases from vipassana to Tonglen to Chod, the ego's typical response to life—act, separate from, defend—is challenged. Alternative perspectives produce the liberating experience of not being driven by narrow self-concern or fear of negativity.

Of course, sometimes meditation might just help us relax. If I am so tied to my thoughts that they will give me no rest, the ability to watch them and thus to separate from them can be a profound relief. If my anger or grief feels out of control, Taoist fusion's exercise of focusing on them and then replacing them with more positive emotions might feel like a blessed respite. But relaxation and emotional uplift in and of themselves are not the goal of spiritual life. We may relax before going on a bombing run—as the pilots who were taught Transcendental

Meditation (focus on a mantra or sacred sound) during the Vietnam War may have done. We may relax on the meditation cushion and then return to a life of ostentatious consumption or arrogant privilege.

Like yoga and prayer, meditation is an element within, and not the defining heart of, a spiritual life. It gives us knowledge of ourselves and teaches us to be attentive to our thought patterns. It can underscore our wish to follow God's teachings or to feel our connections to life. But its ultimate value depends on what happens once we stop meditating and go on to our other activities and relationships. Does greater awareness of my pattern of compulsive accomplishment make me more able to refrain from pushing myself or others so much? Can I replace anger with kindness when my wife or a colleague doesn't reward me for all my hard work? Can I take the calmness of an hour of focusing on meditative music into my next doctor's appointment, even if he has bad news? For someone else, the question might be: Does the love I feel after concentrating on Adonai, Jesus, Allah, or Vishnu shape how I deal with a difficult in-law or face my money problems?

In the World

Ancient teachings are very clear on how essential and difficult meditation is. As Nagarjuna put it, "Without the discipline of guarding the mind, what use are any other disciplines?"[36] And in the *Bagavad Gita* (6:34), Arjuna laments that the mind is "more difficult to control than the wind." But whatever spiritual aspirants faced 2,000 years ago is nothing compared to the chaos of today's media-saturated, cell-phone-using, computer-based, iPod-wearing, six-CD changer in the car while driving, 227-channel satellite radio (slogan: "everything, all the time") using, Facebook and Twitter always in touching, fragmented, and often downright nutty mental state. We are blessed and cursed with choices and information, overwhelmed by a glut of interesting, engaging, enticing stimuli. We are trained to go fast, faster, fastest; to respond to all the offers before us; to be online, in touch, and up-to-date. Calm, quiet focus is simply not on the agenda.

Almost without exception, this media invasion is profoundly unspiritual. Even in purely psychological terms, ADD and ADHD have reached epidemic proportions. Reliance on multitasking is both compulsive and, many studies have shown, unproductive and inefficient.[37] If we cannot slow down and reflect, we simply cannot get a critical distance on the life we have been leading and the values we have been taught. If we cannot focus our minds, we cannot overcome the behavior or beliefs that are damaging us, even if we want to.

And so while it has always been of great importance in virtually every religious tradition and many contexts of eclectic spirituality, meditation is even more important now. History has changed our daily lives, moving meditation from being desirable, useful, and helpful to absolutely necessary. We *all* ought to meditate more.

And in desperate enough circumstances, when people are willing to confront their internal sources of unhappiness, practicing meditation can profoundly change the way they experience their lives—and therefore the way they live them. Consider these descriptions from participants in an intensive 10-day course (11 hours of meditation a day, starting at 4:30 A.M., in a residential setting, with three highly experienced instructors) in vipassana meditation in 2002:

> "My life was in constant turmoil. But when I took the Vipassana course, it changed my thinking. . . . I can now say that I am okay with my situation spiritually and mentally. I still struggle, but I am not so caught up."[38]

> "I now feel a wholesome attitude in my life. I previously couldn't get there. I couldn't feel it. I didn't have it. Now I feel it. Something has changed in me."[39]

> "Vipassana has offered and continues to bring peace of mind to me, even and especially in times of seemingly total despair. I've learned to adjust my way of thinking to a life as it is, and not as wanted."[40]

The remarkable thing about these reports is that they do not come from what we might think of as the usual suspects. These are not middle-class alternative types from some liberal college town who search out exotic spiritual practices and bring their cloth shopping bags to Whole Foods. These are inmates at Alabama's maximum-security Donaldson Prison, a place for men convicted of murder, armed robbery, drug dealing, and rape. These statements and dozens more can be found in the fascinating account of teaching vipassana in this setting, *Letters from the Dhamma Brothers*. In 2002, after extensive preparation by prison management (including, remarkably, sending several of its staff to take a 10-day meditation course in Massachusetts to familiarize themselves with the process) and commitment by 20 of the world's more unlikely meditation students, the 10-day process began.

The technique was based in the classical instruction of Indian Buddhist S. N. Goenka. For three days, the students were simply to focus on the place at the base of the nose where breath enters the body. And then, when a modicum of balance and ease had been achieved, they were to mentally sweep through the body to notice any and all sensations, thoughts, or emotions. They were not to judge what came, but simply be aware of it.

Some of the men had earlier experiences with meditative and self-awareness techniques, and some had not. They were all serving very long sentences for very serious crimes, many with no chance of parole. Almost all had suffered their own traumas before they turned criminal: physical, sexual, or emotional abuse, abandonment, desperate poverty, racism.

The Alabama experiment followed other entries of meditation to prison. Goenka had brought it to India's most violent and intimidating prison in 1975, with remarkable results. A minimum-security facility in Washington had a similar positive experience. Films about those experiences were shown so often at Donaldson that some of the students had literally memorized them.[41]

Meditation retreats require great discipline. The physical demand of 11 hours of sitting a day is itself an enormous challenge. Except between students and instructors, conversation is not allowed. Most important, the students had to face the contents of their own minds and be willing to apply Buddhism's basic values of self-awareness, acceptance, and compassion to themselves. Throughout the course, the powerful, intimidating men would come face-to-face with decades-old grief, guilt, regret, and unfettered rage. After years of projecting hypermasculine toughness and invulnerability, many openly wept.

This letter is from a man facing life imprisonment for a series of drug and burglary crimes, sent to prison authorities in support of the program:

> It ain't easy, being "face to face" with your own reality. Each student must face their own mental formations and start realizing the attachment that brought them suffering with painful entanglements. But as you continue to practice…these barriers start to dissolve. There is then a radiant sense of happiness with a freedom from the addictive attachment that brought suffering; then comes courage to be at peace with the truth as your reality and with the sincere wish for happiness and wellbeing of others.[42]

The Donaldson experience reveals many common features not only of meditation but also of all spiritual practice. Most important of these is the fruitful tension between social support and individual commitment. The religious tradition that made the practice available originated millennia ago and had to be taught and maintained over the centuries. Although the barriers to making it available to prison inmates are unusually steep, almost every practice any one of us might learn has come to us through a process of collective human creativity and transmission. It is the rare spiritual genius who thinks up something new—and even that will always be based in earlier forms and techniques.

As well, and crucially, the students, teachers, and supportive prison staff created a novel social setting, one in which previously alien norms of behavior, belief, and expectation were the rule. Physical aggression, emotional withdrawal, and fierce individualism gave way to peacefulness, emotional openness, vulnerability, and sincere interpersonal support.

Finally, a shared set of beliefs through which the process of meditation could be interpreted was necessary. The moment-to-moment experiences could be used by the prisoners only if they had some broader framework in which to understand them. Buddhism provided the framework at Donaldson. In other places and with other practices, it might be some other religion or less formally organized spiritual convictions. Spiritual practices, no matter how powerful the experiences they offer, do not stand by themselves but are always surrounded by beliefs about what they mean and why they work.

All aspects of this new social reality were essential to the creation of a new personal reality, but the core of the process was the commitment and just plain hard work of each single person: to sit, *again*, for another 90 minutes; to be witness only to one's own mind, with no physical movement, mental distraction, conversation, book, or TV; to experience every wrenching memory of abuse, each devastating, self-inflicted loss. All this took enormous courage and faith—in the process, the ideas behind it, and ultimately in one's own capacity for change. The faith is keyed not to God or heaven, but that one's present tortured reality can give way to something else. Ultimately, this is the element of faith that spirituality demands— that another life is possible.

As the experience of the Dhamma Brothers shows, the practice gave what it promised. The inmates developed greater self-acceptance and control, more feelings of peace, less bitterness and isolation. Among vipassana students, recidivism is significantly down, and the quality of their behavior in the prison is way up. Their reality, externally so unchanged, has been transformed by a deep spiritual shift within themselves. Above all, they learned, as S. N. Goenka said when he joined them on the final day of the course, that "deep inside everyone is a prisoner of his unwholesome behavior patterns at the depth of the mind."[43]

Beyond the Self, Within the Self

In one of the earliest accounts of Buddhist meditative practice, a monk tells a fellow seeker that he has had an experience of Nirvana—of the end of suffering and indeed of personal identity itself. "During that time," he says, "I had no sense of 'I am this, this is mine, this is my self.'"[44] Throughout the centuries, many people have reported the dissolution of personal identity through spiritual practice and mystical experience. A person feels filled with light and bliss, one with God, or part of nature's infinite play. Such mystical encounters can be the foundation of a deeply spiritual life. As possible fruits of spiritual practice, they represent a powerful contrast to the decidedly unspiritual experience of our ordinary mind of individualism, consumerism, competition, and group hostility. Most of the time, we are *very* aware that "I am this" and what is mine; do not even feel united with an inefficient coworker or a noisy neighbor, let alone the infinite play of nature; and think ourselves as "part of" an ethnic group, family, or the fans of a sports team a good deal more than God.

In just this way, the experiences generated by spiritual practice—meditation that dissolves the ego, fervent prayer in which we lose ourselves, intellectual contemplation, or physical movement of the body or voice—can remind us that the daily routine of desires, frustrations, and attachments are not all we are.

By contrast, Judaism offers the *Mi Sheberakh* ("may the one who blessed"), a prayer that asks for healing "of the body, mind, and spirit." When we think of our own health problems or those of family members, friends, or even inspiring public figures, we say a *Mi Sheberakh* for them. Or consider something as simple as the Lord's Prayer, which asks for "daily bread" and forgiveness. In such prayers, which may be among the most heartfelt of spiritual utterances, there is no attempt to transcend our ordinary mind or conventional social position. We do not see ourselves as filled with light, but as parents trying to endure our children's suffering. We are not conscious of ourselves as divine, but as people who have trespasses that need to be forgiven. We remain firmly fixed in our usual identity, and there is no question of our being anything but what we are. All we can hope is to acknowledge our limitations before God so that we can improve without being racked by guilt or sooth our fears about someone's health so that anxiety and grief do not damage our ability to function.

On this spectrum, meditation tends (though not always) to be on the first end and prayer (though not always) on the opposite side. The widespread idea of single-minded focus that is frequently part of a meditative exercise naturally leads, if only during the practice itself, toward an experience of the eradication of social identity. Prayers, so often an embodiment of powerful emotions and intense yearnings, are typically more tied to our everyday selves.

Yet there are many ways in which these two dimensions can connect. Chanting can begin in emotion and gradually eliminate the sense of self. In the most personal forms of prayer, the words themselves can morph into psychic realities in which our egos lose themselves. Alternatively, we might focus on the most abstract of mantras or mandalas, only to find compassion for suffering or acceptance of our daily lot. An intense yoga practice that begins with a comparatively impersonal sense of bodily movement may trigger long-suppressed and intensely personal emotions.

In this way, all forms of spiritual practice contain within themselves the double demand of the spiritual path: on the one hand, we are instructed to rise above ordinary mind, relationships, and forms of life. On the other, it is also taught that spiritual life is simply a kinder and gentler version of the perfectly familiar. And of course, given the enormous variety of personality types, cultures, social situations, and time of life, different people will tend to connect to different points on this spectrum. There are people for whom spirituality is modestly rooted in being a little more compassionate and self-aware; there are others who will taste the heady elixir of the dissolution of the ordinary self into the divine or the cosmos. Some will expect only that they will increase their patience and compassion. Some will hope that they will feel God's presence.

Is It a Spiritual Practice?

There are many other practices people often associate with spiritual life: tarot cards, the *I Ching*, psychic readings from people who claim access to extraordinary sources of knowledge, the use of crystals or distillations of flower scents (the Bach Flower remedies, aromatherapy). If some descriptions of vipassana meditation seem to verge on psychotherapy (dealing with repressed material, coming to accept one's hidden feelings), these activities lean toward the occult: a deck of cards that will give you life advice because the cards reveal a hidden reality that somehow the cards understand, rocks with healing power undetectable by scientific methods.

Such practices are thought of as spiritual, I suspect, in the sense that they are not defined by a scientific or technologically mechanical understanding of the world or the self and often use a vocabulary centered on personal development, psychological transformation, inner awareness, and the search for equanimity.

From my point of view however, taking advice from cards or a book, no matter what their cultural style, are in and of themselves no more inherently spiritual than consulting a competent dentist or financial planner. These, too, may involve listening to experts and may, if they really are experts, make one's life healthier or more success-ful. Do what your dentist tells you, and your teeth will last longer. Get a good planner, and your retirement prospects will get a little brighter. Yet in any of these cases, if the response does not involve a positive effort toward spiritual virtues, it is not spiritual.

Still, crystals and tarot are not necessarily unspiritual either. It all depends on how they are used. Consider, in particular, the tarot—an ancient card collection divided into major and minor face cards and four suits somewhat analogous to the modern playing card deck. Each card has a rich, evocative image, and while there is some vague similarity in the way the particular cards are represented in the hundreds of different versions that exist, there is enormous variation. The fool, the queen, or the seven of swords might be a person, a geometric design, animals, flowers, or objects, in any one of countless artistic styles. As well, the written guide that accompanies the deck to explain the import of each card will bear the personal stamp of a particular tarot teacher. The emphasis could be on women's liberation, our relation to nature, Christian faith, or psychological growth.

The tarot is most often used as a tool of divination. A seeker raises some par-ticularly important question about how to understand or deal with his life; he or an experienced card reader lays out some of the cards and "reads" their meaning. At which point a reasonable question arises: how could a bunch of cards tell me how to live? Whatever someone thinks the cards mean, why should I take their meaning seriously?

Consider this advice from Joan Bunning, a noted creator and interpreter of tarot decks:

> Meaning is a truly mysterious quality that arises at the juncture of inner and outer realities. There is a message in everything...trees, songs, even trash...but only when we are open to perceiving it. The tarot cards convey many messages because of the richness of their images and connections. *More importantly, tarot readings communicate meaning because we bring to them our sincere desire to discover deeper truths about our lives....*
>
> If there is a meaning in a reading, where does it come from? I believe it *comes from that part of ourselves* that is aware of the divine source of meaning. This is an aspect of the unconscious, yet it is much more. It acts as a wise advisor who knows us well. It understands what we need and leads us in the direction we need to go. Some people call this advisor the soul, the superconscious, or the higher self. I call it the Inner Guide because that is the role it plays in connection with the tarot....
>
> When you reach for your tarot deck, you signal to your Inner Guide that you are open to its wisdom. This simple act of faith allows you to become aware of the guidance that was always there for you.
>
> We are meant by nature to rely on the wisdom of our Inner Guide, but somehow we have forgotten how to access it. We trust our conscious minds instead, and forget to look deeper. Our conscious minds are clever, but unfortunately, they just don't have the full awareness we need to make appropriate choices day by day...
>
> When we know how to access our Inner Guide, we...have the certainty and peace that comes from aligning our conscious will with our inner purpose. Our path becomes more joyous, and we see more clearly how we bring together the scattered elements of our lives to fulfill our destinies.
>
> I use the tarot because it is one of the best tools I have found to make the whispers of my Inner Guide more available consciously. The ideas, images and feelings that emerge as I work through a reading are a message from my Inner Guide. How do I know there is a message, and it's not just my imagination? I don't, really. I can only trust my experience and see what happens.
>
> *You do not really need the tarot to access your Inner Guide.*[45]

Spiritually speaking, the crucial concepts here are the ideas of meaning and wisdom. The seeker is spiritually oriented because she is trying to find some significant insight into how she ought to be living. She is questioning the norm, the habitual, the taken for granted. And she is oriented to answers that will lead her where she needs to go. But "needs to go" for what? For inner tranquility, long-lasting happiness, and unselfish joy, in short, the spiritual virtues and what they offer. If this is the orientation of the seeker, however, she still will have to make the difficult choice to give up the short-lived but very tempting pleasures that are the opposite of wisdom and inner peace. While the cards may focus her attention on serious questions, enable her to understand her spiritual tasks more clearly, and crystallize her aspiration for spiritual development, they could never substitute for the work this change requires. Properly interpreted, they may give excellent spiritual advice—but so might a competent meditation teacher, priest, rabbi, sensitive friend, empathic therapist, or wise book. I find the tarot, filled with archetypical images that can be taken to mean a host of insightful things about relationships and life choices, valuable at times. Certainly, if I get a reading that reminds me to beware of my tendency to focus on work and responsibilities at the expense of my inner life, a morning's use of the cards can prompt me to up my daily dose of meditative introspection.

In just this way, the truth or reality of tarot cards and of what Bunning calls the Inner Guide, together with other instances of semioccult practices, are very much like belief in God. Whether the divinity is real and is even calling me, I still have to respond to that call, determine what the message is, and decide whether a godly life is what I really want. And this decision must be lived out, or God's reality, no matter how cosmically true, means little for me. The same goes for all the good advice of a tarot deck, the crystals that promise to aid my inner healing and grounding, or the soothing smell of organic, wild-crafted, lavender aromatherapy oil.

7

Why Now?

WHAT IS THE source of the enormous interest in spiritual ideas, values, and practices in today's society?

It is, I believe, the failure or, at best, very partial success of many of society's leading values and authorities. There is widespread disenchantment with consumerism and the market, science and technology, professional expertise, organized religion, and reformist political movements. In terms of other historical developments, an interest in spirituality is also a by-product of religious pluralism. On the whole, spirituality's emphasis on psychology and morality over metaphysics matches a widespread cultural trend away from, in one historian's words, "the metaphysical and cosmological" in favor of "the human, the historical, the empirical"[1] and is part of what philosopher Charles Taylor calls "the massive subjective turn of modern culture"[2] away from roles, duties, and rules and toward a focus on "how people experience their personal lives."[3]

Limits of Wealth

Perhaps most important, there is the simple fact of the poverty of affluence. The enormous range of consumer goods, the remarkable powers of the new technologies, our longer lives and bigger houses and ease of communication—these are not making us happy. Instead of calm enjoyment, we are gripped by ever increasing desires only temporarily satiated by new purchases. The Christmastime orgies of consumption leave a lingering sense of emptiness. Obsessions with career success and wealth never seem to be placated. Instead of the promised happiness, we find varieties of despair—which may turn to panic as the structures of consumption are threatened in a persistent economic downturn and we are forced to work harder for less.[4] Those doing "well," simply getting older, or seeing how splendid McMansions and neurotic discontent coexist may wonder if all these possessions and powers can really bring us anything but the most fleeting of pleasures. In the words of one commentator, we may come to realize that we are "rich, free, and miserable."[5]

Most long-term studies of America show a general decline in satisfaction and a rise in boredom, anxiety, and depression. The need for—or at least the use of—psychiatric medications (which some believe to be contributing to rather than alleviating our emotional ills) has spread from adults, through adolescents, to grade-schoolers. This phenomenon is not limited to the United States. China's meteoric rise in wealth has seen a corresponding rise in depression and suicide.[6]The World Health Organization projects that by 2020, depression will be the second leading cause of health-related problems in the world.

Spirituality has always been a response to suffering. From Buddha's promise of an eightfold path that will lead to the cessation of misery, to the 23rd Psalm ("Though I walk through the valley of the shadow of death, I will fear no evil"), to present-day spiritual promises to relieve our anxiety or grief, it is the task of spirituality to lead us to a more contented life. Yet in earlier centuries, many sources of suffering seemed inevitable: widespread poverty, high rates of infant mortality and women's death in childbirth, the vagaries of weather or crops, infectious diseases, and political domination. These realities have been greatly mitigated in the developed world and among the rising middle classes in the developing nations. Yet instead of widespread happiness, we have the reverse. Thus while it is not hard to connect the emotional distress of the poor, underfed, and oppressed to their social situation, how do we explain it among the comparatively well-off and socially respected?

When emotional suffering goes along with historically unprecedented material wealth, the basic premises of spirituality seem to be confirmed. If, in Bill McKibben's phrase, "more no longer equals better," the quintessential spiritual question—what is a truly good way to live?—comes to the fore.[7] And thus the global market, touted by its supporters as the only rational way to organize economic life, comes into serious question. Above all, the market defines people as consumers and producers and makes the center of human relationships a monetary exchange aimed at bettering the lives of disconnected individuals. The result, many argue, is that the winners of this exchange end up with lives of rich emptiness, the losers are ground into poverty, and nature is irrevocably damaged.[8]

In response, tens of millions of people, sometimes termed "cultural creatives" or holders of "postmaterialist, expressivist" values, tend to reject at least some of the dominant values of wealth, power, and status in favor of more spiritually oriented values of time for friendship and family, love of nature, practices of self-reflection, and the pursuit of inner meaning.[9] They seek an economy based in local, organic, self-sufficient, limited, sustainable consumption, in which values of modesty, connection, compassion for all of life, and self-awareness shape work, recreation, family, and use of the physical world. Their sense of reality, spiritual social activist Charlene Spretnak suggests, is based in an essential sense of interrelatedness, rather than in autonomy and separation.[10]

Authority, Diversity, Freedom

Serious doubt has also been cast on the adequacy of science, technological development, and the general goal of the domination of nature, thus creating further
openness for spiritual insights. This doubt is particularly significant because science and technology, many social theorists believed, would eradicate religion's
social influence and usher in an era of human contentment. Instead, we have seen
gas chambers, the hole in the ozone layer, gushing oil leaks at the bottom of the
Gulf of Mexico, and infants born with a 190 toxic chemicals in their bloodstreams.
Experts in engineering, social policy, medicine, and psychology fail to solve problems from heroin addiction to ADHD, childhood depression to global warming,
or their projected solutions create new problems.[11] In medicine, frequent revela-
tions show that touted treatments for illnesses are not working or have disastrous
side effects and that the original research that justified the use of tens of billions of
dollars of new medications was inadequate, slanted, or consciously misrepresent-
ed.[12] Earlier in the last century but still relevant for those on the political left are the
scientific pretensions of Leninist Communism, with its ideal of central economic
planning managed by experts to usher in a golden age of freedom and happiness,
which instead led to political dictatorship and economic collapse.

Such failures open practical space for knowledge based not in objectification
and domination, but in self-awareness, empathy, and introspection—the basic
stuff of spirituality. In a variety of forms—humanist and feminist therapy, positive
psychology, holistic medicine—models of health and well-being deny the adequacy
of objectification and emotional detachment typically valued by a culture rooted in
paradigms of traditional natural science and technological control. Ironically, positive psychology, which offers itself as a scientific and empirical method for studying and attaining human happiness, employs several spiritually oriented words in
its basic self-description, including *love, forgiveness, spirituality*, and *wisdom*.[13]

Since the 1960s, there have been other profound changes in attitudes toward
authority, all of which create further space for spiritual alternatives. Activist movements challenged racism and sexism, aggressive foreign policies and the use of
nuclear weapons, colonialist or communist tyranny. A global movement—often
with a strong spiritual aspect—has been calling for a global response to the environmental crisis. All in all, since that time, "The notion of institutional moral
authority would...remain a problematic, precarious ideal, more often interro-
gated than not and never taken for granted again."[14] While the consequence is not
always a spiritual turn, at times it is.

Comparable resistance to "the establishment" was common within institution-
alized religion itself. There was the watershed, near-revolutionary Second Vatican
Council (1963–64), which introduced elements of self-criticism and openness to
the value of other faiths; Jewish Renewal's call for an increase in spiritual intensity

within a moribund Judaism; the passion for a personal encounter with God of evangelical Christianity; and the social commitment of engaged Buddhism. All these demanded a more personally authentic, deeply felt experience and practice of faith.[15]

Even within the progressive or radical political community, one that since Marx had been generally (though far from exclusively) antireligious, there developed a growing interest in the merging of political and spiritual ideas. Some activists were struck by the failures of secular radicalism in the world socialist and communist movements and the general tendency for radical groups, after an initial high tide of enthusiasm and effectiveness, to degenerate into in-fighting, verbal or physical violence, self-interest, and dogmatism. The lessons of political campaigns led by explicitly spiritual leaders like Gandhi, King, and Latin American liberation theologians were studied not just for their tactical success but also for their embedded values of nonviolence, respect for the opponents, and attention to the spiritual maturity and care of the activist.[16] Spiritual values, it turned out, might be essential to beneficial political change rather than a distraction from it.

Some political activists also came to see that spiritual traditions could aid in responding to pain that is not caused by injustice and requires acceptance rather than struggle. The birth and growth of children, the death of parents, the pain of debilitating illnesses—such experiences can be overwhelming if we do not approach them with the spiritual resources of patience, mental and emotional clarity, and compassion for ourselves and others. These are essentially spiritual virtues, which people who are trying to change the world for the better need as much as anyone else.[17]

There was as well an increasing experience of religious diversity, one that struck American consciousness more strongly in the 1950s than ever before. In the face of this diversity, many self-consciously religious people accepted the spiritual premise that there were numerous paths to the divine.[18] Within religious diversity, it was easy to find shared spiritual virtues. Gratitude, generosity, humility, and compassion were valued by all religious groups.

Finally, the spiritual freedom to pick one's own path to the sacred reflected a capitalist marketplace geared to consumer preference. In religious scholar Robert Wuthnow's words, people now "seek" for spiritual truth rather than simply "dwell" in an established and settled religious community and identity.[19] It is no accident that more than half of self-defined religious people in the United States report that they changed their religion at least once or that alongside a countermovement of fundamentalism stressing religious orthodoxy, there has grown up within organized religions themselves a vital interest in experientially oriented practices like meditation and spiritual retreats.[20]

Confronting all these limitations of a society based in the dominant worldview, people are now asking a series of questions that challenge that view: What if, beyond a certain basic level, happiness is not connected to wealth? What if the market is no longer a basis for social progress, but a source of alienation and exploitation? What if self-knowledge, family, and community are more important than shopping? What if in some way we must respect nature besides using it? What if healing requires self-awareness and a holistic reorientation of beliefs, emotions, and the body as much as it needs medical authority? What if progressive political change has to include spiritual insight and discipline? What if the essential meaning of religion is the cultivation of a loving heart, not the acceptance of certain descriptions of God? Answers to these questions are taking many forms, but a significant percentage lead toward the spiritual ideas described in this book.

PART II

Why It Matters

Spiritual life is a personal choice. As separate individuals, people find charismatic teachers or inspiring texts and discover that they can be calmer and more loving (or a little less miserable) if they are compassionate and mindful. As well, it is one of spirituality's hallmarks that it is often disengaged from the constraining world of organized religion, orthodox creeds, and even, in many cases, a defined community. Although people may get solace and offer support to others on the path, the ultimate guide is the individual's own sense of spiritual progress. Further, when we seek a spiritual life, we separate ourselves from a good deal of society's common beliefs and pursuits. The central values of spirituality oppose those of the marketplace, the nation-state, the army, and the football field. The disciplined pursuit of mindfulness, acceptance, gratitude, and loving connection (as opposed to career success, comforts just for my particular family, wealth, or really tight abs) is a distinct form of life—one that stands out from, and against, the rest of social life.

This, at least so far, is the dominant message of this book.

In part II, the focus shifts dramatically. Here we look at three universal human realities: the worlds of illness and healing, of nature, and of politics. No one can choose to always be well; to be disconnected from air, water, earth, and other life forms; or not to be part of the collective ways in which we distribute social power, status, property, and rights. In part II, we will see that spirituality matters not only because it helps individuals face their personal suffering but also because it has something positive, perhaps irreplaceable, to offer in these wider contexts. It is an important resource for health, it can help heal our connection to nature at a time when nature faces unprecedented threats of humanity's own making, and it offers a distinct approach to political change—even as it is itself changed by politics.

8

Spirituality and Healing

WHAT IS A spiritual approach to healing, and why does it matter? Consider some examples.

- Psoriasis is a painful and disfiguring condition in which large patches of skin turn red and are covered with gray scales. It is thought to be caused by an autoimmune system disorder that leads to the overproduction of skin cells and produces extreme itching and discomfort. One treatment for psoriasis is exposure to ultraviolet light. For brief but frequent periods, patients in a hospital setting are stripped naked, except for protective goggles, and exposed to special lamps. Treatment side effects include drying the skin, burns, nausea, headache, itching, and even skin cancer.[1] Jon Kabat-Zinn of the University of Massachusetts Medical Center, one of the pioneers of the medical use of mindfulness meditation, wondered if psoriasis patients might be helped by learning how to meditate while undergoing the treatment. Initially, the goal was simply to enable patients to face the difficult process in a more relaxed and focused way. Yet what Kabat-Zinn and his colleagues found was that for patients who had learned the basics of meditation and who practiced it during their treatment, their "skin cleared on the average much more rapidly than in the case of non-meditators—in many cases as much as four times as rapidly."[2]
- Many army veterans returning from Iraq and Afghanistan suffer from a variety of stress-related psychological and physical problems. Often grouped under the heading of posttraumatic stress disorder (PTSD), these problems may include insomnia, sudden and uncontrolled anxiety, disorienting flashbacks, and physical pain. In the face of this serious problem, Air Force Major Jon Greuel, a flying instructor and certified yoga teacher, teaches yoga to active-duty military personnel in Iraq. The goal, Greuel says, is to develop proactive stress management to avoid developing posttraumatic stress disorder: to teach effective strategies to enable our troops to transition more easily from battle-ready, in preparation or response to a threat, back to a normal state of arousal once the requirement for vigilance has passed. Yoga has also been

employed in programs for vets in Florida, Massachusetts, and Wisconsin.
The "Yoga Warrior" method, says its creator from central Massachusetts,
"integrates concepts from yoga therapy, traditional yoga philosophy, psychology, and sensory integration theory with current scientific knowledge of the
body and mind to promote health and well-being." Many of the vets who have
been through the postwar yoga program report less physical pain, emotional
reactivity, and insomnia.[3] Sue Lynch, vet and yoga teacher in the There and
Back Again yoga for veterans program in Charlestown, Massachusetts, claims
that "Yoga is calming.... You develop the ability to feel safe and in control,
to be aware of what's going on. If you feel an intensity of sensation in your
body, you can work with it. You don't have to take it on if it's overwhelming."
Paul Zipes, an experienced Navy diver, has been teaching yoga to veterans in
Florida. One of his first students was a returned soldier who had seen multiple deployments in Iraq. "He saw bad stuff," said Zipes, and "had been in
therapy for injuries and stress, physical pain and insomnia." A week after his
first class, the vet told Zipes that "he had the best night of sleep in a couple
of years." Despite a slew of medications for sleep and anxiety, "nothing made
him feel as good as yoga."[4] "Real men, combat-weary guys," says a Vietnam
vet and counselor, learn from yoga that "to be aware and to be mindful is the
solution to many of their problems."[5]

- Sat Bir Khalsa, assistant professor at Harvard Medical School and director of
  research at the western Massachusetts yoga retreat center Kripalu, believes
  that yoga "may contribute to benefits above and beyond those provided by
  traditional therapies." The Department of Defense has taken claims of people
  like Lynch and Khalsa seriously, funding a 10-week study of the effect of yoga
  on veterans.[6]

- A female cancer patient, diagnosed in her mid-50s, spends months frantically searching for a cure. Despite her best efforts, it eventually becomes
  clear that the illness is terminal. Yet one day she turns up at her therapist's
  office, her face expressing a dramatically different emotional state than her
  earlier desperation and fear. "I'm going to die pretty soon," she tells her therapist. "But I'm okay. I'm better than I have ever been in my life. I'm healed."
  The therapist reflects: "I have often seen people go through a similar series
  of phases: shock, a mad search for a cure, and the acceptance. More than
  that, the illness does something positive for them. They find strength and a
  depth they never had before. People," he suggests "are sometimes *healed by
  their illness*."[7]

- A couple's 11-year old daughter suffers from a host of medical problems: devel-
  opmental delay, partial deafness, loose ligaments and joints, muscle weakness,
  metabolic and emotional disorders, asthma. Worst of all, she has a severe and

worsening case of scoliosis, a curvature of the spine so great that if unchecked it could eventually destroy her ability to breathe. The orthopedist has all but insisted on surgery to fuse the vertebrae of the spine, but the potential consequences of unsuccessful surgery include paralysis and death, and the surgery's outcome is questionable in any case. So the family has taken on a complicated and demanding alternative program of nutritional supplements, exercises, wearing a back brace 23 hours a day, extensive chiropractic care, and electrical stimulation of the spinal muscles. The father (along with his work) is frantically managing the program, while his wife is taken up with endless phone calls to doctors, therapists, and insurance companies, managing the daughter's activities at her special school, earning a living, and parenting their other child. At times, the daughter is actively engaged in the back program, but after a while, the stress, discomfort, and out-and-out pain become too much. The father becomes increasingly demanding, pushing his daughter to comply with the regimen. Periodically, the two of them dissolve into screaming conflict. The mother takes her husband aside. "What are you doing?" she asks, compassionately but firmly. "I have to get her to do the program, or else," he replies grimly. "Or else, what?" "Or else we'll have to do the operation—and from that, she could die." "Well," his wife answers, looking directly into his eyes, her love for her daughter and for him shining in her face, "then she will die."[8]

These examples reveal three different dimensions of healing. First, the problem of illness itself: physical or mental malfunctioning or abnormalities in conditions such as cancer, arthritis, diabetes, substance abuse, and Alzheimer's.

Second, there is the question of a person's understanding of and response to her illness. Is there any way to stave off the anger, grief, and depression that would seem to be the natural response to chronic pain, incapacity, and untimely death?

Third, there is the role of the caretakers who are serving the sick and trying to help them heal. While this category includes everyone from hospital staff to the daughter caring for her aging mother to the daughter's (hopefully) nurturing psychotherapist, I focus here on parents of children with special needs. Of all caretaking relationships, the parent-child relation is the one where the idea that as parent I must guarantee the well-being of another person is often taken not as pretentious overreaching, but as a basic norm.

Let us look at each of these contexts in turn to see if spirituality in the form of practices like Hatha Yoga and meditation and attitudes such as mindfulness, acceptance, gratitude, and compassion can help us heal. We will also ask: To the extent that they help, are they still spiritual? And when they are part of the healing process, do they change the meaning of healing itself?

Spirituality in Integrative Medicine

There are many names for it: complementary, mind-body, alternative. The one that seems to be sticking now is "integrative medicine," defined by a consortium of 46 of the nation's most prestigious (Harvard, Johns Hopkins, Duke, Columbia, Vanderbilt, etc.) medical schools as "healing-oriented medicine that takes account of the whole person (body, mind, and spirit), including all aspects of lifestyle. It emphasizes the therapeutic relationship and makes use of all appropriate therapies, both conventional and alternative."[9] For example, along with medical treatment and advice, Duke University's Integrative Medicine offers "mindfulness meditation, nutrition, supplements, acupuncture, movement and exercise, therapeutic massage, and mind body techniques." Their staff includes teachers of mindfulness-based stress reduction, yoga and massage therapists, and an exercise therapist who believes that "understanding the complexities of motivation, emotion, and spirit are critical in order to achieve optimal health."[10]

Such offerings are widely repeated elsewhere. Mindfulness-based stress reduction, in which Buddhist vipassana meditation is used to aid patients suffering from everything from high blood pressure to diabetes to depression, is taught in more than 250 hospital settings. Hundreds of clinical studies of the effects of yoga and meditation have been undertaken—and many more are underway. Some insurance plans support yoga classes and meditation as tools of illness prevention or wellness. Even teams of the National Football League, whose players routinely go from magnificent physical specimens to limping patients, have hired yoga teachers for prevention and rehabilitation.

Why do yoga and meditation help us heal?[11] If I have high blood pressure, which puts me at risk for heart disease, if my immune system doesn't function very well and I get a lot of colds, if I have poor digestion, chronic neck pain, or suffer from the effects of chemotherapy to treat my cancer or medications for AIDS, why would sitting in a cross-legged position on the floor (or in a straight-backed chair) and focusing my attention on my breath do anything for me?

A too simple answer is that my ego is making me sick, or my ego is making me sicker than I need be and is limiting my recovery. Anxiety, selfishness, constant anger, unexpressed grief, and despair, together with a lack of awareness of these, are bad for my health. Sometimes, indeed, they can be lethal.

Yet for a long time most of western medicine and much of the common sense of our culture was predicated on the idea that beliefs, emotions, and physical health were unrelated. We assumed that it is the mind that believes, wants, and experiences emotions and that our bodies digest food, move around, and have beating hearts and painful bunions. To better understand the dynamics of illness and healing, this presupposition that cognitive, emotional realities and physical ones are separate has been reexamined. Now we know that there is an intimate and powerful connection between the mind and the rest of who we are.

Sometimes the connection is comparatively unimportant. If I have a toothache, blisters from too-tight hiking boots, or a skin infection, I can probably do just fine without altering my mental processes at all. A competent root canal specialist, bigger boots, Band-Aids, and antibiotics often do the trick. In contexts like infectious diseases, emergency medicine, dental restoration, and orthopedic surgery, western medicine has had remarkable success, often without paying any attention to our beliefs or feelings.

Yet in other contexts, the model of body-mind separation is dramatically limiting. The track record of standardized medical treatments for back pain, insomnia, depression, allergies, and high blood pressure, to name but a few, is problematic at best. Some symptoms are resolved for some people, many symptoms are not resolved for many, and the standard medications often have dangerous side effects. It is here that we may speak of the need for "treating the whole person," "holistic health care," "mind-body medicine," "participatory health care," and "integrative medicine." It is here that changing the way we think and feel can dramatically impact the course of an illness.

As we have seen, meditating can significantly improve as simple and seemingly mechanical a treatment as sitting in front of UVA lights for psoriasis treatment. A growing body of research also suggests "meditation may be an effective intervention for cardiovascular disease, chronic pain, anxiety and panic disorder, substance abuse, dermatological disorders, reduction of psychological distress and symptoms of distress for cancer patients; and reduction of medical symptoms in both clinical and nonclinical populations."[12]

Yoga, taught as a combination of asanas, breath control (*pranayama*), and meditation has had positive effects in countless conditions, including anxiety, arthritis, asthma, back pain, depression, fibromyalgia, hypertension, insomnia, and irritable bowel syndrome.[13] To take one remarkable example, yoga is now being integrated into the management of the degenerative nerve disease multiple sclerosis. Benefits may include "increased body awareness, release of muscular tension (thus relieving spasticity), increased coordination and balance, increased flexibility and strength, control over fatigue, increased tolerance to heat, improved circulation and breathing, improved organ function (including bowel and bladder), enhanced alertness, better management of stress and an overall feeling of well-being."[14]

Over the last 30 years, researchers have investigated several ways in which what we think and feel has direct effects on physiological processes. The most well-known example of this connection is in the fight-or-flight response. "Facing what we perceive to be a dangerous situation, an ancient physiological response kicks in. Up to 80 percent of the blood leaves our forebrain, stress chemicals pour into our bloodstream, primitive stress response emotions sweep over us, and we proceed through another day in the modern civilized world with the biochemistry of an early ancestor in mortal danger."[15] Fight or flight is valuable. It prepares you for extraordinary physical exertion, selfless heroism, and tasks that would ordinarily be far beyond you, but at a price. Although the price may be right for immediate physical threats, it is way too steep for today's long-term, repetitive stress that simply wears us out.

Stress is costly because there are direct connections between our understanding and experience of the world and a complex network of bodily responses. As we see a loved one and feel affection, get the news we've been fired, or remember being raped, our love or fear, anger or depression includes physiological changes: muscles tighten or loosen, heart rate goes up or down, and cells throughout our body respond to particular chemicals that are being released by the nervous system. It is the whole person, not just her thoughts, "saying": "this is important to me and every part of me has to respond." And the world to which we are responding can be a remembered past (as in PTSD) or an anxiety-inducing future.

For example, the experience of emotion connects to our immune system's production of the white blood cells that defend against bacteria, viruses, and other foreign bodies.

> All our leukocytes (white blood cells)—which fight off infection from bacteria, viruses, and foreign proteins—have receptors located on their outer surface specific for certain peptides. These peptides are molecules released from the brain that tell the rest of the body (and specifically our immune cells) how we are "feeling."... When we are feeling happy, we secrete higher concentrations of endorphins than when we are depressed....If you're sad or depressed there's less stimulation of white cells than normal and you literally become immunosuppressed.[16]

As a result, too much stress lessens the immune system's ability to defend the body. This means, among other things, more susceptibility to infectious diseases like the flu, slower recovery from injuries, and greater difficulty in handling the side effects of cancer or AIDS treatments. Also, consider that cancerous cells are generally found in countless places throughout the body. We generally have microscopic tumors all over the place, but they do not develop because our immune system eliminates them. A weakened immune system is less able to perform this essential preventive care. Overall, a stressed-out person is more likely to experience a variety of emotional, behavioral, and even physical symptoms, such as insomnia, headaches, digestive problems, fatigue, and overly tight muscles leading to injury and chronic back pain. Anxiety, depression, and other mood changes are common. And too often people who can find no healthy way to deal with stress make their health worse by medicating themselves with drugs, alcohol, or extreme risk-taking behavior.

It goes on. The bodily systems that respond to stress and the immune system interact. Immune cells dampen the effect of stress, slowing down the production of stress hormones. And in a healthy equilibrium, stress hormones keep the immune system from too much activity. But chronic stress can lead to the opposite of the stress response: the inability to mobilize a stress response because the key glands—the adrenals—have been overworked by chronic stress already. The result is an out-of-control immune system that starts to attack its own body, thus leading to immune system diseases like arthritis, psoriasis, asthma, allergies, and hives.[17]

This is just one pattern of mind-body connections. There are others. For example, depression, hostility, stress, and loneliness, it turns out, condition the functioning of the heart. High stress levels in general, responded to by an overactive sympathetic limb of the nervous system, can stress the heart dramatically enough to cause death and in less dramatic long-term ways increase the likelihood of cardiovascular illness or lessen the ability of the body to recover from it.

Some researchers believe the correlate is likely: "While specific mechanisms are still under study, a growing body of evidence suggests that certain brain-heart signals can be influenced by intangible factors that are typically part of the yoga practice, such as relaxation, mindfulness, prayerfulness, meditation, and group support."[18]

Like negative emotional states, positive emotional states are associated with particular physiological responses. These responses arise in the brain and in the vagus nerve complex running from the brain stem to several central organs and can have beneficial physiological effects. To illustrate, the forced exhalation that is part of laughter eases the stress response and allows a kind of brief detachment from the social connections that make stress-inducing demands on us. In one study, people who were taught a six-week program of mindfulness meditation, including loving-kindness toward others, "showed enhanced immune function."[19] In stimulating the vagus nerve, compassion opens receptors on that nerve for oxytocin, which is an internally produced chemical associated with equanimity and pleasure, and slows down the rapid breathing that fuels the stress response. Some researchers have found that cooperative behavior in general prompts release of the feel-good chemical dopamine and that "giving or helping offers deep psychological benefits."[20]

The general principle of both the negative and positive cycles is summed up by Candace Pert (whose research into neuropeptides helped fuel the detailed knowledge on which mind-body medicine is based). She defines *emotions* as essentially both physiological and experiential: "emotions exist in the body as informational chemicals, the neuropeptides and receptors...and they also exist in another realm, the one we experience as feeling, inspiration, love."[21] In short, emotions are neither physical nor mental; they are both.

In these ways, there is a positive feedback loop of compassion that is the counterpart of the negative one of stress. Instead of more emotional upset leading to more health problems and more stress, we have a positive, generous, trusting emotional state leading to a better functioning immune system, a dampened-down stress system, and a further increase of feelings of love and trust.[22] There is an observable, structural basis to this pattern. Studies have shown that meditation practice changes the brain so that the part responsible for feelings of ease, happiness, and optimism lights up more often than the part that holds worry and unhappiness. And this pattern is not only experiential and temporarily biochemical. Even after a comparatively short period of meditation practice, differences in the left frontal regions of the cerebral cortex can be measured. In highly experienced, long-term meditators, this part of the brain is unusually developed.[23]

Finally, there is recent evidence that spiritual practices like meditation or focused prayer, invoking what pioneer body-mind researcher Herbert Benson has long called the relaxation response, can alter our body on the most basic levels. In one remarkable example, they affected the actual function of our DNA. Genes, the coded instructions for bodily construction and ongoing physiological processes, are greatly influenced by information from both their external and internal environment. Recent advances in laboratory detection allow us to analyze a person's entire genetic makeup and see which genes are operating and which are not and even to make preliminary judgments about how well or ill they are functioning for our overall health. Initial results suggest that use of meditative techniques alter the behavior of the 200 or so genes responsible for the stress-immune connection and that both "short and long-term practitioners" can benefit from a "genetic expression" that is more balanced and health preserving.[24]

How It works

A mind that leads the self to suffering, emotions we cannot tolerate or manage—these manifest in our cells as well as in our consciousness. Because they are both physical and experiential realities, they are, in ways that are increasingly physically measurable, bad for our health. Spiritual practices and values help in healing because they help manage and balance our emotional patterns and help us find a critical distance on the beliefs that may be stimulating our emotional overreaction. Having an active meditation practice can focus the mind and temper our emotions. Following the paradoxically straightforward and no nonsense counsel to accept our limitations, look on the bright side and feel grateful for what we have, choose love and compassion over envy or contempt, and feel at home in the universe rather than isolated and alienated helps us to be healthy.

There are a number of reasons that Hatha Yoga can be beneficial as well. For one thing, our emotional state can be directly influenced by what the body is doing. As stress leads to a raised heart rate, tensed muscles, and sweaty palms, so a lowered heart rate and relaxed muscles can calm us down emotionally. Studies have shown that as simple a fact as whether we are standing, sitting, or lying down can increase or lessen anger and hostility. Along with other cues, bodily states are interpreted by the mind as a signal of how we feel. This is probably one reason veterans suffering from PTSD, insomnia, depression, and rage at the Center for Investigating Healthy Minds at the University of Wisconsin reported better sleep, less anxiety, and more positive emotions after practicing yoga.[25]

But as we have seen, yoga is more than a particularly balanced and constructive set of physical exercises. When you teach yoga, says Carol Krucoff, certified nurse and yoga instructor at Duke Integrative Medicine, there is something else. People may come "just to stretch and strengthen," but "the first thing is the breath—which is really a form of our Spirit. By deepening, and consciously using the breath one comes into the present moment—and learns to let go of doing, planning, organizing, of all the chatter that we live with all the time, to hear the messages of the heart." It is the combination of asanas, *pranayama*, and meditation that promotes our awareness, and this awareness, Krucoff believes, is a foundation for spirituality. Yoga therapy, she says, is based in the belief that physical problems have emotional and spiritual components. "If you come in with back pain, it is not just a problem of your disc, but of how that disc is affected by your attitudes, your response to stress, the tension you carry in your back muscles. It's all connected."[26]

Harvard Medical School instructor and researcher Sat Bir Singh Khalsa, who has investigated the positive role of yoga in the treatment of insomnia, offers a related view. He believes that the spiritual dimension of yoga can lead to a more profound state of consciousness, a unitive mystical experience of our connection to the rest of the universe. Along the way, it increases our ability to respond to stress and supports particular organs (e.g., yogic breathing increases lung functions). Further, the bodily awareness so central to the practice of yoga, which tends to be ignored or short-changed in conventional exercise (especially competitive sports), helps make us aware of both the negative effects of unhealthy habits and the more positive experience of wellness. Yoga can therefore generate a greater appreciation for the person's own role in maintaining health and can lead to greater compliance with doctors' recommendations for medication and lifestyle change.[27]

To underline the difference between spiritual practices and more conventional medical techniques, I asked Krucoff, Khalsa, and Jean Van Gemert (a psychotherapist colleague of Krucoff who teaches mindfulness-based stress reduction) a simple question: "Suppose we develop a pill that treats the problem for which you are using yoga asanas, *pranayama*, and meditation. The new medication takes care of back pain, insomnia, or high blood pressure" (conditions with which they are all familiar). "Do we still need yoga and meditation? Would anything be lost without it?"

All three responded in a way consistent with the basic premises of mind-body medicine. If they just took a pill, "they would be losing a lot," Van Gemert said. "Conditions like hypertension happen for a reason, a reason that connects to the rest of your life. If you develop your mindfulness, there's a chance you can see what that reason is. Elevated blood pressure or cardiac difficulty is your body trying to communicate, and it behooves you to listen now so the body doesn't have to speak more loudly."[28]

Khalsa agreed: "You would not be treating the underlying cause, which is liable to come back and haunt you in other ways. With the pill, without the yoga, you simply don't get the skill set that yoga provides: how to manage stress, how to be aware of your body and mind. You also don't get the experience of self-efficacy and empowerment. Yoga training provides a sense of mastery and confidence in relation to your own health."

"If you just had a pill," Krucoff added, "you would lose the opportunity to learn about yourself. Yoga is a practice of self-discovery. A form of self-action. Instead of being dependent on a pill you can learn to prevent problems in the future."

At this point we need to ask: "It may be *healthy*—but is it *spiritual*?"

Take mindfulness based stress reduction (MBSR) as an example. First developed at the University of Massachusetts and now offered in hundreds of other health centers, the program defines itself by basic Buddhist practices and teachings. The meditation technique offered is standard vipassana meditation—more or less the same technique used by the Dhamma brothers, a basic Buddhist tool for centuries. The beliefs underlying the technique are familiar Buddhist fare: grasping and attachment breed unhappiness, it is essential to develop our capacity for detachment from destructive mental patterns, and mindfulness is the key to that detachment. Those who teach in the program are instructed to learn to "meet our own suffering and that of others with attention, resilience, transparency, and compassion" and advised to develop a "daily practice of mindfulness meditation and on-going participation in silent, teacher-led retreats." Strong emphasis is given to education in Theravadan Buddhism "because the spirit, practices, and attitudes of MBSR are reflective of this tradition."[29]

But are they? Is this blend of goal-oriented (end the addiction, lower the blood pressure, heal from psoriasis faster) medicine with techniques originally aimed at overcoming all attachments really an authentic appropriation of these techniques? Is this "Buddhist spirituality in action" or just the opportunistic use of one part of Buddhist teaching for a goal—health—that has no necessary relation to any religion?[30] We could, after all, be using our health for a large number of activities, none of which are necessarily connected to the Buddhist purpose of stringently moral enlightenment. We could seek to be healthier dishonest politicians, insider traders, or bank robbers. Can the spiritual insights that created meditation and that direct us to a fundamental personal change be limited to simply making life a little healthier and less painful while we maintain our same long-term goals? After people go through the mindfulness training, lower their blood pressure, recover from chemotherapy more quickly, and have less anxiety and better digestion, does it make any difference what they do with their lives? Have they truly undergone a *spiritual* healing if they are still pursuing self-centered, even socially destructive goals—but doing so now with better self-care? How Theravadan is that?

To make the question starker: Pete, an army major from the U.S. Special Forces who is a veteran of Iraq and Afghanistan, tells us: "Yoga, at its best, not only improves performance as a soldier, but facilitates your life as a whole."[31]

What does it mean to be an improved soldier—that one is better at killing people and breaking things, for is that not the purpose of a solider? Can this be the unitive consciousness of which Khalsa speaks or even approximate the nonviolence that is part of yoga's traditional moral teachings?

These questions about the ultimate meaning of spiritual practices used in (seemingly) nonspiritual contexts are difficult ones. Even raising them presupposes a set of moral judgments that many may find alienating. Who am I, after all, to say that someone's work life or identity as a soldier is a violation of spirituality? If people are less tense, more aware of themselves, and more balanced, if their stress response is not playing havoc with their immune system and their mental activity is less obsessive, isn't that enough?

From the standpoint of most (though not all) spiritual perspectives, it is not. Theravadan Buddhism's eightfold path includes a category of "right livelihood," traditionally defined as nonviolent, nondestructive work. One is instructed very clearly not to leave the meditation hall and go back to immoral work in the world. Similar ideas can be found in other religious traditions and in the ideas put forward by the vast majority of eclectic spiritual teachers.

Spiritual development may certainly include the kind of calm and focused energy yoga helps produce or the mental relief offered by a steady meditation practice. And certainly self-awareness and extended periods when we are not tense, overly excited, or obsessed with our desires is essential to spiritual life. But ultimately what we are after is not just such experiences but a life defined by awareness, gratitude, compassion, and loving connection. There is a problem when spiritual practices are used simply to make it easier for us to get what we want, rather than changing the basic pattern of wanting altogether.

However, there is another way to think about this dilemma. If there are to be warriors in the world, and there can be no doubt that there will be for a very long time, it is better that those warriors be "peaceful." If yoga improves the "performance" of a soldier (as Major Pete said), that might mean more accurate shooting or better use of explosives, but it might also mean less panic leading to unnecessary violence, fewer civilian deaths, and a more humane attitude toward prisoners. If meditation does not automatically make people kinder or more socially responsible, it may at least allow us to turn down the noise in our heads so that the possibility of kindness and social responsibility arises. There is, after all, no guarantee that any practice, belief, or teaching will make us moral. It is not guarantees that we seek, but ideas and practices that are more or less likely to gently nudge us in the right direction.

As I suggested in chapter 2, spirituality is not and can never be an absolute state of being. Whether a practice, teaching, attitude, or belief is spiritual for a particular person depends on the wider context of their lives. A Wall Street inside trader, a bomber pilot, a prison inmate, an abusive spouse—any of them may move a little bit toward greater spirituality by seriously practicing yoga and meditation. They will, in all likelihood, be a little less out of control, a little less reactive, a little more aware of their own physical and mental patterns and of the difference between healthy and self-destructive forms of life. And whether they are vice president of Goldman Sachs or an Army sharpshooter, they are likely to do that job a little more calmly, gently, and with a little less damage than they would have before. At the very least, they are likely to be more open to such a change in the future. They will have developed something of an awareness of the effects of destructive passions like greed, anger, and arrogance. Of course, they may not significantly act on that awareness. But just having the awareness is a step in the right direction. In an analogy offered by yoga teacher and scholar Gary Kraftsow: yoga can be a launching pad, propelling us to a fundamentally different experiential and spiritual form of life, or it can be a life raft that simply keeps us from drowning. Clearly, one is closer to the launching pad if one is *not* drowning, even if the life raft simply takes you back to the way you've been living.[32]

The point is not that any form of life in which you meditate and do yoga is spiritual, but that any form of life in which you go from not doing them to doing them is at least likely to become more spiritual than it was before. Of course, we can wall off everything we do on the meditation cushion and the yoga mat, forgetting their lessons as soon as we go back to work, family, or community. But this kind of contradiction can arise for any religion, secular moral code, and political ideology. We can always say one thing and do another, limit our application of the teachings when they make real demands on us, or find convenient reasons not to take any of this too seriously.

How did traditional societies, lacking scientific research methods, double-blind clinical trials, and knowledge of bodily processes based in microscopes and molecular biology develop such powerful and effective tools for health? It is clear that they did not know many things, so what is it that they did know?

First, Indian yoga, Buddhist meditation, and comparable practices drawn from China such as tai chi and chi gong are rooted in premodern understandings of the self in which body, emotions, beliefs, and spiritual attainments are interconnected. The *nadis* (pathways) and *chakras* (energy centers) referred to in Ayurvedic (traditional Indian) medicine and yoga, like meridians and energy centers in Chinese medicine, link physical structures, organ functions, and emotional states. To act on any of these physically—for example, by shaping the breath and adopting a physical posture—is from a traditional point of view simultaneously to affect how we feel, how we think, and how well our bodies function. Medicine in these settings was always integrative, since it was part of cultures that always had integrated conceptions of the self.

Second, these integrated conceptions of the self reflect religious perspectives that tend to lack the body-soul dualism of the western religious tradition. In monotheism, we tend to identify the soul with the mind and thus make a categorical distinction between mind and body. In eastern traditions, by contrast, the mind is just a subtler version of the body. While yoga, for example, is not without its own dualism—distinguishing between *purusha*, the ultimate, true or divine self, and *prakriti*, the manifest world—for yoga, the mind is part of *prakriti*. This difference may explain why Judaism, Christianity, and Islam have not created the kind of fusion of physical discipline, meditation, and spiritual aspiration that one finds in yoga or chi gong. Insofar as Hinduism, Buddhism, and Taoism sought a kind of ultimate well-being for their adherents, they would necessarily seek practices that simultaneously promoted that well-being for body, emotions, and mind.

Third, when medical practices are rooted in a spiritual understanding of health, they are tied to a critical perspective on the goals, passions, and compulsions of ordinary life. Such practices seek to interrupt the ego's—and the surrounding society's—usual messages of what we are supposed to do and be to bring us a countermessage from the perspective of enlightenment, spirit, or God. Whatever we may think about the objective truth of the metaphysics of Hinduism or Taoism, they serve a vital purpose in the context of health: a rest from the ego's usual drivenness. Physically and emotionally, such a rest is often precisely what we need.

Living with Illness

All too frequently medical treatments of whatever kind do not work. If, as Job said (5:7), people are "born to trouble as the sparks fly upward," we are also born to get sick, lose functions as we age, have accidents, develop incurable degenerative diseases, and die before our time.

So far I have emphasized practices that affect things like heart rate, breathing patterns, glandular secretions, and genetic expression. Now the emphasis shifts to understanding reality in a new way rather than changing it, on values rather than practices. These values offer a framework to help us face our pain and nevertheless find some comfort. Since our society so values autonomous accomplishment and pleasure, can spiritual teachings help us see the life of a sick person as anything other than suffering and untimely death?[33]

Overall, a spiritual understanding of illness has two sides, seemingly opposed but in reality no more in conflict than the fact that sometimes we are awake and sometimes we sleep. There is an integrated clinical approach combining medical expertise and self-care in the form of practices like yoga and meditation. At the same time, however, we are also taught to make peace with a fundamentally new life reality. It is about controlling what can be controlled and letting go of what cannot.

When we get seriously sick or injured, we may be so deeply changed that we hardly recognize ourselves. We can no longer run five miles, earn a living, read a newspaper, digest our food, or hug our children. These losses can lead to denial, rage, depression, and crippling fear, but they can also provoke a response in which the mysterious malleability of the self is a springboard to spiritual freedom. As religion scholar Mircea Eliade put it, illness can be a kind of "initiation"—a process that breaks our established boundaries. Inevitably altering the definition of the self, it allows something previously unknown to come into existence.[34] The process will almost surely be marked by pain, distress, and loss, but a new life is possible at the other end.

In a way, the spiritual task of facing illness is not essentially different from other difficult life situations. But now the stakes are much higher, the tasks that much more difficult, and the results potentially more life enhancing. The aim is to develop our awareness and acceptance of our situation, have compassion on ourselves and our caretakers, and find joy, or at least appreciation, in whatever life has left us.

Talking of mental illness but potentially referring to any illness, a Zen Buddhist psychotherapist suggests: "Depression offers us an opportunity to deepen our spirit, our lives, and our hearts."[35] Illness can require that we alter old habits, help us rise to challenges we would have thought were beyond us, and show us that life can have meaning even though we do not have things we thought were essential. Because of what it teaches us and despite what it takes away, we can become more whole. Or in the words of a neurosurgeon: "Every major surgery or illness is filled with moments of potential and even actual spiritual transformation. Health-related crises produce windows of vulnerability and susceptibility. They call into question everything we've achieved, pursued, or dreamt.... When the air is knocked out of us, we grasp the meaning of breathing."[36]

Medical professionals of all types often distinguish between curing and healing. In the first, says Dr. Nedda Hobbs of Boston's Children's Hospital, whatever problem you are facing is either solved or managed. Cancer is in remission, the heart now works fine, and the broken arm has knit. Or at least the previously unchecked diabetes, asthma, or seizures are now reasonably controlled, and you can more or less return to life as before. Healing, by contrast, has to do with making meaning of your suffering, accepting the changes in your life, learning whatever lessons it has to teach you, and connecting to the bigger picture of existence.[37] Buddhist teacher Stephen Levine, who has spent decades comforting people with fatal illnesses, describes it as learning "to touch with compassion that which before we faced with fear and aversion."[38]

One critical spiritual lesson of illness is the simple truth that human life is based in dependence. Everything we think we are—successful professionals, great skiers, political activists, spiritual writers, carpenters—is rooted in countless factors over which we have no control. From the sun's energy to the nitrogen-fixing bacteria that enable plants to grow, from the evolution of culture that provides us with language, art, and science to the countless workers who build our houses, grow our food, produce our energy, and make our clothes, from each of our cells and organs doing its appointed job to the hundreds of millions of bacteria that live within us and do what our cells cannot, we depend on others.

It is a great illusion of liberal political thought in general, and modern technologically driven capitalism in particular, to think of dependence as something we are free to choose, a matter of smart contracts and rational calculations of best advantage. The illusion that dependence is always a matter of choice is shattered by illness. We discover how dependent on this organ or that physiological process we have always been and how much we now need a hospital, a respected specialist, a network of alternative healers, kind friends, expensive medications, and accommodations mandated by the Americans with Disabilities Act.

Further, illness can be a powerful reminder of the spiritual lesson that life is change. Today, we may feel pretty good. Tomorrow, we may be in a car crash or develop a cough that just won't go away. Today, we can run and dance. Tomorrow, next week, or next year, the legs stiffen, the knees ache, and our heels simply can't take the impact. Today, we have health; tomorrow, or next year, we won't. Whatever the condition of our body and mind now, the only certainty is that it will not last.

And now another spiritual paradox arises. On the one hand, spiritual wisdom instructs us to celebrate whatever good fortune we have. If we didn't get the dream job or the love of our life just married our best friend, we can still appreciate the gifts of eyesight, being able to walk, hear, and reason. If we have simple health, we can delight in it. Yet, here is the tough part: can we both celebrate these simple and precious gifts and face their deterioration and loss? The spiritual teachings of traditional religions have been clear that, as Solomon tells us (Ecclesiastes 3:2): "There is a time to be born, and a time to die." Students of Buddhism have long been instructed to meditate on corpses or on what their own body will look like in a hundred years. Every traditional Jewish prayer service includes a prayer to be said by mourners. And there is a wonderful story in which a famous rabbi tells his followers that repentance, which traditionally one is supposed to do for more than a month before the critical holiday of Yom Kippur, must be done for one day only, the day before one's death. "But Rabbi," asked a confused disciple, "how are we to know which day it will be?" "That," the rabbi replied quietly, "is the point."[39]

Finally, illness is a teacher because if we respond to it spiritually, we realize a powerful and probably undreamed-of freedom: the ability to know enjoyment of life, gratitude, and compassion even as we suffer. We might remember the fictional Ivan Ilych, in his last moments able to think of others with compassion for perhaps the first time in his adult life. And we can find corroborating reports from people who have grappled spiritually as well as medically with illness that some kind of breakthrough—if only for a few minutes at a time—is possible. In this breakthrough, they tell us, the sick find themselves grateful for life, overwhelmed with compassion for their loved ones who are suffering by their side, and able to generate flashes of humor and delight.

It is natural for people to think at this point: "For God's sake, I have cancer (or heart disease, or steadily worsening glaucoma, or the early signs of dementia), and I have a right to be angry at this awful fate." Surely they are right. And surely no spiritual teacher, no teacher worth his or her salt in any event, would say they do not.

But a spiritual teacher might ask: what is the good of such a response? Will the rage dissipate, leaving us cleansed, or turn to hostility and bitterness? Will self-pity, fear, or a sense of deep loss over what is slipping away turn into calm or simply leave us in anguish? Indeed, no spiritual teacher wishes to take away your right to feel as lousy as you want—if that is indeed what you want. But is it? Or is it what you think is the only possible response to your condition? Reflecting on the fate of the Tibetan people, the Dalai Lama once said: "The Chinese have taken so much from me, I will not also give them my peace of mind."[40] Replace *Chinese* with the name of your ailment, and you find the heart of a spiritual response to illness.

This response offers an alternative way of perceiving the situation, a gestalt switch in which realities like pain and heightened dependence add up to something other than despair. While the negatives remain, there is now a sense of possibility: finding what is absolutely essential in life, connecting directly and honestly to people now that conventional roles and responsibilities have been shaken, finding as much pleasure in the tiniest aspects of life rather than (as is so often the case) getting as much as you can and still looking for more. In this way, spirituality offers not just practices like meditation and emotionally oriented values like compassion, but a radically different way of thinking about the ineluctable realities we face.

In *Speak the Language of Healing*, a book about how to face cancer "without going to war," a woman writes: "It is the very transience of life that makes it precious. If we all expected to live forever, life would not amount to much. It would become very cheap.... Given the reality of death, how do I find peace of mind?... Knowing that I will die—perhaps in a year or two, perhaps this afternoon—is exactly what makes me savor life."[41] A richly spiritual engagement with a life-shortening illness may change it from life-shortening to, strangely, life-enhancing. For one thing, many spiritual writers have suggested that time is an illusion, or at least a product of mental perspectives. The future is a mental construct based in the assumption that things will continue. One can have a shorter life only if the mind constructs an image of some other life and compares it to this one. In fact, the only time we actually have is the present. If we can engage in the present fully, neither past nor future will exist, because we no longer compare the *reality* of what we have with the *thought* of something else. In a present unmarked by comparison or limit, it is possible to find a deep sense of peace no matter what the state of our health.

Reaching that state of mind is not easy. All the pressing demands of ordinary life militate against it. Yet illness can be a spiritual teacher precisely because it makes ordinary life impossible. Like a meditation retreat on steroids (or chemotherapy), illness makes the old routine and the old attachments almost impossible to maintain. Another author of *Speak the Language of Healing* says: "I believe we arrive in this life as spiritual beings, and one of our tasks here is to learn to be human. For me, cancer has been my greatest teacher and my greatest gift. In four difficult years following the diagnosis, my heart embraced a life lesson that breast cancer survivor Adrienne Rich shared in her poetry: I came to see the damage that was done and the treasures that prevail'"[42] Another author lists her "treasures": learning to accept the reality of her limits and imperfections; to face her fear; to fulfill her own need for nurturance. Having learned these lessons, she can tell us that the "real measure of my healing would not be about a cure in my body. No, healing would happen in my heart and soul." When that happens, she is ready to say, "I do not yearn for the old breast, the old life. If cancer was the price I had to pay to make the transition to a place of peace, I would do it again in a heartbeat."[43] Such personal accounts of people undergoing all sorts of dire illnesses abound. It is not the party line of people writing books on spirituality, but sincere self-descriptions from people who may have been secular, conventionally religious, or at best only mildly interested in spiritual ideas before their illness began.

"What are these stories from breast cancer victims," a skeptic might retort, "but people damaged by environmental pollutants, cancer-susceptible genes, and bad luck who are clutching at illusions?" It is always possible that people are claiming a spiritual peace they do not really feel. Yet note that the kinds of response shown do not depend on traditional *religious* comforts. These women are not basing their sense of healing in faith-oriented claims like "God has a plan" or "Soon I'll be in heaven with Jesus." If they are bound in illusion, it is not the illusion of a reality that is, for us on earth, always elsewhere and for which there is, all things considered, not much evidence. Rather, a spiritually oriented response to illness allows them to tell a different story about their lives, to find comfort smack in the middle of their suffering. This may remind us that *everyone* is telling a story about the meaning of their lives, and all we can do is decide which ones we prefer. Saying that breast cancer is *only a tragedy*, a loss, and a defeat is just as much a story as saying that it is a teacher. Each account is equally compatible with the facts; neither can be proved as more rational than the other. However, it is not hard to see which one will give us a meaning that we can live and die with and which one is more likely to leave us bitter. These women are not denying the reality of their pain. They are saying they have found ways to think about their experiences that allow them some real happiness despite it. A paralyzed victim of neurological degeneration declares simply: it is "better to know and grow from the experience than to remain aloof and have no basis for wisdom."[44]

If such achievements are illusions, they work too well to be cast aside. These illusions allow us to resist our culture's typical understanding of illness: that it is only pain, loss, and helplessness. Susan Wendell, a philosopher suffering from extreme chronic fatigue syndrome, maintains: "In the societies where Western science and medicine are powerful," people with disabling conditions "are constant reminders...of the inability of science and medicine to protect everyone from illness, disability, and death. They are 'the Others' that science would like to forget"[45] Wendell, like the women struggling with breast cancer, must work through despair if she is to make sense of her life. This she does by valuing what she has, rather than simply missing what is gone forever.

> When I look back on the beginning of my illness, I still think of it, as I did then, as an involuntary violation of my body. But I now feel that such violations are sometimes the beginning of a better life....The state of my body limited the possibilities in new ways, but it also presented new kinds of understanding, new interests, new passions, and projects. In this sense, my experience of illness has been profoundly meaningful.[46]

Esthers

One Friday evening at the Reform Jewish temple I attend, instead of the usual rabbi's sermon, my family got up to talk about our experience of having a child with severe disabilities. My then 14-year-old daughter Esther, who suffers from cognitive limitations, weak muscles, partial deafness, anxiety disorder, severe scoliosis, and a metabolic disorder, spoke last. At one point, she raised her head from her carefully prepared text, looked directly at the 500 or so people gathered for the service, and said: "To you parents who have kids with special needs, I have one thing to say. Don't blame yourselves; it's not your fault."

If parents of handicapped children don't feel it is our fault, as Esther suggested we might, very often we feel that it is our responsibility to fix it. And if we can't, we wonder how it is possible for us to live a life of anything but anguish when our children are in pain, terribly limited, socially isolated, endlessly frustrated, or dying. Spirituality properly teaches us to find the good in life by being detached from our desires. But what does it mean to detach from the suffering of others, especially if the other is my child?

In conventional terms, disability is simply a profound failure. As a friend said to me soon after Esther was born—actually trying to be supportive!—having a child like Esther is "every parent's worst nightmare." Occasionally, of course, we see a TV drama in which there is a heroic triumph over all odds: the one-legged girl who runs the marathon, the charming boy with Down syndrome. These images only emphasize how bereft are all the others who are not special, who do not beat the odds, who are not at all cute. When acquaintances casually talked about how I will feel "when your kids finally go away to college," it was a small but painful matter to remind them that college was not in Esther's future. The awkward silence that followed only emphasized that those of us with disabled children inhabit a different country, a different universe, than the norm. When youth, physical beauty, career success, and a well-ordered portfolio are the ideal, children who cannot read or walk seem simply to be a loss. As the mother of a developmentally delayed son in the poignant documentary *Best Boy* says: "If you want to know heartache, have a retarded child."

The negatives of disability are all too obvious: thousands of hours spent in doctors' offices, searching online for alternative treatments, meeting with special teachers, and interviewing home health aides; lost sleep, friends, money, vacations, and career possibilities; and witnessing our children's suffering. And there is a kind of stigma. In a culture with a profound inability to tolerate pain, suggests theologian Stanley Hauerwas, the disabled will be shunned.[47]

Is there anything else? Can parents of children with disabilities find a spiritual rewrite of the dominant social narrative when miraculous cures do not materialize? Even with the best medical attention, 25 holistic healers, home study programs, encouraging her to exercise before she gets to watch TV, purchasing 37 overpriced computer learning programs, and doing Hooked on Phonics together, Esther has remained Esther. She is sweet, emotionally wise far beyond her IQ, a surprisingly not bad shot with a basketball from seven feet out, and in many ways very, very impaired.

A spiritual reinterpretation of the value of Esther's' life, can, I believe, begin with a spiritual reinterpretation of my own as Esther's father. This will first of all be rooted in an honest acknowledgment of what is possible. Who, after all, told me that I had the power to heal everything that is broken in the world? At the same time, I cannot walk away from the obligations that have been placed before me. I must do what can be done, even while knowing that a good deal of what I do may accomplish little. Many of the world's traditional spiritual teachings focus on this dilemma. The warrior prince Arjuna, hero of the Hindu religious poem *Bagavad Gita*, is instructed by the God Krishna to fulfill his social duty but release his attachment to the results of his actions. Buddhists counsel us to realize that the problem is not that the world is uncontrollable, but that we do not accept this fundamental truth. They emphasize it is essential that we show compassion for all who suffer, no matter what else we cannot do. Kierkegaard said flatly that to avoid despair, we need to give up our attachment to "world-historical" accomplishments and concentrate on living principled ethical lives. The Talmud, stressing the intention rather than the accomplishments of love, teaches us that "to save one person is like saving the whole world." It suggests that even if we cannot save the one person, our efforts make a difference in "other realms."[48] Countless traditional and nontraditional spiritual voices have said that whatever healing, helping, and social improvement we perform is God working through us, not the fruits of our own individual abilities or powers. Even without a belief in God, this is a realistic assessment of the effects of our action, so much of which depend on countless factors over which we have no control.

We cannot *cure* the Esthers. But we can *love* them because they, too, are made in the image of God, because they suffer and deserve compassion, because they were given to us, because we can see how hard they are working at life, and because they have their own gifts. We can train ourselves to convey to them that we believe in the meaning of their lives, no matter how restricted those lives are. We can have faith, not necessarily in an all-powerful God who has hidden plans, but in the value of what is right before our eyes: a smile, a laugh, and children who crawl because they cannot walk, coo at us because they cannot talk, and will themselves to keep going day after day despite everything. With such a spiritually rather than religiously oriented faith, my parental responsibility has a clear purpose. A mother of a deaf child says, "Having a child with a disability makes you slow down and enjoy him or her, perhaps more than most parents whose children are not disabled. I'm not saying I am a better parent, just that I am more appreciative of this little creature of God."[49] If this is not easy, and a good deal of the time feels nearly impossible, this is another reminder that the extreme rewards of spiritual life come at an extreme cost.

If we can love our limited children, perhaps we can also find some well-deserved self-acceptance as well. For don't all of us have limitations, disabilities? Aren't there many things others can do that we cannot? Many lessons we just don't seem to be able to learn, insights that don't stick, bad habits we can't shake? Thus in learning to appreciate my disabled child, I can perhaps learn to appreciate the disabled father that I am—my plethora of physical limits, emotional immaturities, and spiritual shortcomings notwithstanding. Esther is far from perfect. So am I. If learning to accept Esther teaches me to do the same for myself and other people, is that not a precious gift? If I can be accepting and compassionate to Esther even though she has multiple disabilities, perhaps I can do the same for myself, even though sometimes I am nasty, not as successful as I'd hoped, or just plain dumb.

A spiritual response to cancer or heart disease is twofold: actively use all possible resources, including meditative practices and spiritual attitudes, to support recovery and also accept what cannot be cured and find a spiritual meaning for pain and loss. The same is true for any parent of a handicapped child. Typically, there is much to be done that will help our children function better, enjoy life more, or at least be in less pain. But in the end, the only aspect of Esther's life that I can really control with any degree of certainty is the part in which I offer her love and give up my desperate attachment to "results." In this dimension, the task is not to cure her, but to accept the value of my own love, even if it won't cure her.

And there can be surprising moments of grace. A mother tells us that having an autistic child means both a "bleak realization that a mother's love isn't always enough" and an "unexpected joy at the smallest of life's mercies: a crooked smile, a shirt buttoned, a word remembered, a name scrawled uncertainly on a piece of paper."[50] Philosopher Eva Kittay writes that Sesha (her multiply handicapped daughter who cannot walk or speak) is a "teacher of love."[51] Michael Berube argues that the ultimate value of having his son with Down syndrome mainstreamed is that the other children will learn to understand and value difference and approach their own differences with less fear or shame. In this sense, his son has as much to offer the normal school setting as it has to offer him.[52] Esther herself can be funny, caring, and emotionally insightful. When asked what she thought the secret of life was, she replied without hesitation: "To love people."

In several collections of writings by parents of children with disabilities, this basic spiritual response to disability is repeated.[53] The pain is not erased, but it has a different meaning, and this meaning is not hopelessness. "The most important things I have learned since having a disabled child," says the mother of a cognitively limited, severely epileptic daughter, "is that the whole purpose of our existence is to love and be loved."[54]

Thus love is the one sure ticket out of the cul-de-sac of despair that disabilities can cause. It is only love, in the end, that we can control. From Rumi to Jesus, from the Bodhisattva to Gandhi, is this not the quintessential spiritual lesson? If we are to find a way out of despair, says Miriam Greenspan, it can only be through listening to its insistent message that we need to change our expectations and attachments.[55] The father of a child with autism assures us: "The sorrow, although unwelcome, can be a pathway to an unconditional love that grows from a realization of the intrinsic beauty of each child's existence. We parents of children with disabilities can feel fine about ourselves when we grasp this and give up superficial achievement-based values."[56] This process is complex and multifaceted,

marked by pain that cannot be discounted. From the mother of a child with multiple handicaps:

> Sometimes I feel burned out, other times, completely inspired....I realize
> that I am a better person for having gone through this struggle. But I also
> know that my lost innocence was the price I paid for this enrichment as a
> human being. This is not to say "I would have chosen illness, or a disabled
> child." After all, I didn't have a choice. It is to say, "I can use this for good
> and not just for ill."[57]

"All the things taking place," Chogyam Trungpa reminds us, no matter how disturb-
ing, "are helpful. As long as we have a sense 'that we are treading on the path.'"[58] With
that sense we can live with our pain, rather than fearing that it will destroy us.

This need to undergo and understand our suffering and to change toward new
values is a basic narrative core of world spirituality. The Jewish experience of slavery and liberation, the crucifixion of Jesus, the acetic wanderings of the Buddha,
Muhammed's flight through the desert—in a spiritual sense, all these are about
a kind of death and rebirth, about a profound anguish that makes possible a life
deepened by love, broadened by compassion, and illuminated by appreciation
for the beauties of daily existence. These stories are most emphatically not about
a life in which nothing is lost. Jesus had his moments of despair on the cross.
Joseph had to be sold into slavery before he could become Pharaoh's assistant.
"Suffering," C. S. Lewis declared after his wife died of cancer, "is God's wake up
call."[59] But what is it we are to wake up to? To accepting that a life that we cannot
control, that may be enormously painful, is still a life worth living.

From a spiritual point of view, each person is of infinite value, because each
person, if looked at properly, can help us with the infinite important task of finding our true nature, loving God, or reaching enlightenment. Unlike the SATs,
baseball games, or Wall Street, in this context disability is no handicap. If we pay
attention, *anyone* can be our teacher. That is one reason human beings deserve
love—and the respect and care that love entails. And if despite fatigue, frustration,
and disappointment, we can raise ourselves to answer that call, we can heal.

One summer afternoon, Esther is practicing basketball with our portable
hoop, taking shot after shot, which I rebound for her in our driveway. Bright sun,
85 degrees, and Esther is sweating and red-faced in her special undershirt, thick
plastic back brace, and T-shirt. For a moment she stops, looks up at the cloudless
sky, and shakes her fist. "God," she yells, "I am really angry at you. Why did you
give me these special needs? Why did you give me so much pain? I'm sick of it.
I just want to be normal." She shakes her fist one more time, motions for me to
pass her the ball, and shoots again: swish! She gets it in. Now her arms are raised
in joy.

9

Spirituality and Nature

To be Hopi is to embrace peace and cooperation, to care for the
Earth and all its inhabitants, to live within the sacred balance.

DENNIS WALL AND VIRGIL MASAYESVA[1]

Shall I not have intelligence with the earth? Am I not partly
leaves and vegetable mold myself?

HENRY DAVID THOREAU[2]

If only you could hear the song of this grass! Each blade is singing out to God for no ulterior motive, not expecting any reward.
It is most amazing to hear their song.

REBBE NACHMAN[3]

STRUGGLING WITH ISOLATION, endless rushing, and the fear of death, facing the
failures of the isolated nuclear family, consumerism, and technology, confronted
by a lurking sense that life has no meaning, that our losses are too great to bear,
and that all our powers and accomplishments add up to little of real value, some
people go within to meditative states, some go backward in time to fundamentalist religion, and some go outside to a river or a night sky, the rainforest or a single
tree in a public park.

It is perhaps a cliché, but nevertheless a heartfelt one, that a great many people feel closer to God or spirit in nature than anywhere else. That is why there
are so many descriptions of mountains or forests in religious terms—as cathe-
drals, temples, or sanctuaries. The spiritual quality of nature resides in the sense
that our connection to it is truer than our social identity, ego-bound desires, and
conventional priorities. As intense meditation leads us beyond a sense of "this is
mine, this is myself," as fervent prayer may lead us closer to God, as our bodies
and breath blend in yoga or we lose our attachment to individual success in spiritually oriented service, so the experience of nature brings many people back to
their essential selves. In this way, our relationship to other life-forms can serve the

same function as human-centered practices: teaching us similar lessons and inviting us to bring those lessons to the wider world.

People have been soothed and inspired by nature for a very long time, yet now nature possesses both a unique importance and a unique vulnerability.[4] Understood as life-forms and support systems (e.g., fish and water, trees and soil) that function without human control or interference, nature is now virtually banished from the earth. Having altered the planet's climate; produced chemicals that permeate air, water, earth, and the tissues of almost all species; and changed the very chemical balance of the ocean, we have pretty much eliminated nature. Climb a mountain and find a cell phone tower; walk a deserted beach and get tar balls from oil spills on your feet; gaze on a flowered spring meadow and hear a chain saw or see broken glass. Planes, snowblowers, leaf blowers, and highways make a moment's peace a rare and often quite expensive commodity. If a spiritual hunger for experiences of nature is a permanent feature of human psychology, that hunger is a lot more unsatisfied than it used to be. Because experience with this natural Other is essential to our mental health, ecopsychologists tell us, we suffer from a "nature deficit disorder" that verges on a kind of madness.[5]

Thus nature spirituality in the modern age contains within itself the seeds not only of a personal but alsoof a social transformation. If the personal ego can make us sick as individuals, our collective ego of reckless industrialization and unrestrained consumption can make us ecologically sick as a society. If yoga and meditation are helpful responses to individual maladies of modernity such as high blood pressure and anxiety, so a spiritually oriented relation to nature may be our best response to the collective maladies of pollution and climate change.

Connection and Reenchantment

A spiritual bond with nature can deeply affect our sense of who we are. In place of an ego-oriented understanding of ourselves as limited, separate, and tragically mortal, we perceive fundamental connections to other life-forms and to a dynamic process that will continue long after our individual deaths. These connections encourage a kind of universal concern for other beings, take us away from obsessions with possessions or desires, and balm our grief. We sense a naturalistic expression of the ancient Buddhist idea of interdependence expressed in the jewel net of Indra: an infinite net in which each juncture of filaments contains a precious jewel—and each jewel reflects all the others.

Yet for nature to support spiritual virtues, it cannot be understood just as a playground or an aesthetic display. A walk in New England's autumn foliage of spectacular orange, yellow, and red leaves against a perfect blue sky, accompanied by a gentle breeze, is delightful. But the pleasant, no matter what its source or degree, is not in and of itself spiritual, for spirituality is not essentially about pleasure.

If, however, this pleasant experience leads toward greater appreciation of life, less compulsion to succeed or consume, and a gentle acceptance of our common mortality—then nature will have done its spiritual work. More broadly, as James Gibson suggests, in the modern world the "reenchantment" of nature—once again seeing it as inherently meaningful, valuable, even sacred—often supports a critical attitude toward social realities like the uncontrolled market and the scientistic reduction of nature to inherently valueless matter. An enchanted nature is much more than raw materials for industry, a background to human political and military pursuits, or an amusement park.[6]

This enchanted understanding of nature can be found in traditional religion, poetry, and art; in personal experiences; and in a variety of distinctly contemporary cultural expressions from Disney movies to animal theme parks and surfing culture.[7] Theologians identified with different traditions—Catholics Meister Eckhart and Thomas Merton, Protestant John B. Cobb, Buddhist Thich Nhat Hanh, Muslims Rumi and Sayyd Nasr, Rabbi Arthur Green—celebrate the power of nature to bring us closer to God or spiritual truth.[8] Pagans, followers of Wicca, deep ecologists, ecofeminists, and many environmental activists assert the essential sacredness of nature and the distinct attitudes and forms of life such sacredness requires of us.

Even ostensibly secular groups, far removed from what is generally understood as religion or spirituality, reflect this sensibility as well. For example, longtime Greenpeace-USA spokesman Christopher Childs asserted, "There is broad acceptance among Greenpeace staff that the work is quintessentially spiritual, though definitions of what is meant by the term vary."[9] The "Principles of Environmental Justice" were created in 1991 by people of color environmental activists seeking to integrate ecological and social concern, conservation of endangered landscapes, and protection of minorities suffering disproportionately from pollution. It begins: "Environmental justice affirms the sacredness of Mother Earth, ecological unity and the interdependence of all species, and the right to be free from ecological destruction."[10] In these and many other instances, we find that a deeply felt personal connection to nature leads directly to environmental social activism.

Modes of Spirit

*Apprehend God in all things, for God is in all things. Every
creature is a word of God.*

MEISTER ECKHART[11]

The spiritual quality of nature tends to be asserted in three different ways. For American environmental activist David Brower, Wicca teacher Starhawk,

American conservationist John Muir, ecophilosopher David Abram, and naturalist and novelist Brenda Peterson, nature is important just because of what it "naturally" is. "Nature," wrote Brower, "just is God." We connect with the Goddess, says Starhawk, simply by connecting to rocks, trees, animals, other people, and ourselves.[12] Muir counsels us: "Climb the mountains and get their good tidings. Nature's peace will flow into you as sunshine flows into trees. The winds will blow their own freshness into you, and the storms their energy, while cares will drop off like autumn leaves."[13] "Magic," David Abram suggests, "is the experience of living in a world made up of multiple intelligences, the intuition that every natural form one perceives—from the swallows swooping overhead to the fly on a blade of grass and indeed the blade of grass itself—is an experiencing form, an entity with its own predilections and sensations, albeit sensations that are very different from our own."[14] Growing up in the national forests of Oregon, Brenda Peterson remembers, "I assumed that the trees were our ancestors. They were here before us. We were their children."[15]

Second, a more animistic, shamanic orientation finds the spiritual value of nature in spirits that inhabit or express themselves in natural forms. Some indigenous tribes may believe that one can converse with a hawk, receive instruction from a bear, or be morally inspired by a mountain. Cree hunters offer prayers to their prey's spirit before a hunt, and aboriginal Australians believe that their use of fire to increase biodiversity is properly applied only when they are instructed by the land itself.[16] Here is an illuminating anecdote about a western pharmacologist's encounter with a native conception of nature's spirit. The resesarcher asks the local shaman to explain to him which plants can be used for which ailments. The shaman collapses in uncontrollable laughter, then calls some other tribespeople over, and repeats the researcher's request, and they all break down in mirth. When the westerner asks what is so amusing, he is told: "If you want to use it, the spirit of the plant must come to you in your dreams. If the spirit of the plant tells you how to prepare it and what it will cure, you can use it. Otherwise, it won't work."[17]

Third, nature can be seen as a sign of the handiwork of a divine power. Traditional Protestant theology often described God's revelation as being found in two books—the Bible and nature. The image is brought up to date in scientist George Washington Carver's reflection: "I love to think of nature as an unlimited broadcasting station, through which God speaks to us every hour, if we will only tune in."[18] Alternatively, contemporary Catholic ecotheologians Thomas Berry and John Hart believe that everything in nature, and indeed the universe as a whole, is "sacramental"—a way in which God discloses the divine presence.[19]

There are real differences among these three perspectives, but in a spiritual sense, they all point in the same direction. Whether the forest is sacred because all of life is sacred, because in some sense the trees possess distinct spirits and even some form of consciousness, or because the complexity of the forest ecosystem is part of God's gift of creation, the result is that the forest is our kin, part of the miracle that is life. The mutuality we feel with the forest and with all other parts of this miracle means that we are always surrounded by what is, in only the mildest of overstatements, a family. If life is the basis for our kinship, we can recognize and celebrate our shared aliveness. If we see spirits in the forest, the forest becomes kin because we, too, are spirits. If we believe that God is the source of all creation, then even if there are real differences between us and snails, we also have something—perhaps the most important thing—in common.

This sense of kinship can engender spiritual virtues.

For example, if one believes that on this planet we have been given a truly marvelous source of beauty, sustenance, and inspiration, we may face our personal disappointments and losses with greater equanimity. We may find the marvels of nature in the spectacular—lightning in the night sky. Or the minuscule—the way an ant can sense as little as a single molecule of a scent. Or the intriguing: a species of rainforest tree has a bark that grows at some distance from the trunk, allowing a particular species of ant to live in the space. The ants in turn attack any animal that seeks to feed on the tree's leaves or bark. An appreciation of such facts can support values often lacking in the purely human realm of social relationships.

There is also a spiritual lesson in the fact that life is not a product of humanity's knowledge or conscious choice. Billions of years of physical changes and evolution have led us to today. The accomplishments of these natural processes may induce a kind of quiet humility that is a vast spiritual step up from human-based arrogance over our goals and powers and foster a corresponding modesty about our own individual capacity to accomplish or control. The world happened without our ego, and much of our own existence—our heartbeat, ability to digest food, perception of sights and sounds—exists without our ego as well. This brings forth an essential spiritual message: there is more to life and more to our identity than what we can consciously choose, desire, and control.

In addition, nature offers, as nineteenth-century British essayist William Hazlitt observed, a kind of constant and profound egalitarianism. Nature gives to us without "hypocrisy, caprice, nor mental reservation."[20] This generosity—the flip side of which is the way nature is an equal threat to all people—can provoke an awareness of that aspect of our identity that is not tied to social concerns. Wealth or social position, good grades or fame, ideology, and philosophy are simply irrelevant to a birdcall, the feel of warm ocean waters, or the smell of wild lavender.

In this way, nature models a kind of authentic and persuasive reciprocity and a universally fair interdependence. Oak leaves fall to the forest floor and provide food for worms, rodents, and microorganisms, who in turn nourish the soil on which the trees—and future leaves—depend. The oceanic food chain goes from microorganisms up to whales, whose decaying bodies feed the tiniest of creatures in what

Rachel Carson called a kind of "material immortality" of the flesh.[21] Humans are so dependent on this reciprocity that if the forests don't give us oxygen in return for carbon dioxide, if the rains don't fall at the right time, if the bees and bats stop pollinating, we will be in deep trouble.

This universally distributed reciprocity suggests a moral perspective quite different than the usual compulsive ranking of the really important (famous, rich, accomplished, etc.) and the merely ordinary and may weaken decidedly unspiritual attachments to self-importance, individualism, and selfishness. In nature, quite often the smaller the being (e.g., bacteria in the soil), the greater the role (making it possible for plants to absorb minerals from the soil and thus for us to have vegetation at all). For a spiritual seeker, bland injunctions to humility are made concrete when we realize how much of our food depends on earthworms to aerate the soil and bats to pollinate fruit trees. Independence and autonomy, those supposed hallmarks of the mature ego in modern times, take on a new and rather dimmer light in the face of our actual ecological situation.[22]

Often, spiritual views of nature refer to its "perfection." But what does that mean? Certainly it does not lie in the fact that nature gives any of us exactly what we want. The earth is not an eternal heaven where every desire is met or a perfect enlightenment where we never feel any angst. Rather, the earth's perfection is rooted in the rhythms of birth and death, eating and being eaten, and in a beauty that is ever changing just because all of us are fragile and temporary. These beings with whom I share the earth do not need to be eternal or perfect to be sacred. The leaping trout, the redwood tree, the shockingly red cardinal with his insistent spring mating call outside my window—these are enough just as they are. I know that this is not Eden, birth is still irrevocably tied to death, flesh still subject to a host of ills, and viruses, tornadoes, and locusts can still make mincemeat of us. But if all of it is a miracle, then all of it, just by being what it is, praises God, finds the still point of meditation, or is part of the great truth of being.

Native Nature

Spiritual relationships to nature have been essential to human culture for a very long time. Even when human powers were dwarfed by drought, famines, or rivers too wild to cross, nature was nonetheless identified as a source of inspiration and spiritual insight.

From the Zen poets of Tang dynasty China, over 1,000 years ago, we hear:

> *Spring has its hundred flowers,*
> *Autumn its moon,*
> *Summer has its cooling breezes,*
> *Winter its snow.*

> *If you allow no idle concerns*
> *To weight on your heart,*
> *Your whole life will be one*
> *Perennial good season.*[23]

Does this not remind us of Psalm 19?

> *The heavens declare the glory of God;*
> *the skies proclaim the work of his hands.*
> *Day after day they pour forth speech;*
> *night after night they reveal knowledge.*
> *They have no speech, they use no words;*
> *no sound is heard from them.*
> *Yet their voice goes out into all the earth,*
> *their words to the ends of the world.*

Or of Rumi's advice?

> *The breeze at dawn has secrets to tell you.*
> *Don't go back to sleep.*
> *You must ask for what you really want.*
> *Don't go back to sleep.*[24]

And of course, from Jesus (Matthew 6:28–29): "And why do you worry about clothes? Look at how the lilies in the field grow. They don't work or make clothes for themselves. But I tell you that even Solomon with his riches was not dressed as beautifully as one of these flowers."

Openness to learning from nature and the sense of kinship and reciprocity such openness entails are the essential themes of indigenous spirituality. Despite marked and significant differences, native tribes throughout the world typically value and respect their natural surroundings. This moral focus shapes their hunting and agriculture, their attitudes toward water and land. And it does so because the indigenous understanding of nature has a spiritual effect on their egos, that is, on the part of native people that (as in everyone) tends to greed, competitiveness, and self-indulgence.

Although native groups may have made serious ecological mistakes at times (e.g., overhunting large game in prehistoric North America),[25] those mistakes may well have shaped the later culture toward ecological balance. Overall, the indigenous environmental record, if hardly perfect, is far, far better than ours. And this difference did not stem from a simple lack of technology. There were environmental catastrophes—for example, in Babylonia and ancient Israel—long before the industrial revolution.[26] These catastrophes unfolded in religious cultures that privileged male sky gods over both the earth and any feminine principle of natural fertility and rarely supported a respectful approach to the human-nature relationship.

By contrast, cautions against ecological greed and recklessness permeate indigenous traditions. For one example, there is a widely told Native American story of Gluskabe, who uses trickery to lure all the living animals into his game bag so that hunting will be easy. "You have not done well," his wise old grandmother tells him, for in taking so many animals, "Our small ones, our children's children, will die of hunger."[27] In the words of a tribal leader from the Amazon region: "We Indians consider ourselves citizens of the forests."[28] Clearly, to be a citizen of the forest, you need to be able to sublimate your desire to triumph over it, use it without limit, or turn it into a condo complex. This is a far cry from traditional global religions' advocacy of dominion over the earth, rejection of it as a merely temporary abode that prepares us for the eternity of heaven or hell, or fear of it as a source of mistaken attachment.

Buddhist, Islamic, or Jewish teachings often show the destructive interpersonal effects of, for example, greed or envy. Genesis explores what happens when we cannot deal with our disappointment over lacking God's favor (Cain and Abel) or our desire for status in the family leads us to betray a sibling (Jacob and Esau). Buddhist instruction on meditation emphasizes the benefits of mindfulness and the drawbacks of its lack. From legends of native peoples, we get a corresponding emphasis on the importance of living in balance with the earth. As trust in God is the antidote to Cain's envy or Jacob's ambition, so trust in the encompassing community of life can offer indigenous peoples a comforting sense of belonging. A Brazilian Tupinamba Indian said to a colonialist:

> I see that you're all mad. You cross the seas, suffer all sorts of upsets, and work so hard to amass riches, that you leave to your sons and those who live on. Don't tell me that the land you feed couldn't also feed you? We have our fathers, mothers, and sons that we love, but we believe that when we die the earth that has nurtured us will also nurture them. That's why we rest easy.[29]

This confidence in a reciprocal balance with nature is part of an entire way of life and requires far more than a simple belief in nature spirits. To live according to spiritual virtues in their relations with nature, natives must be scrupulously mindful of the effects of their actions. They have to develop a kind of disinterested compassion so that they do not privilege human comfort over ecological balance and the health of other species. They need factual knowledge of how the world works, as well as an ability to manage their own emotions, applying spiritual values to how they dwell, raise crops, tend flocks, and use water.

Consider a Native American on a vision quest hoping to encounter a power animal from whom he can receive moral guidance. The animal, we may suppose, will be uninterested in the ego side of the native, such as his attachment to being a better warrior than his brother or his purely verbal expression of respect for the river or the elk. The wisdom of nature can come in only as the standard manifestations of the ego go out—if not completely, at least to some extent. That is why before one seeks out animal guides, rituals of purification—fasting, physical feats, isolation—are undertaken. Just as extended periods of meditation can undermine the normal mind, so can extreme physical experiences. Only after that undermining occurs can one actually intend the words of a Navajo song: "The thoughts of the earth are my thoughts, the voice of the earth is my voice."[30]

Finally, both the purification and the encounter (the "vision" part of a vision quest) are not intended to take a person out of the world. Indigenous peoples do not have community-supported monasteries or religious figures who are excused from the demands of ordinary life. Rather, as with prayer, meditation, study, or selfless service, the true goal is to function spiritually in ordinary life. For the native, this means to manage the tribe's relation to its natural surroundings with humility, grace, and restraint. In modern, far more complicated settings, it requires that we keep our ecological relations in mind as we buy food, earn a living, raise children, build our dwellings, and (as we will see in the next chapter) take part in politics. Despite the differences between indigenous spirituality's defining relation to nature and that of both traditional religions and contemporary teachers, the problem remains the same: how to live without violent attachment or the attempt to escape.

Balance, Restraint, Listening

Virtually every form of spirituality has a way of understanding what is wrong with a life dominated by ego and offers images (enlightenment, grace, wisdom, stilling one's mind) of the spiritual solution to these problems. Nature spirituality typically invokes an image of balance in which each being gets and gives and the system as a whole supports them all.

This is why the deep pleasure we can get from nature—the beauty of a sunset over the beach when the weather is good and the blackflies haven't come out yet—is not really the point. The question is, rather, what kind of self is getting this pleasure, and what does the pleasure mean to us? If it is treated like most pleasures, then it will support neither spiritual progress nor ecological balance. We will enjoy it, lust for it, try to own it (*this is my private beach house, trespassers will be prosecuted*), and feel disappointed when it starts to rain or the traffic is heavy on the way—the usual. The point is that just as we cannot reach enlightenment or God with a rampant ego, so we cannot reach or maintain ecological balance either.

Spiritually speaking, the pleasures of nature are there to teach us something—and the teaching is meant to get us to change our lives in a certain way. These are lessons of reciprocity, humility, and gratitude understood not primarily as felt emotions but as ways of being in the world.

If it was easier to practice such virtues in small tribal societies, where negative ecological impacts were immediately noticeable and technology did not amplify mistakes to frighteningly destructive levels, that does not mean we do not have much to learn from what these cultures can teach. It was easier to be moral in the time of the Buddha or Christ, since life was simpler, technology did not amplify the effects of our everyday lives, and the state did not complicate our relationships with each other.[31] Certainly, many aspects of moral and spiritual life are now more complex, perhaps more difficult, than they were. But the essential insights remain valid, even if it will take a great deal of work to apply them to our current situation.

In particular, a spiritual engagement with nature now requires a critical attitude toward modern technology's goal of absolute domination of the earth. In the words of Rachel Carson, whose earlier evocation of the ocean's biological and spiritual dimensions created the public recognition that helped publicize her later (and historically groundbreaking) critique of pesticides, *Silent Spring*: "The 'control of nature' is a phrase conceived in arrogance, born of the Neanderthal age of biology and philosophy, when it was supposed that nature exists for the convenience of man."[32]

Is this not similar in many ways to spiritual traditions that emphasize mindfulness, gratitude, and compassion in human relationships? You cannot relate spiritually to other people if you seek to dominate them, make them do your bidding, and compel them to give you what you want with no return from you. In the context of our relations with nature, this is similarly true, even though it is in some ways more complex; for after all, we can continue to live only if we control nature to the extent of getting the necessities of life. Even the most enlightened of gurus turns on the heat on a winter morning—or one of his disciples does. In the same way, human relations always involve some amount of mutual use, whether it is by the people who fix the roads and grow the food or the way we get a fellow diner to pass the salt.

But there is a profound difference between respectful reciprocal interaction and domination based in political, economic, or cultural inequality. The same is true for our relation to nature. Nature can be used—for shelter and clothes, food and art and recreation—without being irrevocably diminished, poisoned, or stupidly wasted. Forests can be responsibly managed so that lumber is taken out but biodiversity remains.[33] Food can be grown biodynamically. Technological innovations can be evaluated carefully and very slowly. But using nature responsibly requires self-awareness, restraint in desires, and the ability to enjoy life without excessive consumption. Exactly how much use is enough and how much is too much is certainly not an easy question, but the same difficulty arises in our relations with people. It is often difficult to distinguish between just and exploitive economic relationships or to know what forms of political power respect and which violate human rights.

One way to understand how a spiritual approach to nature contrasts with dominant cultural messages can be found in environmental journalist and activist Bill McKibben's wonderfully astute *The Age of Missing Information*.[34] The book compares the "information" McKibben got from watching 24 hours of programming on 150 cable TV channels to his experience of 24 hours on top of a small mountain in the Adirondacks. The respective messages, McKibben suggests, are very different. Constantly reiterated in a variety of forms, the dominant lessons of our media system are that your needs, desires, and well-being are the most important things in the world. There is an entire world geared to making you happy, healthy, and beautiful. And there is no limit on how big our economy can grow to satisfy you. More roads for more cars for more malls for more "needs"—this is as natural as the sunrise and as patriotic as Mom and apple pie.

The mountain, not surprisingly, offers different messages. Observe any of the creatures—squirrels, rabbits, hawks, small pine trees—and it is soon obvious that they have limits. If birds grow too large, their wings will not support them; a too tall pine tree on top of a mountain would be highly vulnerable to wind. Moreover, the mountain, like the swamp, the river, the meadow, the ocean, and the earth itself, is a system of interrelated parts, no one of which has precedence over any other. Each part does something keyed to its particular structure. And no matter how big, powerful, or beautiful, every individual is dependent on countless other beings.

This last insight is expanded by psychologist James Hillman's lament that in a world robbed of its soul by being reduced to materials for scientific research, industrial production, and individual pleasures, our own selves are haunted by the fear that we, too, will be as "dead" as nature. Therefore, we feel a relentless pressure to perform, achieve, and amount to something, as well as the loneliness that comes from "living in a graveyard."[35] In related accounts, critical theorist Max Horkheimer and Buddhist David Loy argue that taking nature purely as an object of control is motivated by an "endless and self-defeating search for security" (Horkheimer) or a psyche caught between fear of isolation and terror of dissolution (Loy).[36] Dread of loss, meaninglessness, and death are expressed as the endless quest for more power over the world. Since human beings are part of the world, the domination of nature soon turns to the domination of people. Countless public, political tyrannies have sought to socially engineer human beings the way we build bridges and railroads. The psychological basis of marketing soap or presidential candidates and the false promises of plastic surgery and antidepressants all embody the notion that nature—in these cases, human nature—exists to be controlled, "improved," and used. Nature spirituality, by contrast, seeks peace with its own limits, knowing that the soul can be truly at home only in a world that has inherent value and in which great care is taken before anything is changed.

Interdependence, limits, respect, and care are spiritual insights. A long line of thinkers have told us about them, and they are the common stuff of native traditions. But there is no guarantee that people will take such spiritual insights from McKibben's mountaintop or Rumi's early morning breeze. In exactly the same way, people can find in the Qur'an either peace and humility or jihad against the unbelievers, and the biblical prophets can be read as preaching love of justice or contempt for transgressors.

This lesson is beautifully illustrated by John McPhee's fascinating *Encounters with the Archdruid*, in which leading U.S. environmentalist and wilderness lover David Brower was taken on three expeditions (down the Colorado River, in the Rocky Mountains, and on an undeveloped island) with men who made their livings controlling, dominating, and domesticating precisely the areas Brower hoped to keep wild.[37] All the men listened to the same wilderness, but only Brower heard lessons about human limits and reciprocity. Unlike the developers, Brower was inspired to environmental activism when:

> the mountains talked to me through…the jay's complaint, the kooka-burra's laugh, the coyote's howl, pines answering the wind, fallen leaves answering our shuffling feet, and the lilting notes of a stream, hermit thrush, or a canyon wren completed the symphony.[38]

Spiritual Subjectivity

There is a further message beyond what McKibben or Brower heard, one actually present in traditional scriptures, though many who hold those scriptures sacred tend to ignore it. The message is that creation is not only a generous gift from God or a field of relationships from which we can learn spiritual lessons about acceptance or humility. Nature also possesses its own spiritual subjectivity. It celebrates, worships, and has a presence that is not reducible to what it reveals about God or teaches us about ourselves.

Consider these excerpts from biblical psalms, essential writings for both Judaism and Christianity:

> *Let the heavens rejoice, let the earth be glad;*
> *let the sea resound, and all that is in it.*
> *Let the fields be jubilant, and everything in them;*
> *let all the trees of the forest sing for joy.*

Let all creation rejoice before the Lord. (96: 11–13)
Let everything with breath praise God. (150: 6)

Or recall that in Psalm 148 we find the assertion of a remarkable equivalence between humans and the rest of creation: *all* of us should praise God because we are all—sea creatures and snow, fruit trees and wild animals and cattle—God's creations.

How literally are we to take this? When the Qur'an (40:57) states: "The creation of the heavens and earth is greater than the creation of mankind, but most of the people do not know" and (6:38) that all other species are "a community like yours" that will be "gathered" by Allah, the message seems clear. Everything counts.

Precisely this same sense of the subjectivity of nature, of its inherent capacity to express its own relation of the sacred, can be found in essentially secular (in conventional terms) nature writers like Barry Lopez:

Whatever evaluation we finally make of a stretch of land...no matter how profound or accurate, we will find it inadequate. The land retains an identity of its own, still deeper and more subtle than we can know. Our obligation toward it then becomes simple: to approach with an uncalculating mind, with an attitude of regard....To intend from the beginning to preserve some of the mystery within it as a kind of wisdom to be experienced, not questioned. And to be alert for its openings, for that moment when something sacred reveals itself within the mundane, and you know the land knows you are there.[39]

The idea comes through once again from Thomas Berry, a Catholic priest and one of the visionary thinkers of religious environmentalism: "The natural world is subject as well as object...the maternal source of our being...the larger sacred community to which we belong."[40]

Yet unlike that of people, the spiritual subjectivity of Lopez's "land" or Berry's "sacred community" will not be expressed in a language. What then is it that the natural world does that would count as praise of God? Since we have no direct line on God's perspective on this, the question becomes: how do *we* have to see the world so that we can see *it* as praising God or knowing that we are here?

We would, I believe, have to experience it from a perspective not defined by our own pursuit of profit, military conquest, pleasure, or power (e.g., in sport hunting, mountain climbing, or genetic engineering). Our seeing would need to suspend or transcend economic, social, and ideological identity. In doing so, we might encounter a reality that, as is often the case with spiritual or mystical experience, transcends ordinary language, for the standard language speaker is the standard ego. We typically talk and listen from the standpoint of "me" and "mine," from a set of desires and beliefs conditioned by our social position and attachments. To experience the spiritual subjectivity of nature, something else is needed.

This something else requires that we remember we are beings that breathe and eat, sense the sun, feel the wind and rain, and experience love, fear, and pleasure in our bodies. As trees root to the earth, so do—in rather more mobile ways— our own legs. If the earth's surface is 80 percent ocean, so are our own bodies. Human children develop through play, just like young lions. Ants and beavers work together to build their homes, as we do. The trees breathe out, we breathe in—and vice versa. Our eyes have evolved to see this landscape, our ears to hear these birds and rustling leaves, our tongues to taste the food that grows here.

Rooted in something other than conventional social identity, we may sense the wondrous and mysterious reality we share with the rest of the earth: that plants arc toward the light and dig deep for water; that river currents swirl around rocks; that there are colors instead of just varying shades of gray; that birds sing, wolves howl at the moon, and waves make patterns in the sand; that each of us has been born to dance upon the earth. And most important, we are all here together—being rather than not being. And if *being* by itself is the source of wonder and the sacred, then *beings* can be of value, even if they do not have language or personal experience. The oak tree, the beetle, and the star do not have to talk about themselves or feel pleasure and pain to exist and to be awe-inspiring. Sensing all this we can follow religious poet W. H. Auden's invitation to "bless what there is for being."[41]

To remember all this, we have to surrender, if only for a little while, our politics and our theology, our social status and the list of books we have written. And we will have to directly engage with the natural Other. Such engagement may take a wide variety of forms: visiting one particular tree for a few minutes a day—for years, watching animals give birth and die, farming in a way that doesn't damage the soil, studying the intricacies of nature without seeking profit or power.

Consider this suggestive example. Jim Nollman, who among other things likes to outfit a boat with underwater speakers and jam on his guitar with humpback whales, offers the concept of "interspecies protocol."[42] This is a form of etiquette, or mannered respect, that requires us to develop careful and detailed acquaintance with, for example, lions; that we get to know them as individuals, not just types ("this is just what 'lions-in-general' do") and take their actions as a sign of a reasonable intentionality. For an example, Nollman tells a story of how a particular tribe of African Bushmen had learned to share a local waterhole with a pride of local lions. Each group knew when during the day was their turn; encounters were extremely rare and always benign—until new settlers arrived and failed to observe the schedule, and a lion mauling resulted.

Interspecies protocol, Nollman emphasizes, is far more than simply admiring the beauty and grace of lions or of being moved by the wonders of nature. It requires an active practice of relationship in which we are willing to be affected by what we encounter without reduction or objectification. As Nobel Prize–winning scientist Barbara McClintock put it, we must see each ear of corn, each cell, as an individual and not just as an object that exemplifies universal laws.[43] Here the similarity to other forms of spirituality arises again. Compassion requires us to respect the freedom of others to respond as the particular being they are. When we seek to limit their response, impose our vision on them, or stop listening to what they have to tell us, the possibility of authentic compassion is ended.

The Ecofeminist Body

There is never a good reason to be greedy or violent, but we do have to displace and use other beings to survive. We may give up much of our conventionally social ego and survive, even flourish—but we cannot stop eating, drinking, or keeping warm.

In some versions of spirituality, our essential need to consume, sexual instincts, and socially expected standard of living are considered so dangerous that we are called on to virtually end them through practices such as severe fasting, celibacy, and extreme poverty. A good deal of traditional spirituality in Hinduism, Buddhism, and Christianity[44] takes a dualistic attitude toward the body, contrasting it with the soul, God, or spiritual insight. Patanjali, the most important source of the religious understanding of yoga, can be read this way, especially when he says that "purity" can give rise to "dislike" of one's body (II. 40) and when he identifies spiritual development with "freedom from the body" (III. 43).[45] In Buddhism, there are meditations in which the body and sensory experience are represented as fragile, a great burden, or even disgusting.[46] Comparable expressions in theistic religions are easy to find.

Yet such traditional anti-body attitudes need not reflect a primordial fear of the material in and of itself so much as fear of an all too common human inability to relate to the material without relentless attachment. On this view, it is not our physicality that is the problem, but what we make of it. Perhaps that is why, along-side their disparagement of our bodily nature, religious traditions also offer celebrations of the physical. In one place, they may denigrate the senses or sexuality, but soon after, they may advocate a spiritually oriented acceptance, joyfulness, and compassionate engagement with them. That is why Buddhism has a rich literature of poetry in which nature is an image of enlightenment; why Jesus could tell us to learn the spiritual lessons of flowers and children; why the Song of Songs, called by the revered Jewish sage Hillel the most important book of the Bible, is an extended celebration of springtime, the beauties of nature, and sex; and why serious and traditionally oriented yoga masters like Sivananda talk of the importance of the body as a vehicle for the soul to reach God.

What these more positive views of the body suggest is that our physical urges are no more evil than work in the world, love of family, or enjoyment of a fresh strawberry. Only when our connection to them turns to compulsion and addiction are they damaging. The fact that this kind of turning is so widespread does not mean that we must give up the body, but that through spiritual practice, we must learn to hold its urges comfortably rather than destructively.

Such an integrated balance, rooted in celebration rather than denigration of the body, is perhaps the central message of cultural ecofeminism, which maintains that the bodily existence we have in common with the rest of life is the basis for spiritual identity. Grace Paley describes this as a "revolutionary understanding that we call feminist and ecological, in which we share the world with all creatures and all living things and know that their stories are our own."[47] In this form of understanding, Charlene Spretnak adds, the "distinction between inner and outer mind dissolves, and we meet our larger self."[48] In the larger self, we "deepen our experience of communion with nature" and "discover that the divine is immanent" in the world.[49] And in Carol Christ's words, the divine is "the whole of which we are a part... earth and sky, the ground on which we stand, and all the animals, plants, and other beings to which we are related."[50]

If the bodies of trees and mosquitoes and turtles are of spiritual value, so are ours. If the world, if nature, is divine—so are we. If dolphins and wild irises can coexist with other fish and other plants, surely we—smart as we are (though that may be our undoing)—can as well. With these reflections, ecofeminist spirituality overcomes the familiar split between the body and the soul, the material world and consciousness.

And it is not only that a body-despising spiritual dualism is mistaken, spiritual ecofeminists argue, but that it is inherently oppressive. Devaluing the body and nature and privileging the mind or soul has been the ideological basis for a comparable denigration and then subjugation of women, nonwhites, and colonized peoples. All these groups have been represented as more "natural," primitive, unreasoning, and unspiritual in comparison with men, whites, or colonizers. In all these cases, the pattern of justification is the same, as is the resulting "defilement of earth's body" and the defilement of women's bodies.[51]

The rejection of the body may also be rooted in a fear of mortality. The emphasis on spiritual reality as eternal, the sense that what is wrong with the body is that it changes, dies, and decays, may reflect the ego's desperate attachment to its current form far more than a spiritual yearning for the divine. And this desperation may be based in a profound misunderstanding.

Why can't *we* live forever? Why can't *our* souls dwell in eternity? Quite simply because that is not who *we* are—at least, not as we actually experience ourselves. We rejoice in new life and mourn for the dead. We sense the preciousness of our own sentience and, in the face of our approaching dotage, acutely feel what will be lost as that sentience diminishes. We know ourselves as beings who have learned from experience and change over the years. We defend ourselves from assault, watch our children grow, and buy an awful lot of vitamin pills to slow down the aging process. Outside of the occasional profession of faith in our immortal souls, we talk and act like the very mortal creatures we are. If there is a part of us that is immortal, it is known only very fleetingly and through a much darkened glass, and it is an image sparked by the ego's fear of loss as much as by any authentic spiritual aspiration. Spiritual freedom is not exemption from transformation, but the ability to joyfully accept it.[52]

Social Questions

Having learned the spiritual lessons of nature, Canadian ecologist David Suzuki suggests, we no longer ask, "How do we reduce the deficit?" or "How do we carve our niche in the global economy?" but instead "What is an economy for?" "How much is enough?" and "What are the things that provide [real and lasting] joy and happiness, peace of mind and satisfaction?"[53] In this way, there is, he believes, a natural movement from love of nature to a deep questioning of the social order that is destroying it.

In one telling example, consider how Howard Zahniser, who spent seven years crafting the Wilderness Act to preserve large areas in the United States untouched, was self-consciously moved by spiritual as well as practical goals. Zahniser believed that the "most profound" of wilderness values was the way it could support a person's ability "to sense and see his own humble, dependent relationship to all of life." Wilderness was able to provide a uniquely powerful sense of the reality beyond the individual self, a sense enormously necessary in a society dominated by consumption and technology. At the core of this spiritual sensibility was "the recognition that we are interdependent and obligated members of this larger community of life."[54]

Thus as meditation enabled the Dhamma brothers, men with violent pasts and decades of incarceration, to choose lives of greater peacefulness, self-acceptance, and compassion, so a spiritual sense of nature has led people to become engaged in ecological activism. This is shown by the self-descriptions of countless ecological activists from Brower and Zahniser to the leaders of Greenpeace and world-class biologists. In one compelling instance, we find Kenya's Wangari Maathai, who received the Nobel Peace Prize for her work in reforesting Kenya, offering this understanding of her work:

All of us have a God in us, and that God is the spirit that unites all life, everything that is on this planet. It must be this voice that is telling me to do something, and I am sure it's the same voice that is speaking to everybody on this planet—at least everybody who seems to be concerned about the fate of the world.[55]

Rick Bass, writer and environmental activist, tells us:

> Somebody's God put the spark and light of peace and joy and worship and
> awe in my heart, when I stand in a cathedral of ancient cedars, or when
> I am far back in the distant mountains, so close to the sky and a scale of
> time greater than my own brief stay—and that spark tells me that for me,
> activism is a form of prayer, a way of paying back some small fraction of the
> blessing that the wilderness is to me; a way of celebrating and protecting
> that creation, and a way of giving thanks.[56]

If gratitude can lead to charity, humility to peacefulness, and mindfulness to less
compulsion and addiction, so in our era of environmental crisis, the felt reciprocity with nature can lead us toward social change.

Just because nature spirituality has inherent social implications, it raises some
difficult questions.

Rachel Carson's rejection of the control of nature, Gibson's demand that we
reenchant the world, Native Americans' horror at the white man's commodification of the earth—in a time of environmental crisis, all these have an undeniable
appeal. When air, water, earth, and our own bloodstreams are polluted, when we
are rendering a species extinct every 10 minutes or so, something else is desperately needed.

Yet haven't we needed, or at least thought we needed, a culture of disenchantment, objectification, and commodification? If treating nature like an object rather
than like kin is so bad, what has made so many of us so eager to do it for so long?
Has this all just been one big mistake? (Note that every spiritual perspective has to
face some form of this question. If we really are children of God or pure detached
awareness, how have we gotten so misled into thinking we are something else?)

The simple answer is that control-oriented science and technology have enabled
us to deal with illness, food production, transportation, and childbirth (to name
a few) in immediately beneficial ways. Seemingly small advances like eyeglasses,
birth control, and refrigeration can make monumental differences in ordinary
life. The rainforest, modern environmentalism's symbol of threatened ecological
interconnection, is a place where many tribes suffer from near-starvation, relentless parasites, and early death. It is not hard to see why at least some of them
have bought into modern conveniences like antibiotics ("anti-life"!), aspirin, and
plastic water jugs.[57] In the real world, nature, we might say, is not pretty, not (as
Buddhist ecologist Joanna Macy suggests) a "lover,"[58] but a dangerous place where
everything from tigers to viruses would like nothing better than to eat us alive.
This is why some complain that all the talk of nature's spirituality is just romantic
nonsense based in the privileges of wealth and modern technology—a view possible only after nature has been tamed.[59]

In the same vein, we may ask any nature lover who seeks cooperation rather than control: what will you give up? Jet travel, indoor plumbing, anesthesia, or the (remarkably energy-hungry) Internet?

In answering these important concerns, we can begin by noting that they mirror, though perhaps in a much more difficult way, spiritual dilemmas about how to live a life of compassion and selflessness and still hold a job, live in a house, and pay off your Visa card bill. Certainly we can answer with superficial generalities about not taking more than your share, appropriate technology, and sustainability. But the concrete details will not come so easily. If the response is that we can keep all we have, we just need better technology, it might be remembered that nonpolluting, non-resource-exhausting versions of most modern conveniences are very far off and will in all likelihood be far too expensive for most people.[60] I am not saying that there is nothing to be done right now. There are many things, from energy conservation to local food to being a lot more cautious in allowing new chemicals in the air and water. I am saying that these complex and difficult questions will be with us for a long time, and many have no easy answer whatsoever.

Yet a sense of kinship with nature, while it may take a particular form in a technologically advanced society, is certainly not purely a modern creation. Zen haiku from the thirteenth century, the celebration of the beauties of spring in the Song of Songs, the delight in other creatures that is so prevalent in indigenous traditions—all these coexisted with high infant mortality, low life expectancy, punishing winters, and having to carry water on your back.

A second difficulty has to do with those who love (or at least say they love) nature and yet are not too fond of people, whose joy in forest or stream coexists with, as in the case of the highly influential twentieth-century German philosopher Martin Heidegger (1889–1976), a morally fatal attraction to aggressive nationalism and anti-Semitism. Though couched in often impenetrable philosophical jargon, Heidegger's understanding of nature actually resembles those found in Zen poetry, Hasidic rabbis who celebrated the spiritual power of meadows at midnight, and even some indigenous peoples. As well, his critique of modernity's reduction of nature to a mere resource for purely human ends anticipates many of today's ethically, politically, and spiritually oriented forms of environmentalism. How could he have combined two such seemingly opposite ways of understanding the world?

Heidegger's profound political misjudgment of Nazism, alongside his long-term interest in finding something spiritually special about Germany (its culture, its soil, its blood), show that simply loving nature will never be enough. And not only was Heidegger far from the only Nazi to have this deep contradiction in his understanding of the world[61] but also similar moral and spiritual failings can be found throughout the history of much of the world conservation movement. For many years, environmental concern focused on the preservation of pristine wilderness

and lacked any systematic awareness of the human costs of pollution and especially of the racial and class inequality of exposure to environmental toxins.[62]

Ultimately, however, these moral failings are hardly the special property of those
who find spirit in nature. Many members of traditional religious groups have been
similarly self-interested, morally hypocritical, or blind to the social effects of their
actions. And this goes for the secular world as well. It is all too common to see
selfless revolutionaries turn into oppressive bureaucrats, talented engineers not
ask what their inventions will be used for, creative entrepreneurs make money off
physical or cultural poison, and otherwise kind and generous souls cheerfully eating the flesh of animals raised in the most horrible conditions. The difficult truth
is that we can never be sure of the overall moral stature or spiritual development
of a person based on a single issue. We can be humble yet lack mindfulness, kind
yet wasteful, politically correct and verbally aggressive, adept at meditation and
arrogant.

Finally, the great advantage of certain forms of spirituality is often the comfort they bring, a comfort based in the notion of an all-powerful personality to
whom we can turn or a universally valid method of enlightenment we can practice. Yet nature, or at least the earth, is in rough shape. There is no guarantee
that it will pull through in anything like its present already severely compromised
form. Nature is sacred and awe-inspiring—and simultaneously vulnerable and
under attack. Oneness with God, complete enlightenment—these are states of
the soul that promise an end to suffering. But to become one with a clear-cut
forest, an ocean choking on plastic waste, or a frog born with organs outside its
body because of pollution—this is a kinship with suffering, not an escape from
it. In this way, spirituality tied to nature, while often similar to other forms, has
its own distinct trials. Yet just because of these, it has its own particular potential
strength. Developing spiritual virtues in the face of global environmental insanity
and our own moral sloppiness, technological distraction, and attachment to ease
is a daunting challenge. It takes us far beyond the dualisms of self and world,
spirituality and politics, and personal life and our effects on the entire earth to the
point where all these are seen as indissolubly fused. In just that way it can enrich
our spiritual life as perhaps nothing else.

IO

Spirituality and Politics

*At the risk of seeming ridiculous, let me say that a true
revolutionary is guided by great feelings of love.*

CHE GUEVARA, LEADER OF THE CUBAN REVOLUTION

*Question: What about Gandhi's life and message has most
influenced you?
Answer: Many of us can be so holy, you know, but we don't get
very much done except satisfying our own personal needs. But
Gandhi did what he did for the whole world.*

CESAR CHAVEZ[1]

*We must cry out against injustice or by our silence consent to it.
If we keep silent, the very stones of the street will cry out.*

DOROTHY DAY[2]

*When the deepest and most grounded spiritual vision is mar-
ried to a practical and pragmatic drive to transform all existing
political, economic, and social institutions, a holy force—the
power of wisdom and love in action—is born.*

ANDREW HARVEY[3]

TO TALK ABOUT the place of spirituality in the world of politics, and the place of politics in the world of spirituality, we may begin with the environmental crisis.

Environmentalists, said Aldo Leopold, "walk alone in a world of wounds."[4] I am not sure about the "alone" part, but a "world of wounds" sounds right. From the disappearing rainforest to the pollution-caused dead zones in the Gulf of Mexico, from the melting glaciers to the rising rate of childhood cancer, the wounds are all around us—and are a serious challenge to spiritual virtues.

Consider, for a start, mindfulness—a rock-steady, nonreactive awareness of ourselves and the world. In the face of environmental issues, this means taking in a host of complicated, difficult details[5] and being mindful of the painful emotions all this knowledge brings out in us: fear, despair, anger at "those responsible," and the numbness that comes when we avoid or deny the ever-growing devastation.

Next, however, spiritual teachings prescribe peacefulness: acceptance of our fate and gratitude for the beauties of life. It is one thing to feel at one with God or spiritual truth in a tastefully decorated meditation room, a nicely appointed church with the sun streaming through stained-glass windows, or a yoga retreat center in Costa Rica. In these places, peacefulness comes, if not easily, at least without the lurking sense of doom that we might feel reading any serious environmental magazine. Is peacefulness even appropriate when we hear about a mountain turned to rubble for yet more coal or a tribe poisoned for yet more oil?

Then there is compassion. As a feeling, this is a heartfelt desire that (in the Buddhist formula) all beings might be at peace, happy, and free from suffering. As a form of life, it means a gentle, persistent kindness extended to all. Can this "all" include public relations firms who knowingly try to confuse the public about the science of global warming or pesticides and the bought politicians who cut special deals for toxic industries? These people are responsible for a kind of long-distance, slow-motion murder of humans and of countless other species as well.

Finally, there is the ethical question. Virtually all forms of spirituality emphasize the nonnegotiable need to refrain from harming others, stealing, or bearing false witness and to ease the sufferings of all sentient beings, care for the defenseless, and build a society where "justice rolls down like the waters, and righteousness like a mighty stream" (Amos: 5:24). Yet as difficult as moral life has always been, the vast and intricate interconnections among human beings today make much of morality almost impossible as an individual. In our everyday lives, we steal from future generations by consuming nonrenewable resources and daily use products that hurt the innocent. Can we be moral if we are not trying to alter all this?

To make the point more concrete, it is certainly a spiritual moment to behold the beauties of a sunset over a breathtaking mountain range, thanking God or spirit or the mystery of life for the vibrant colors, the slowly shifting patterns of clouds, and our deep feelings of peace. But surely the spiritual character of the experience becomes somewhat problematic if we are watching the sunset from the deck of our $2 million chalet, high on the cliff of a gated community for which a highly skilled security team keeps the riffraff out. And it is even more problematic if we have bought our clifftop villa with money made from a factory whose cheap labor we help guarantee by supporting the local dictator who keeps the workers in line. Gratitude does not stand on its own but exists in a broader moral and political context in which we determine whether we actually have a right to that for which we are grateful. The *spiritual* authenticity of gratitude is therefore at least in part a political question of justice and rights, one that must be seriously confronted if our spirituality is not to sink into self-interested moral favoritism.

These reflections apply to the full range of social and political problems: violations of human rights; the oppression of women, homosexuals, or ethnic and religious minorities; and unconscionable poverty in the face of arrogant affluence. These realities pose profound difficulties for mindfulness, peacefulness, compassion, and morality—and for God as well. How we are to feel God's presence—or, indeed, any authentic spiritual emotion—as we behold so much needless suffering? With or without belief in God, as a Jew or a Christian, a Buddhist, pagan, or freelance eclectic spiritual type like Thoreau, how can we keep our sense of spiritual presence from simply evaporating as we behold—or directly experience—a concentration camp, a starving child, or the screams of someone tortured by the secret police?

More than a decade ago, I wrote a book exploring these questions—*A Spirituality of Resistance: Finding a Peaceful Heart Protecting the Earth*. The short answer I gave then was that to be authentic, spiritual peace requires active social, political, and moral resistance. In this chapter, I build on that discussion, together with my argument in a book called *Joining Hands*, that the worlds of politics and religion, though often seemingly opposed, actually have much to teach each other.

Connections between Politics and Spirituality

When our social relationships are organized justly and rationally, people's rights are respected, individuals and groups are treated fairly by social authorities and receive respectful recognition in the wider culture, and precious human and natural resources are used with foresight and good judgment. When injustice and irrationality prevail, we have exploitation and oppression. Minorities are persecuted, women are relegated to social inferiority, dissidents are suppressed, the earth is poisoned, and the rich get endlessly (and sometimes obscenely) richer.

Politics is the realm of thought and action in which we determine how just and rational our societies will be.

Do spirituality and politics have any connection—besides the fact, that is, that they exclude one another? Politics, after all, is bound up in mass movements, struggles for power, and competition over wealth, property, cultural recognition, and political independence. It is expressed in public conflicts that aim at fulfilling the ego's demands for power, autonomy, and a reasonable standard of living. Moreover, political life is about what is happening right now: this election, that fight to depose a dictator, looming budget cuts, a referendum about gay marriage. And it seems that politics is usually a zero-sum game: Republicans versus Democrats, doves versus hawks, supporters of Israel versus supporters of Palestine, my country-gender-ethnicity-party-way of life versus yours.

In stark contrast, we usually associate spirituality with an inner quest for mindfulness and compassion and a questioning of the ego's demands. Spirituality focuses not on current conditions but on timeless truths, not on struggle but on gratitude. In spirituality, everybody wins, because spirituality is essentially concerned with the virtues that promote a better society by promoting better individuals.

To many spiritual seekers, political people are angry, aggressive, and not in touch with the fundamental problems of social life, which have to do with emotional immaturity, distorted consciousness, and mistaken values, not laws and institutions. Unless we open our hearts and develop our awareness, many spiritual teachers counsel, no change of political leaders or property relations will have any significant effect. One oppressive group will replace another; the new system will be as ultimately unfulfilling and violent as the old one. Only when we change ourselves from within will we be able to change the world.

To the politically oriented, spirituality often seems a narcissistic escape made possible by a refusal to confront social reality. Emphasis on spiritual experiences tends to ignore the question of the social conditions that make those experiences possible. The stress on internal and individual change virtually guarantees blindness to one's own position of privilege. As well, the consumerist gloss on many contemporary spiritual forms—claims of near-instant personal growth, tacky self-promoting by self-proclaimed spiritual masters, expensive fees for access to priceless wisdom—indicates that spirituality is nothing more than another slickly marketed fad. The whole thing is a kind of meditating while Rome burns that ignores the root problems of human suffering: institutional structures of power, ownership, and privilege.

If each side here tends to caricature the other, political types ignoring the vibrant history of spiritual social activists like Gandhi, King, or Aung San Suu Kyi, and spiritual aspirants turning a blind eye to the great love (not to mention courage and self-sacrifice) that have been part of political movements for national independence, human rights, and social equality, well, there is also a fair amount of truth in each side's critique of the other. Political movements are often violent and self-serving; spirituality is often escapist and, well, self-serving. Spirituality can be an avoidance of reality; political activism can simply up the privileges of one group at the expense of others. Like science, which often sacrifices truth to personal advancement and human welfare to military power or profit, or art and literature, which can be merely trendy, both politics and spirituality have long records of narrowness and ethical inconsistency.

Yet that is not the end of the story, not by a long shot. At least in certain forms, politics and spirituality actually have something in common besides their flaws. At their best, they share a persistent and deeply meaningful dissatisfaction with the status quo.[6] Both offer a critical response to suffering, because both are based in the belief that taken-for-granted structures that shape our lives can be radically improved. If for politics these structures center on ownership and social position, and for spirituality on attachment and mistaken self-understanding, they nevertheless agree that what we have now is not the best we can get and prescribe fundamental change as a response: political change, even revolution, for one; personal change, a near-total self-transformation, for the other. We might say that for both the fundamental enemy is complacency, a resigned acceptance of sufferings that in fact can be overcome. As German Christian Dorothy Soelle writes, in phrases that could equally describe many secular political movements, spirituality's rejection of the social order "begins with our not being at home in...a world founded on power, possession, and violence."[7]

It may be that spirituality and politics, far from simply being enemies, have something to learn from each other.

Political Lessons for Spiritual Life

Let us look first at some reasons why spiritual life requires political awareness and action.

Our lives, no matter how intimately *personal*, are not *individual*. Every time we turn on our computers or drive a car, we use energy that has effects on the global climate. We live in cities, states, and nations controlled by centralized governments whose laws we obey and whose policies our taxes support. Our social status and privilege depend on taken-for-granted norms in which certain groups receive more respect, recognition, and opportunity than others. Some, perhaps a great deal, of what we have, we have only because others do not.

If we are part of, and support, a social order that is essentially unjust, how much spiritual development is possible for us? Can the self be liberated spiritually if it tacitly supports a government that is subverts democracy (as the United States has done in Guatemala, Iran, and El Salvador), ignores the oppression of minorities (as racial segregation was ignored for decades), or uses products that are toxic (as are most people's cleaning products, computers, and cell phones)? If these realities are part of the social order that sustains us, do we not have to take seriously the task of changing them to achieve a moral minimum in our own lives?

Here is another way to put this point. To exercise spiritual virtues like compassion, many traditions teach, good intentions are not enough. Knowledge and moral judgment are also required. Traditional Buddhism called the first *upaya*, "skill in means." To be compassionate, for example, requires that we extend ourselves not only gently and lovingly but also in the most appropriate way. It would not do, for example, to offer a very hungry Orthodox Jew a ham sandwich. But realizing this requires knowledge of Orthodox Judaism's dietary laws. One of the first socially oriented modern Buddhist teachers warned: "To be Dhammic [in line with

Buddhist Teaching], besides being honest and virtuous, also requires knowledge.
If one's knowledge is incorrect, no matter how honest and virtuous, one will not
be able to make it Dhammic. They might make laws which go against nature and
which create suffering and danger."[8]

Moral judgment is essential because we need to respond fairly to the suffering we wish to ease. If a person is suffering because his slaves have been freed or
because the sight of two women getting married upsets him, a moral judgment
is required that whatever our compassionate response to his suffering is, it is *not*
reinstituting slavery or outlawing gay marriage. In this way a moral code, which
writ large is a theory of justice for society as a whole, needs to guide even the most
heartfelt and intuitive compassion.

Part of our responsibility, then, is to determine whether the way we earn a
living and the privileges and status we enjoy are just or unjust, rational or needlessly destructive, and what is a morally justified way to respond to socially based
suffering. If we determine that we are part of an unjust or irrational social order,
we then need to ask ourselves how things can be made better. When groups are in
conflict, individually oriented concepts of suffering and kindness are not enough.
The actions we take and the social changes we support will be determined by our
beliefs about what is just and how best to achieve justice.

These are all political questions—no more capable of being answered by the
vast majority of spiritual teachings than how to program a DVD player. Responding
to them requires a developed perspective on what a just society is and a political
strategy that recommends actions most likely not simply to lessen misery in any
particular circumstance, but to reduce the overall, long-term tendency of a particular social order to create pain. It is not about healing the sick but changing the
social conditions that promote disease; not about being nice to people who are suffering but making sure that they have rights, are treated fairly by social authorities,
and receive respect even if they are racial or ethnic minorities or poor. Spiritual
groups can be socially involved by doing charity or relief work, and this is certainly
a fine thing. But such work is often politically neutral in relation to the ongoing
structures of oppression.

As a concrete example of the way a political perspective helps us encompass the
full reality of the world in which we live, consider the deep spiritual relationship
with nature discussed in the last chapter. For many people, this relationship led
to a sincere desire to create natural areas—protected reserves where fellow living
creatures could be free from human threats.

There is actually some question about the initial motivation of many of those
who helped create many of the world's national parks,[9] but even if we attribute
to the founders the best of intentions, their spiritual attachment to wilderness
too often coexisted with an oppressive blindness to local people who had been
using these wild areas for generations. To preserve nature, native tribes had to be

expelled—often at gunpoint and to their cultural or physical death. This has been true for U.S. national parks and for comparable areas throughout the world. The result is millions of conservation refugees whose human fate has been forgotten while others' spiritual needs for wild nature have been met.[10] Without a political understanding of the way dominant races or nations often ignore the interests of the powerless, this kind of moral mistake will be all too common.

Overall, in the modern world an absence of political awareness is really only possible at the cost of denial and avoidance. For better or worse, probably everyone reading these words has access to newspapers and TV, the Internet and a library. It is possible not to comprehend, at least in outline, the basic facts of our collective political situation only if we refuse to look at it. That refusal requires at least a little bit of knowledge about what we are intentionally not seeing: the ecological consequences of our lifestyle, what the government does with our taxes, or the shapes tyranny takes throughout the world. But to the extent that spiritual life rests on willful ignorance and moral inattention, it will be deficient. We cannot be mindful and compassionate, "save all beings from suffering," or love the divine in every person without an awareness of—and a response to—the political realities that encompass our lives.

The Spiritual Gift to Politics

But the story does not end there. Although I would be only too happy to see every spiritual seeker, convinced by the force of these reflections, rush out and join the liberal to radical political groups I favor, there is another side to the matter. Not only do spiritual seekers need political understanding and engagement but also political movements desperately need spiritual wisdom. While responsible for some pivotal improvements in the human situation, activist groups and political theorists have also exhibited serious deficiencies. A spiritual involvement in political activism can help redress those weaknesses, particularly political penchants for being self-serving, internally divided, blind to the effects of trauma, and bound by culturally limited ideas of what a truly liberated society could be like.

Far too often, political groups, whose battle cry had been some variant of the French Revolution's original "liberty, equality, fraternity," create their own repressive dictatorships or at least take for themselves precisely the privileges and power they decried in the old ruling group. This was the disastrous history of communist movements and can be found in many nationalist revolutions as well.[11] On a smaller scale, one can see the evolution of self-protective and self-interested union bureaucracies or leaders of gender and racial movements. This recurring pattern gives rise to the spiritual critique of politics as simply the wrong way to go about making social life better and the common claim that we need a "revolution in consciousness" before we can have one in the streets.

Besides an out-and-out betrayal of their original goals, political movements have a disappointing history of partiality. The Declaration of Independence's claim to uphold the rights of "all men" left out those who were propertyless, female, or African American. After the Civil War, the movement to gain the vote for African Americans abandoned a similar quest for women. Nationalist movements in formerly colonized countries often disregard the rights of tribal groups. Unions seek decent wages and working conditions for members but may be racist or sexist and unconcerned with the fate of nonunionized workers. Political radicals in the early 1960s had virtually no sense of their own oppressive treatment of women or contempt for politically conservative workers. In all such cases the inspiring values of political movements—freedom, equality, human rights, universal respect—are applied with a disheartening selectivity.

Political movements are also frequently rife with infighting, invective, and hostility toward those who disagree. The entire social world becomes divided into the just and the unjust, the victims and the oppressor, the exploited and the exploited. Not surprisingly, a mind-set that sees the wealthy, the government, men, whites, colonialists, or imperialists as simply "the enemy" is all too easily reproduced within the political group itself. And then fellow activists with a different perspective or who favor a different strategy become the enemy in turn. Because encounters are understood almost purely in terms of absolute moral categories, compromise, mutual understanding, and empathy for another's life experience are in short supply. Destructive internal struggles of otherwise hopeful political movements result.[12]

Of course, it is true that in some contexts compromise and mutual understanding are impossible. Corporations committed to polluting without penalty, dictators who shoot union leaders, or imperialists destroying native cultures may simply be unreachable. But there are other political settings—for example, civil wars or struggles between ethnic groups—that are shaped as much by mutual trauma as by any simple division into oppressors and oppressed. In this dimension, a too simple view of either side's moral standing usually engenders new injustice, with the traumas of violence and victimhood reproduced from one generation to the next. Here the most hopeful goal is not the triumph of the oppressed over the oppressors, but reconciliation between people on both sides who carry painful memories and urgent fears, one that allows the present community and its descendants to live without continuing carnage. Much of political theory and the movements based in its claims have a difficult (if not impossible) time conceptualizing such situations.[13]

Finally, the goals of political movements too often take the conventional social ego for granted and see the benefits of consumerism, acquisitiveness, and a dominating attitude toward nature as unquestioned goods that simply need to be distributed more fairly. The result is a too limited horizon of political possibility.

Disenfranchised groups get the vote, but their political support is keyed to narrow self-interest or militant nationalism. Incomes are raised, but poverty gives way not to enduring satisfaction but to driven consumerism and environmental reckless-ness. Sexual freedom turns into cheapened pornographic sexuality rather than a grateful joy in our capacity for pleasure. Political critique focuses on public waste and injustice but frequently has too little to offer in their place.

Spiritual virtues can be of great help in overcoming each of these weak-nesses of conventional political movements. Nonviolence, compassion, and mindfulness-based self-awareness can be antidotes to political violence and a knee-jerk dualism that understands political conflict only in terms of heroes and villains rather than in terms of the mutual sufferings of traumatized groups. Universal compassion for all sentient beings or a belief that we are all made in the image of God may soften political movements' tendencies to favoritism. Spirituality's hallmark critique of attachment to material objects, social status, and public accomplishment may add some needed depth to what we do after national independence, social equality, or "the revolution."

So far, my discussion of the connections between spirituality and politics has been long on abstractions and lacking in examples. Thankfully, however, there is a rich tradition of spiritual social activists engaging in struggles for human rights, social justice, peace, and sustainability. They have done so without rigid attach-ment to a particular religious tradition, with a great emphasis on spiritual virtues such as compassion and self-awareness, and with an encompassing love of life. As we examine some illuminating case studies, we will see how spiritual social activ-ism can enrich both spirituality and political life.

Engaged Buddhism

Engaged Buddhism is the application of

> Buddhist teachings to the resolution of social problems—[it] has emerged in the context of a global conversation on human rights, distributive justice, and social progress. Inasmuch as these concepts have had few parallels in the classical formulations of early Buddhism... "Engaged Buddhism" is unprecedented... a new chapter in the history of the tradition.[14]

Created in Southeast Asia by the Vietnamese Zen Buddhist monk Thich Nhat Hanh and Thailand's Theravada Sulak Sivaraksa, Engaged Buddhism subse-quently developed a significant presence in the west, particularly the United States. A global umbrella organization, the International Network of Engaged Buddhists, lists a wide variety of relevant focus areas, including gender, human rights, peace, alternative development, and climate change.[15] Despite a broad diversity of social settings and issues, the many manifestations of Engaged Buddhism share a number of common themes that provide paradigm examples of spiritual social activism.

The overriding principle, which Nhat Hanh reports aroused considerable dismay among his fellow monks, is that the place of the Buddhist monk or serious layperson is not in a monastery pursuing socially isolated forms of intense meditation and other austerities.[16] Devout Buddhists, rather, need to engage with the common people of their society to respond to the fundamental sources of suffering beyond individual attachments.

The source might be war, in which case the Buddhist task is to gently advocate for peace. It might be extreme poverty, and then the Buddhist will in a respectful but clear way support the well-being of the peasants, workers, or unemployed. It might be unsustainable deforestation, in which case monks might (as indeed they did) "ordain" trees in Thailand's rainforest to keep them from being cut down. Confronted by the threat of nuclear war, environmental recklessness, or the dangers of nuclear energy, engaged Buddhists offer public critique and protest: trespassing nuclear test sites, connecting Buddhist values to ecological awareness and modesty in consumption, and focusing attention on the unanswered question of where to put radioactive wastes.[17]

In the context of modernization, Buddhist individuals and organizations in Thailand, Sri Lanka, and Mongolia have opposed models of development that stress export-driven, single-crop agriculture, megadams, and urbanization over traditional subsistence communities. For his primarily Buddhist country, Mongolian Prime Minister Nambaryn Enkhbayar advocated "a pollution free way of living, ability to adapt quickly to the new environment in a broad sense, mobility, a more or less harmonious relationship with the environment, and readiness to give up the demands or things which turn into a burden."[18] This model stands in stark contrast with the emphasis on increasing technology, consumption, and gross national product pushed by large western aid organizations and monetary institutions like the International Monetary Fund and the World Bank.

Home to Sarvodaya (literally, "everyone wakes up"), Sri Lanka provides an instructive example of the positive role of spiritual values in public life. Sarvodaya is Sri Lanka's largest private organization and has an active presence in more than 15,000 of the nation's villages.[19] It began in the late 1950s under the inspiration of A. T. Ariyaratne, a Sri Lankan college science teacher who arranged for student volunteers to aid the poor in the countryside. Out of this simple beginning, there grew with remarkable speed a national organization that has touched the lives of millions of people.[20]

Sarvodaya engages in familiar helping activities, such as flood and famine relief, literacy and sanitation campaigns, peace efforts, and medical clinics, but it does so as part of an overall political *and* spiritual framework that has a very different view of real development than the dominant neoliberal, capitalist model. For Sarvodaya, development takes place "on the spiritual, moral, cultural, social, economic and political levels,"[21] not just the terrain of greater material consumption. Minimal basic needs of water, food, shelter, medical care, and education are essential, but so are a sense of personal and group empowerment, the spiritual appreciation of nature, and holistic ecology.

Sarvodaya was always distinguished by the idealism of its workers, its focus on the poor, and its inclusion of women and members of minority Tamil and Muslim communities. Even more important, however, were the distinct goals that shaped its activities. Ariyaratne personally and Sarvodaya as an organization wanted Sri Lanka to develop into a society governed by broadly interpreted Buddhist ideals, brought about by Gandhian methods of nonviolence, spiritual discipline, and inclusion. Central to this process, they taught, was a subjective awakening to a sense of self-worth, compassion for and cooperation with others, and active engagement in community life. This awakening would create a society very different from the acquisitive, high-technology nation sought by the Sri Lankan government, which has been taken by the dominant institutions of global capitalism to be the hallmark of a successfully modernized country. In a truly radical political and spiritual stance, Ariyaratne flatly rejects this image of success, opting instead for a humanly and ecologically sustainable society in which there is neither western-style affluence nor crushing third-world poverty. "In production-centered society," Ariyaratne says clearly, "the total perspective of human personality and a sustainable relationship between man and nature is lost sight of."[22] A commentator adds, "Sarvodaya's main message is that human suffering cannot be alleviated merely by material means.... All its projects are meant to serve the specific needs of a local community that has be reawakened...to the ancient virtues of interdependent sharing and caring, joint suffering, and compassionate interaction."[23]

Sarvodaya envisaged quasi-independent villages controlled by local citizens through an engaged democracy, in which all basic human needs would be met, many by subsistence labor rather than the marketplace. The result would be a kind of Buddhist socialism, for the goal of economic life would not be continual industrial expansion and ever growing consumer "needs," but balanced support for all facets of a moral and humane life. Sarvodaya's goal of the "liberation of the goodness that is in every person" unfolds in concrete and highly practical actions, such as preventing soil erosion, building schools and roads, purifying water, and conserving biodiversity. For Sarvodaya, the problems of economic development, in fact, parallel those of spiritual development. "The root problem of poverty," argued Ariyaratne, is "personal and collective powerlessness." Yet awakening is not a process of isolated spiritual practice, but something that arises out of "social, economic, and political interaction...interdependent with the awakening of one's local community."[24]

"We believe," wrote Aryaratne, "that poverty, powerlessness, and related conditions are directly linked with affluence imbalances, and injustices in the exercise of political and economic power and other advantages enjoyed by the few over the many. What is necessary is not a palliative, but a strategy for a total, nonviolent revolutionary transformation."[25]

From Sarvodaya' s point of view, development projects such as large dams typically devastated the local ecology and did little for the people who were most closely affected by them. Aryaratne lamented: "By the side of gargantuan dams are parched fields that poor farmers watch disconsolately and with mounting discontent. Under the electricity lines which carry power from the dam to the cities and factories live people who have no permanent structures to call homes and hence are not eligible for that electricity."[26] His goal is emphatically *not* to emulate the west. "Instead, we believe in a spiritual foundation, moral relationships, and small economic and political organizations in a highly decentralized but highly coordinated way."[27] Guided by traditional Buddhist ideals of universal compassion, and applying those ideals through engagement with the critical social problems of his society and nation, Ariyaratne was able to chart a course past destructive models of what third-world communities needed.

Engaged Buddhism rests on three central principles, each of which is a common feature of other forms of spiritual activism as well. First, there is virtually no attachment to a narrowly Buddhist theological framework. The moral and social values Buddhist leaders and groups support are fully compatible with approaches to human well-being in other religions and in secular philosophical and political frameworks. There need be no contradiction between Buddhist values and those of sincere utilitarians ("the greatest happiness of the greatest number"), democratic socialists (human rights and economic democracy), or Deweyan liberals (a social order geared to the contributions and welfare of the entire society). Lack of rigid attachment to metaphysical beliefs or a particular set of scriptures allows Buddhist activists to act in terms of their own views without requiring that Christians, Muslims, Jews, or atheists with whom they work share any but the most universal of moral principles and generalized concern.

Yet, second, Engaged Buddhism is not simply a matter of Bodhisattva's lining up on the barricades. There is a particularly Buddhist tone or style to Engaged Buddhist politics, one based in traditional Buddhist spiritual virtues. For example, there is a kind of gentleness for one's opponent—to whom, as Thich Nhat Hanh once suggested, we should address love letters rather than angry protests.[28] Traditional Buddhist teachings about the need to overcome violent passions of all kinds are relevant here, for, it is believed, a progressive movement motivated by hatred will, no matter what the immediate outcome of this or that struggle or campaign, eventually reproduce the suffering that hatred always creates.

Buddhist activists also preach a kind of gentleness for the self: a meditation-based understanding that activists need to be aware of their own emotional state and sensitive to their own limitations. Day-to-day political activism can be boring, draining, and marked by depressing failures. People hope that their efforts will bring immediate, significant fruits, but more often find that it is one step forward and two steps back, or no steps at all. Realizing how easily this experience can have negative effects, Buddhists offer a mindful practice of self-awareness and self-care, rooted in a spiritually based detachment from the ultimate fruits of one's actions.

Spiritual activists coming from other religious traditions or from a more eclectic spirituality similarly bring their own distinctive spiritual virtues into the political realm, describing those virtues in language congenial to their own background. But like Engaged Buddhists, they almost always include some form of humility, compassion, and self-understanding.

Third, socially engaged Buddhists have to take definite political positions, and in doing so, they inevitably confront complicated questions for which their own spiritual values give them only the most general guidelines. They have to decide whose interests to support to promote social justice, determine which social structures are most likely to promote sustainable economic development, choose which hitherto suppressed social groups (e.g., ethnic minorities, homosexuals) deserve support, ask themselves whether military intervention in a local conflict is ever warranted, and even reflect on the place (or lack of place) of nuclear power in a comprehensive energy policy.

Taking positions on such issues requires joining Buddhist spiritual virtues with theories of social justice—for example, ideas about rights or social equality—and with economic, ecological, and sociological theories about how to manifest compassion and care in real-life situations involving tens or hundreds of millions of people. It is at this point that Buddhists—like Christians, Muslims, Jews, or Goddess worshippers in comparable situations—have to employ ideas taken from very different intellectual contexts.

For example, when Thich Nhat Hanh offers a set of principles he hopes will guide the development of Vietnam and calls for a "willingness to protect the nature and the cultural heritage of our land,"[29] he is depending on a distinct conception of the political value of tradition and nature. In doing so, he places himself in opposition to those who favor western-style modernization and extensive exploitation of natural resources. When American Buddhist Joanna Macy calls nuclear energy the "poison fire" and recommends that an engaged Buddhist spiritual practice might be monitoring disposal sites, she depends on a set of critical beliefs about nuclear power she could not have found in any Mahayana sutra.[30] Criticisms of corporate environmental policy depend on beliefs about global warming or the effects of pesticides. Buddhist demonstrations at nuclear test ban sites depend on a firm rejection of the value of nuclear weapons.[31] Calls for greater government control of corporate behavior depend on a theory of the relation between corporate interests, the government, and the public good.

These contexts exemplify a general rule: whatever psychological and moral brilliance spiritual teachings possess, and I believe they possess a great deal, they cannot be applied in the political realm without being supplemented by explicitly political knowledge and values. If this point is not terribly surprising (take out the word *political* and put in the word *medical*), it is a point that otherwise astute leaders themselves sometimes miss. The Dalai Lama and Thich Nhat Hanh, for example, frequently claim that what they advocate is not political in any direct sense, but simply an application of universal truths about compassion, kindness, and the psychology of human happiness.[32] In reality, however, the particular positions they advocate—peace, moderate ecological development, low consumption—are opposed by many people who believe, for example, that an aggressive military posture, rapid economic growth, and unfettered technological development are better choices. No matter how benignly Buddhist luminaries present their ideas, no matter how amiably they seek to engage with their fellow citizens, they are still advocating for particular positions—ones that necessarily oppose the beliefs and (what are taken to be) the interests of many other people. This is equally true when Martin Luther King Jr. denounced the war in Vietnam, when progressive Episcopal bishops advocate for homosexual rights, or when Catholic spiritual nonviolent union leader Cesar Chavez criticized the health and ecological effects of pesticides.[33]

Feminism

Not only must spiritual social activism utilize explicitly political perspectives but also an encounter with politics may lead to critical changes in basic spiritual values and beliefs themselves. This point is nowhere clearer than in the encounter between spirituality and the secular political perspective of feminism. This encounter has resulted in a fusion between the two in feminist spirituality and in the reverberation of feminist ideas in many other spiritual contexts.

The central issue here is the way spiritual teachers have almost always represented their insights as timeless truths, reflecting ultimate realities of human morality, psychology, and welfare and, for some, of the divine as well. Contingent, limited, merely local truths of culture, history, or personality, we are told, are transcended by the universally valid insights of Jesus or the Buddha, what we learn from serious meditation or shamanistic visions or sacred texts.

The feminist critique argues that significant elements of traditional spirituality do not reflect timeless truths but rather the oppressive features of the local culture; in particular, that culture's devaluation of women and corresponding support for male privilege. "If God is male," feminist theologian Mary Daly trenchantly observed, "then male is God."[34] Because of male power in spiritual communities, spiritual teachings are typically based in men's specific experience of life, including the kinds of work they do and the role they play in interpersonal relationships. This partiality leads them to be unaware of some of their motives and the effects of some of their actions. While they have often prided themselves on their moral purity, they have actually been marked by deep ethical flaws. Through feminism, writes Christian feminist Rosemary Radford Ruether, such "male privilege" gets "reevaluated as sin and evil," and women see that "the entire symbolic universe that surrounds them" is "tainted by hostility to their humanity."[35]

Consider, for a start, how much of the world's spiritual teachings originated in the life experience of people who did not nurture children. Buddha's great spiritual journey started, we are told, when he left his wife and child. The great Sufi masters are known for their relationships with students and their own teachers, not for raising kids. John Muir walking in the Sierra Nevada mountains and writing of nature's spiritual value, Chogyam Trungpa or Shunryu Suzuki teaching Buddhism to Americans, many (not all) great Hasidic rabbis, and even Gandhi, whose spirituality was nowhere less evident than in his relation with his son—all these and countless more spiritual exemplars were completely or mostly exempt from the tasks of parenthood. The domestic routine of dealing with the young and sustaining the family in practical details like cooking and cleaning they left to others.

This is significant for at least two reasons. First, descriptions of the spiritual path are too often based in images of nonrelational autonomy. We are to pray, meditate, wander in search of a teacher, and discover the beauties of nature—by ourselves. Domestic obligations and emotional connectedness are dismissed as distractions and obstacles. But without someone cooking dinner, washing the dishes, and changing the diapers, how will we survive? And where will the next generation of spiritual seekers come from?

Further, if spirituality cannot be found in diaper changing and dinner cooking, but absolutely requires meditation, study, and prayer, then relegating all the spiritual pursuits to men and all the domestic labor to women systematically excludes women from the enormous good of spiritual life. It makes spirituality men's work and household labor women's. But once we realize that men and women are equally capable of loving God, developing mindfulness, and seeing the value of nature, we realize that this sexual division of labor unfairly keeps the goods on one side and the drudgery on the other.

In moving from traditional religion to spirituality, rigid hierarchical roles and rules have to some extent already been overcome. Therefore, it may be less, for example, the Catholic exclusion of women from the priesthood that is the problem. Rather, it is the image of religious life as one necessarily freed from the demands of family. It is not so much that traditional Buddhism gave women no religious authority, but that all too often Buddhism imagines spiritual development as detached and unemotional. Enlightenment for eastern traditions, godliness for western ones—despite their difference, both have often shared a perspective for which a certain disconnection from other people is a basic requirement.

This spiritual emphasis on impersonal emotional detachment not only devalues the culturally female and humanly essential work of family life but also expresses a deep fear of human connection. Succumbing to this fear, spiritual doctrines often presume that intimate human relationships are incompatible with spiritual wisdom.

How could this be? As someone whose experience of family life has often been extremely difficult, I would certainly not suggest that embodying spiritual virtues in a domestic setting is easy. But since when is spiritual life supposed to be easy? Or spiritual wisdom intended to function only in a restricted number of settings—here and here, but not here? Surely the goal is to express compassion, love, awareness, and the rest everywhere people find themselves.

As women become full participants in spiritual communities, they, too, become spiritual leaders and teachers. This change can have far-reaching effects. One of the first female Reconstructionist rabbis suggested: "Women's version of reality is not a hierarchical model where the goal is to move up, to be alone at the top, but rather a network model where the goal is to connect with others, to be together at the center."[36] We might add that the typical male rabbi always needed a wife if he was to have a family. When the rabbi *is* a wife, we are likely to get some new models of both what it is to be a rabbi and what it is to be a wife.[37] Clearly, this has implications for spiritual life of virtually any tradition. A spiritual teacher who has to do the dishes, get up in the middle of the night to change a diaper, talk to his son's schoolteachers, and wait in the ER when his daughter has an uncontrollable fever will be a teacher less devoted to uninterrupted spiritual practice in any conventional sense but much more knowledgeable of the realities of human life and more likely to understand the challenge of manifesting spiritual virtues in the full range of human experiences.[38]

It is not only child raising and emotional connection that spiritual traditions have devalued and even shunned; at times, it is the body itself. This theme came up in our discussion of nature spirituality, and it surfaces again now. Too often spiritual traditions identified women with the body and nature, and spirituality with escape from or transcendence of our earthly nature. Menstruation, childbirth, literally feeding an infant from one's own body—these reminders that human beings are flesh as much as they are souls and spirits were taken as threats to the unvarying purity of the sacred. The body, after all, is weak, vulnerable, changeable, subject to great pain, and extremely temporary. God is eternal and unchanging; enlightenment is a place of perfection in which desires, having been overcome, can never cause us pain. How then could the body connect us to God or enlightenment?

Feminists have taught that renunciation of our bodily nature and devaluation of the feminine through its supposed closeness to the body are symptoms not of spiritual wisdom but of fear. It is the ego trying to avoid pain and find some state of bliss (heaven, enlightenment) in which it will always be satisfied. Alas, this is not to be. Suffering, though not necessarily attachment, is a permanent feature of human life, as is change. Casting out our vulnerability by identifying it with the Other—the female—is simply an expression of our lack of acceptance of this truth. Feminist spirituality, particularly in its ecofeminist variety, takes a dramatically different tack. On this perspective, Charlene Spretnak asserts, "both the Earthbody and the personal body" are "manifestations of divine creativity in the cosmos."[39]

Alongside its demand for equality and celebration of the body, feminist spirituality often involves the attempt to imagine God in a variety of roles and forms and to allow us to use the idea of God without being wedded to any single version. As victims of rigid theology and institutional hierarchy, feminist spiritual teachers almost always stress that multiplicity is not a threat to spiritual purity, but a development beneficial to the entire religious community. For instance, lesbian Episcopal priest Carter Heyward identifies God with, among other things, the erotic connection between loving partners. In doing so, she is not invoking the familiar concept of God and then asking (as it were) for his approval of her lesbianism. Rather, she is expanding the ways in which God can be thought.[40]

If these insights about the sexist limitations of male-dominated spirituality were theoretically possible without a feminist social movement, it is also the case that they were not actual in any significant way until that movement came into existence.[41] Feminist struggles for women's equality and freedom, which can be seen as a continuation of the original struggle for democratic rights against the aristocracy, carried a largely secular, unspiritual origin. But this origin in no way limits their immense usefulness for spiritual life. Unjust powers and privileges will always limit our capacity for spiritual development. The secular political critique of patriarchy, internalized by spiritual traditions, thus enriches these traditions.

Some traditionally oriented spiritual seekers might argue that it is a mistake to allow a secular political ideology to evaluate divine truth revealed by God and taught by a lineage of exalted teachers. Political equality and freedom might be appropriate for a secular social world of differing ethnic groups and political viewpoints, but when it comes to God or enlightenment, truth does not require appeals to democracy. It is always a mistake, the argument would continue, to modify the accumulated wisdom of centuries to fit the political fashions of the present.

The feminist response is simple and effective. It is that these traditions were never purely spiritual to begin with, at least insofar as their doctrines and institutional structures reflected and reinforced male authority over women. They were always political because they always reflected norms for the distribution of power, privilege, and collective respect: regulating who could teach and who had to serve, who would interpret the original teaching and who would merely receive instruction. Just because it has always had a political dimension—and how could it not, since every text, revelation, and insight is shaped by the humans who hold them?—spirituality always requires a political examination and, if necessary, a political critique.[42]

Nonviolence and Spiritual Politics

When compassion, love, and care are manifest in the social realm, they may be understood under the general concept of nonviolence. Here are some examples, each concerning a particular aspect of the central value of nonviolent social engagement.

In the years leading up to the Russian Revolution, V. I. Lenin was the dominant figure in the Bolshevik Party, surrounded by highly intelligent, disciplined, and strong-willed men.[43] Intense conflicts over strategy frequently arose. This was especially true when Lenin, having been exiled to Switzerland during World War I, returned to Russia after the monarchy had fallen. Faced with strategic disagreements, Lenin had one characteristic response: excoriate his opponent and claim absolute rightness for his own views. If those methods failed, he would frequently seek to expel his critics or threaten to resign if his plans were not accepted.[44] Believing that his views had to succeed at all costs, Lenin's basic mode of operation, even within the party, was coercive. In later years, Stalin's totalitarian repressiveness toward his entire nation reproduced on a grand scale the same attitudes that Lenin exhibited within the party.

Like Lenin, Gandhi had a definite political objective and engaged in careful, long-term strategic planning. But unlike Lenin, Gandhi proceeded on certain spiritual assumptions: people shared an essentially divine nature, anyone—himself included—could act immorally or ineffectively, the ultimate goal of all political activity was a society in which each person could freely develop and realize their unity with God, and therefore the correct method of personal interaction and collective change was persistent, active nonviolence.

When disagreements over policy arose among his comrades, Gandhi, believing that nonviolence was the correct method for personal spiritual life and for politics alike, took the exact opposite tack from Lenin. Sometimes his disagreeing associates said they would defer to Gandhi because of their respect for him. No, he counseled, that would be a larger mistake. The most important thing is for you to proceed with integrity on your own beliefs, even if that means you follow a course I think is wrong.[45]

Ultimately, I suspect, Gandhi's approach makes for better politics. It is more likely to bring out the best work in each person, to cultivate younger and less experienced activists, to avoid the political errors of sectarianism and violence, and to allow everyone to recognize errors when they are being made. And while there is no necessary connection between this nonviolent mode of interpersonal operation and spirituality, it is much more likely to stem from spiritual social activists than from purely secular ones.

A second example concerns a tenacious and troubling aspect of contemporary political culture.

Contemporary America is marked by countless examples of deep-seated disagreements that often include dimensions of violence such as acrimonious and seriously unhelpful debates of political candidates, as well as their intentionally dishonest advertising; stark splits over the moral status of abortion, gay marriage, and the stock market; and clearly biased reporting and analysis from news media. Political conversations tend to be composed of invective and sound bites, slogans endlessly repeated, much shouting, and almost no listening. The result is political gridlock, a polarized, often unthinking electorate, and (as in the case of Congresswoman Giffords) violence.

Recognizing how destructive this is, many have called for a return (creation?) of public civility, of conversations where difference and respect go hand in hand. As beneficial as such a development would be, what is missing from such calls is much understanding of *why* people are so eager to address the other side with verbal vitriol and dismissive contempt and how spiritual virtues might help.

The larger social context is instrumental in this problem.

First, certain issues strike us with a kind of gut certainty. I am not thinking of abstract philosophical ideas or arcane policy matters but questions of whether Christianity is true, gay marriage is okay, animals have rights, or abortion is a sin. Here we are often so sure of ourselves that it is hard to imagine those who disagree as being anything but stupid, blind, or immoral.

Further, our beliefs often feel central to personal identity and to family and community. Any disagreement can seem not just like a moral mistake but a deep threat to our very selves and much of what we love. To allow that some other perspective has a point would be a betrayal of everything—or at least a good deal—of what is most important to us.

Yet at the same time, our powerful moral intuitions arise in an unprecedentedly complex and confusing time. Immigration reform, resisting terrorism, ending war, resolving environmental problems, reducing the number of abortions, supporting marriages—all these involve families, communities, nations, and the world economy, political and cultural systems, the distribution of wealth, and the role of new technologies. As the peoples of the world have never been so connected, the social problems we face have never depended on so many interconnected factors.

And here it gets even more anxiety provoking, for the last decades have shown that traditional sources of competence and moral authority are dreadfully inadequate. The Catholic Church continues to reel from the sex abuse cover-ups; science gives us virtually unimaginable power but also creates ozone-damaging CFCs, carcinogenic pesticides, and life-threatening nuclear weapons; democracy is better than tyranny but seems dominated by voter sloth and special interests; individual politicians of all stripes offer change yet produce the same old, same old; the market creates wealth but also poverty, wild financial speculation, and environmental disasters; excesses of rhetoric and corruption darken the bright promises of political organizations on the left and the right; and much of spirituality is marred by narcissistic self-interest.

So the issues are near and dear to our hearts, the problems are incredibly complex, and we have no one to trust—no unblemished ideology, political group, or religious tradition that seems to really know what it is doing.

No wonder we get nasty and shrill, for too often the alternative would be to admit how confused, frustrated, and terribly frightened we are.

Can spiritual values offer an alternative?

I am not sure, and a frank humility rooted in self-awareness might be the most honest response to a good deal of what we face. I do not know how to solve the Palestinian-Israeli conflict, square respect for women's rights with recognition that a fetus is not exactly the same as a fingernail, meet people's legitimate needs and stop polluting, enjoy all our nifty technological toys without getting hooked by them, deal with illegal immigration without hurting children, or find a way to live with either violent religious fundamentalists or those who think the earth is nothing but raw materials to turn into stuff for the mall.

Admitting that we really do not know, as well as how scared and upset we are about all this, might help us listen to people with radically different ideas, even if only to acknowledge that at least some part of what they say makes sense. It would be more truthful if we admitted how little certainty there is, how our pretend certainty is often a cover for our fear, and how at the very least—in this age of global climate change, global economic connections, and global weaponry—we are, really, all in this together. Perhaps we could take it on faith that other people really believe what they say, just as we really believe what we say.

This would not be easy. To engage in what we might call spiritual, nonviolent communication, we might have to sacrifice the pleasures of self-righteousness and cultivate humility, honesty, and openness. We still might end up in drastic disagreement; perhaps in the end we might have to fight it out. But before we got to the end, we could be more respectful, learn something from others, and perhaps find a way to work together on the few things we have in common. Toward this end, the spiritual virtue of mindfulness can help make us aware of our fear and our lack of certainty; that of compassion can show us the comparable emotions gripping those we oppose. Detachment from results may allow us to face even the direst of threats with some equanimity. And cultivating a peaceful heart may enable us to listen to other people's ideas without rage or desperation.

In another setting, we may consider the role of the idea of redemptive suffering in the U.S. civil rights movement—a paradigmatically spiritual movement in the sense that virtues of nonviolence and compassion joined the pursuit of social justice. The ultimate goal, Martin Luther King Jr. taught, was not just the redress of this or that racial grievance, but the creation of a beloved community, a social setting in which love and care were the dominant values. Violence, King believed, always obstructs the development of the beloved community. It was not just that American blacks could never match the power of the white police, National Guard, and army, but that as soon as they engaged in any violent conflict at all, they would have lost the war. The ultimate goal of the movement was not victory, but a society no longer made up of winners and losers of any kind. King did not want to vanquish the oppressor, but to awaken his conscience. And this could only be accomplished by using spiritual strength to compensate for the inequality of social power and to use that strength in such a way as to prevent a repetition of that inequality in a new form. In this struggle, his "army" had "no supplies but its sincerity, no uniform but its determination, no arsenal except its faith, no currency but its conscience."[46]

Most important, King's army had a willingness to endure undeserved suffering. This willingness was not simply an exercise in masochism, but an overall rethinking of the social position of southern blacks. The oppressor's unjust power could now be seen as a weakness, and the lack of money, numbers, or institutional power of the oppressed took a back seat to their moral fervor and capacity for self-sacrifice. It was a typically spiritual redefinition of reality, similar to Jesus' remarkable claim that "the first shall be last," Buddhism's denial of the long-term value of getting what you want, the Bible's assertion that taking care of the powerless is not generosity, but an obligation required by God, and even Hasidism's assertion that ordinary, unlettered Jews possessed religious value.

The force of this revaluation is telling. How can a group subject to long-term humiliation and social subordination feel powerful enough to act? In this case, by seeing true power as coming from a determination to undergo suffering in the pursuit of justice. How could otherwise powerless blacks see white oppressors as vulnerable? By seeing them as fundamentally at odds with their own spiritual nature, in contradiction to their own truest identity.

After four black children were killed in a church bombing in Birmingham, King spoke to the community's grief and rage:

> We must say to our white brothers all over the South who try to keep us down: we will match your capacity to inflict suffering with our capacity

to endure suffering. We will meet your physical force with soul force. We will not hate you. And yet we cannot in all good conscience obey your evil laws. Do to us what you will, Threaten our children and we will still love you ... bomb our homes and ... our churches ... and we will still love you. We will wear you down by our capacity to suffer. ... We will so appeal to your heart and your conscience that we will win you in the process.[47]

This spiritual revaluation is a remarkable source of political strength. Whatever else is true about oppressed people, they can always choose to suffer. But a suffering which is chosen instead of merely endured, invited rather than inflicted by another, is a suffering transformed. As fasting or long hours of prayer produce a kind of spiritual freedom, so people who choose their social suffering are no longer passive victims but active agents. In particular, when hardship is chosen, the person undergoing it has won a crucial victory over fear. The white community's persecution of African Americans—personal humiliation, loss of jobs or bank loans, physical violence—was a strategy of control. Once the persecuted willingly chose to suffer, that control was broken.

Civil rights leader John Lewis, who had grown up terrified of jail, reflected on how his first arrest in Nashville was not crushing, but liberating. "I had never had that much dignity before. ... It was exhilarating—it was something I had earned, the sense of the independence that comes to a free person."[48]

Then there is the charisma of civil rights pioneer James Lawson, one of the leaders of the lunch counter sit-ins in Nashville that in 1960 reinvigorated an otherwise moribund movement. The philosophy of the Student Nonviolent Coordinating Committee (SNCC), which Lawson helped found, was: "Through nonviolence, courage displaces fear. Love transcends hate ... hope ends despair. ... Peace dominates war. Mutual regard cancels enmity. ... The redemptive community supersedes immoral social systems."[49] Lawson's appeal was not based on his social position or any rational guarantee of future success for the struggle, nor in any sense that he would conquer his foes. What struck people about Lawson was his spiritual strength. In John Lewis's words: "He just had a way about him. An aura of inner peace and wisdom that you could sense immediately upon simply seeing him."[50]

This may remind us of descriptions of spiritual "masters" or "gurus"—only now these traits are manifest amid the chaos and violence of an intense social struggle. Politically, Lawson utilized a clear sense of justice and a strategy to mobilize other activists and make effective tactical choices. Spiritually, he relied on a nonrational trust that the ultimate powers of the universe were on his side; that both he and the people he opposed had a fundamental worth that had nothing to do with social position, wealth, or political power; and that he could seek justice nonviolently. Because each human being had an essential connection to God just as he did, they could eventually be reached by a nonviolent appeal to that connection.

Sometimes accompanied by a theistic reliance on God and many times not, a commitment to nonviolence, respect for one's opponent, and willingness to suffer to create a more just society are widespread among spiritual social activists. They are present in the life and work of Aung San Suu Kyi, Myanmar's the Buddhist-oriented leader of that nation's Myanmar's democracy movement; of Cesar Chavez, who brought spirituality into the fierce struggle to create a union for migrant farmworkers and protect them from poisonous pesticides; in Desmond Tutu, whose implacable opposition to apartheid combined with a humble and gentle manner of dealing with the "enemy"; of the community-trained and -supported Mennonite peacemakers who face the wrath of warring groups to try to bring bloody conflicts to an end; of religious environmentalists who work with those of other faiths and no faith, with scientists and secular groups, for a sustainable society; of the many Peace Fellowship organizations inspired by sacred teachings; and of advocates for human rights and the abolition of sexual trafficking.

In many of these cases, spiritual ideas and values have melded with political ones to such a degree that they have become a distinct form of personal and group identity. In this form, the distinction between spirituality and politics is virtually eliminated. For one example, Pete Litster is a director of the Shundahai Network, a Utah-based coalition that seeks to end nuclear testing, prevent the storage of nuclear waste in Nevada's Yucca Mountain, and replace nuclear energy with clean, sustainable power. A spiritual presence, Litster tell us, permeates everything the group does. "Every event, every meeting—starts with prayer. Our peace encampments at the test site begin with a sunrise ceremony and sweat lodges. We recognize the earth as mother and our relations with every living thing as essential to who we are. Contamination is not just bad for people, it's a sin. For us, the spiritual and the political just can't be separated."[51]

Is there any guarantee that nonviolent campaigns (any more than any other spiritual engagements in politics) will succeed in their long-term goals? No. There certainly have been many cases—Indian independence, the U.S. Civil Rights movement, the Philippines, Poland, and recently Egypt[52]—where an essentially peaceful movement led to very significant political change and did so with a comparatively small loss of life. But Indian independence was followed by several million deaths in the creation of Pakistan, American blacks have achieved political equality but still suffer from enormous economic disadvantage, ruling elites continue to dictate life in Poland and the Philippines, and it is still far too early to know what is to come for Egypt. The ultimate fate of all political action is complicated and long-term, and evaluating consequences requires us to balance a host of factors.

Of this, however, we can be reasonably sure. Nonviolence achieves its goals with a minimum of harm and thus a minimum of the traumatic experiences that feed into future violence. The long-standing bitterness and subsequent conflict to which civil wars and armed revolutions often give rise is lessened. Although any serious social change is shocking to those who lose their powers and privileges, a nonviolent change is much less hurtful than one shaped by extensive loss of life. It therefore offers more hope that what follows the revolution will be at least a little better than what it replaced.

The Good Life

Secular movements are often strongest in their critical mode, when they are struggling against various forms of injustice and irrationality: oppression, exploitation, racism, sexism, heterosexism, colonialism, speciesism, the domination of nature, and the pollution of the earth. All these forms of wrong relationship are rightly seen as supported by beliefs, institutions, and social practices that need to be overthrown and replaced.

But after the overthrow, what do we have as replacements? All too often, the positive goals of political movements, what is being striven *for* rather than what is being struggled *against*, are vague, abstract, and lacking in substance. The slaves should be freed, of course, but to do what? Women should have equal rights, no doubt, but what is a humanly fulfilling form for gender relationships? Too often environmental politics defines itself as near-endless injunctions of Don't! No! Stop! But what *should* we do? Progressive politics repeatedly leaves us with a hunger for a substantial, positive image of a rational, moral, fulfilling society.

The answer "let people do what they want as long as they don't hurt others" is the classic response of liberal individualism. It is rooted in the idea that outside of equitable public relationships and protections of freedom dictated by shared human rights, we are free to live our lives as we wish.[53] In many ways, it would seem that spirituality and liberalism are allies. Any spiritual approach to politics would take for granted liberalism's emphasis on freedom, equality, and human rights. And it clearly would embrace liberalism's rejection of religious compulsion. Whatever the separation of church and state means, it certainly entails that political power not be used to enforce sectarian religious belief or practice of any kind.

But liberalism and spirituality part company over the former's agnosticism about what the good life for human beings is. The problem is that in modern capitalist democracies an enormously powerful machine of media and education leave us legally free but all too often psychically enslaved to desires and habits that are emotionally and ecologically destructive. We can do what we want, more or less, but what we want is not chosen with emotional maturity, reflective awareness, or very much wisdom.

For liberalism, the choice of how to live is not only individual *politically*, in that we should be legally free to decide for ourselves; it is individual *essentially*—in that there is no rational way in which we can assert that some form of life is better than another. A spiritual perspective takes a very different approach. It unabashedly asserts that virtues make for a better life—one more likely to lead to lasting contentment and joy[54] and to make a person a more moral and compassionate fellow citizen. Yet unlike a great deal of traditional religion (which is also quite confident it knows how people ought to live), the expression of these ideas could never be something that was imposed on others, demanded of people who don't agree, or backed up with threats of eternal damnation. Insofar as values are spiritual, they can only be realized by a person's understanding and free choice. Thus spiritual values enter the public realm free of both fundamentalism's moral totalitarianism and the false modesty of an anything-goes liberalism.

A spiritual vision of the good social life denies that people's interests are defined solely by their material position and that the goal of political movements is limited to increased and equitable levels of consumption. As Rabbi Michael Lerner of *Tikkun* magazine and the Network of Spiritual Progressives has repeatedly argued, the bottom-line approach to personal or corporate life leads to compulsive growth, unnecessary consumption, and a nagging sense of emptiness.[55] Politics has to do with *meaning* alongside income, with finding a form of social life that can support fulfilling human relationships, not just a good day at the mall. As a (not particularly spiritually oriented) sociologist observes: "The logic of the market—that everything is for sale and we should strive to get as much as we can—has pushed beyond the economic sphere into other parts of our lives. The most important consequence is a deteriorating capacity for meaningful relationships."[56]

As powerful and important as secular movements for social justice and political reform are, they typically do not include this kind of message. They offer rights, equality, an escape from poverty, or generalities like Marx's "from each according to his ability to each according to his needs." And while they may have a detailed critique of the way oppression lessens our abilities or a distorting ideology fills us with false needs, they do not pay nearly as much attention to the positive states of human fulfillment and the modes of personal practice necessary to achieve them. As Martin Seligman's positive psychology—or the much earlier work of A. H. Maslow—counseled psychologists to examine not only human neurosis and suffering but also states of engagement and happiness, so spiritual social activism advocates models of human life based in nontoxic forms of fulfillment.[57]

Since a good deal of spiritual material counsels us not to be attached to pleasures, satisfying relationships, or pleasant experiences, it is somewhat ironic that spiritual activists can offer concrete suggestions for the cultivation of human satisfaction. Yet that is what they do.

Consider meditation. While focusing on our internal mental state may sometimes arouse painful emotions, it can also provide a gentle relief from the restless twitchiness of our normal minds. The delight that sometimes arises in the unfolding of each breath, the calmness that comes when we focus solely on the present moment—these are parts of a fulfilling life that is both fully sustainable and compatible with a just society.

In a more expanded sense, there is the idea of a Sabbath—a weekly time when we celebrate what we have rather than seeking more, enjoy our (even if minimal) bounty rather than try to increase our holdings, and take our ease with friends, family, and nature rather than make smart contacts or exploit natural resources. The Sabbath is defined by the spiritual virtue of appreciation—an unashamed gratitude for life and whatever love and beauty we have. Surely, the gratitude and contentment at the heart of the practice of Sabbath are not easy to come by. They require us to ignore the impulse to acquire or possess new stuff, put aside our (no doubt totally justified) disappointments and resentments, and turn off the cell phone.

Further, a Sabbath enables us to sooth the perpetual sense of lack that our monstrous media machines want us to feel, take life for what it is, and find something to enjoy even in life's imperfection. Doing so requires a positive act of will that can have a long-lasting effect only if it is repeated many times. What we get in return are the pleasures of gratitude and the ability to rest. Advocating for and observing a Sabbath is therefore a potentially quite radical political act. At the very least, it shows what might unfold if we minimized our socially induced addictive consumerism. In traditional Judaism, the Sabbath was a "taste of heaven."[58] In this-worldly political terms, it might be considered a foretaste of life "after the revolution."

Finally, posing spiritual virtues as an alternative to both the dominant forms of an oppressive society or the more negatively oriented social justice movements is not simply a matter of good ideas without a practical role in contemporary society. According to Paul Ray's work on people he calls "cultural creatives," there is a significant segment of the U.S. population, numbering in the tens of millions, who share a collection of beliefs and values that embrace many familiar aspects of spirituality: a belief in the sacredness of nature, modesty in consumption, gender equality, and altruism.[59] Cultural creatives take recycling seriously, resist militarism in foreign policy, support green spaces, and put a high emphasis on psychological and spiritual growth. They publicly support policies and organizations that seek to reshape society in terms of these values. Any casual look at the Green movement in general shows a sizable presence of spiritual values as well. Such virtues have a significant place among large minorities of many developed nations and, as we have seen, have been guiding lights for activist political movements in other parts of the world.[60] In all these ways, the spiritual values, which may seem to be the creation of impractical visionaries, actually generate invaluable practical consequences.

Hope?

Efforts for justice, care, and reason in social life are difficult, partial, frequently defeated, and often reversed. It was a great triumph to end Soviet communism, but that liberation has been replaced by a kind of Mafia mode of production and monumental government corruption. American women have much more equality since the 1970s, along with more date rape and eating disorders. The environmental movement has won impressive victories, but greenhouse gas emissions continue to rise, as does the sheer quantity of toxic waste.

A spiritual approach to politics can help us deal with the grief and despair to which these disappointments give rise. Although spiritual social activists, like every other kind, certainly want to win—pass the better law, overthrow the repressive regime, end discrimination—they also believe what they do has value even if they do not succeed. In standing for the moral truth as they see it, they have faith that they are embodying the same force of life and love that has brought them, and everything else, into existence. This sustaining force may be called God or the Tao, Nature or the Great Mystery or the Goddess.

This faith offers no certainty of ease or happiness—that much is far too clear. God is not like the hero who saves the day at the end of the action movie. But spiritual social activism is not about ease or happiness, though it certainly does strive to lessen unjust pain. Rather, it is about a vital affirmation of existence—that the painful combination of good and evil, justice and oppression, miraculous and horrific is worth loving and fighting for. Even if a particular campaign or battle is lost, even if the entire future is bleak, we will not surrender to the forces of cruelty and insanity. By some mysterious cosmic calculus, it matters what we do. If we believe that, we will have God even in the midst of evil. And we will find God not because of what God does for us, but because of what we try to do for God. In the end, that is all we can be sure of.

As Dorothy Day, a Catholic social activist who combined her earlier communist critique of social inequality, war, and waste with a deeply spiritual model of human relationships, wrote:

We would like to...change the world—make it a little simpler for people to feed, clothe, and shelter themselves as God intended them to do...by fighting for better conditions, by crying out unceasingly for the rights of the workers, of the poor, of the destitute...we can work for the oasis, the little cell of joy and peace in a harried world.[61]

PART III

End/Beginning

Grace and Despair

Think how lucky it is to be born.

RUTH STONE[1]

EVERY SPIRITUAL PERSPECTIVE reflects the sensibility of its creator. And that is certainly true of the one presented here, which has attempted to distill the essential ideas of a wide range of teachings as much as present my own views. My central experience of life—from political activism to academia, from family to staying in shape—is demanding effort. When I have labored long and hard enough, fighting through distraction, anxiety, self-pity, bad luck, and resentment, good things have happened in all these areas. None of them came easily, but they have come. And the same has been true, in spades, of my struggle to make myself more self-aware, grateful, compassionate, and loving. Thus it is not surprising that my description of spirituality stresses disciplined effort. I have downplayed tradition, belief in God, revelation, and even (to a lesser extent) community in favor of the need to energetically and tirelessly act, over and over again, in a more spiritual direction.

Yet from occasional encounters of my own and reports by countless others, I do know that at times something else happens. There is a sudden, unexpected, seemingly unearned vision, an overwhelming sense of being held and comforted by the universe, life, or God. It may come as an upsurge of joy in the face of great loss. We might seem to hear God's voice or feel a sense of divine presence. The compulsions and obsessions that have tormented us—a deep loneliness, anguish over the pain of someone we love, a sense that neither our own lives nor the universe as a whole has any meaning—are suddenly eclipsed by a mysterious burst of trust that love rather than hate or emptiness is the universe's guiding force. What makes us call this grace is that it is a surprising gift, our own little miracle, emphatically not something we have earned or could ever have expected.

Although the vibrancy of grace is temporary, it may virtually catapult those who receive it to a significantly higher stage of spiritual development. It can lead us to be calmer and less self-concerned; more loving, patient, and attuned to the needs and pains of others; and above all, deeply trusting that life matters. Whether because we are children of God, or beings who deserve compassion, or simply we are part of the miracle of life, or all beings deserve compassion, our existence is significant and full of wonder.

Yet what of the grim realities that pervade so much of our world? I write these lines on the tenth anniversary of the 9/11 attacks. As horrific as that day was, it was but one moment of anguish in an endless series. In terms of the sheer number of innocent civilians killed, it is dwarfed by the victims of the U.S. invasion of Iraq or the fatalities of civil wars in Sudan, Bosnia, Syria, or El Salvador. There are also the victims of sexual trafficking, now in the neighborhood of 2.5 million at any given moment; the estimated 30,000 to 40.000 children who, in a world where farmers are paid not to grow food crops and the average American wastes 350 pounds of food a year, die of starvation every single day;[2] and the millions of political prisoners held by repressive governments from North Korea and China to Syria to Iran.[3] Each year, hundreds of millions of animals are brutally exploited in factory farms and labs. By almost any measure—soil degradation, species extinction, sheer quantity of toxins—our environmental situation is abysmal. And despite the efforts of activists the world over, in many ways it is getting worse.

In the face of all this, we may ask: How can spiritual grace coexist with all this suffering? For this suffering is not natural, necessary, or inevitable. The pains of childbirth and old age, a certain amount of illness, accident, and inherited disability—these seem built into the system of life. We would be hard put to realistically imagine our existence without them. But the same cannot be said of rape as an instrument of ethnic conflict or of mild-mannered men tortured for questioning their government's economic policy.

A person wedded to certain religious ideas make might take solace in the belief that this is all God's plan, that Higher Powers are guiding the difficult but necessary process of the evolution of human consciousness toward wisdom,[4] or that since so much of this anguish is caused by unethical human action, it tells us nothing about the universe as a whole, only about what happens when animals possess intelligence, moral freedom, and opposable thumbs.

Given my downplaying of religious metaphysics (God, revelation, etc.), it should come as no surprise that these answers do not comfort me. And even many traditionally religious people find themselves shaken when they confront the Holocaust or the death of a child. Whatever we may believe about God, any morally aware and minimally compassionate person will wonder how such things can be. In the face of that deep uncertainty, the gifts of grace become difficult and doubtful, for some even indecent, and for a time questions such as these darken our sense of life's meaning:

Can we, *should* we, seek God's love or a vibrant sense of spirit in the face of so much pointless wanton death?

Is it enough that God can be found in the concentration camps in the love people showed for each other there? Can we, as Thich Nhat Hanh suggested, celebrate with the one healthy tree, even as we know that nine of 10 are under assault from acid rain? Is it possible to focus on the local tasks in front of us and not get lost in the overwhelming fact of global oppression and loss?

Is the ability to maintain a sense that life matters despite the world's pain the fundamental spiritual virtue—fundamental in the sense that it makes all the others possible and that without it we may not be able to manifest the others very well or for very long?

I do not believe that there are any ultimately satisfying answers to these questions. They can be temporarily solved by theology or poetry, a good bottle of wine or an extended meditation, the exuberance brought on by spring flowers or the helpless laughter of a child being tickled. But they may well return when we hear of some new atrocity, read the testimony of yet another victim, or perhaps feel the lump in our breast and wonder how safe the drinking water has been. Like our own moral, intellectual, and physical limits and the long-term certainty of our mortality, the possibility of despair is a permanent feature of life. For many of us, it is a presence that will never fully depart, and the best we can do is carry it gracefully.

In the face of everything that has been lost, as I write these lines and you read them, what are we to do?

Here is a last, extremely simple thought, one which (I'm not quite sure why) consoles me:

It is enough that it ever was.

And that we were here with it.

It is enough that all the lost life forms and devastated forests graced us with their beauty. It is enough that all the people suffering for someone else's power, profit, or mindless rage did what they could while they were here. The whole amazing show of colors and birdsongs and tiny flowers that fight their way through the snow in March. And people who can be kind even when they are suffering themselves; who can, as they did in concentration camps, make birthday cakes from crumbs and tell each other jokes; who can create exquisite music; who can stand in front of tanks and speak truth to power. It is enough that we were here to be part of it. Enough for me that I get to see it, and taste it, and give my minuscule bit of love back to it. It was always a miracle and even the pain does not change that. The whole of life—all of it together—is grace.

Acknowledgments

I AM VERY much indebted to friends and colleagues who offered instructive comments: Christopher Chapple, Richard Foltz, Sherri Grossman, Mordechai Liebling, Aarti Madan, Richard Schmitt, John Sanbonmatsu, and Donna Semel. And to the busy professionals who gave their time for interviews: Nedda Hobbs, Carol Kruckoff, Sat Bir Singh Khalsa, Jean Van Gemert, and Paul Zipes.

Thanks to Worcester Polytechnic Institute for being my academic home for many years and for its constant support of my research.

And to Cynthia Read, editor at Oxford, for her enthusiasm and engagement.

As always, a special appreciation for my wife, Miriam Greenspan, who possesses a rare combination of deep spiritual wisdom and great editorial skills.

As always, thanks to all the beings with whom I share this life—from the bacteria inside my body to the sun, from the trees next to my neighborhood pond to the seagulls whose wings gleam white against gray clouds—and to all the people who provide food and energy and medical care while I sit at my computer and write about spirituality.

Over the years, I have been blessed to encounter many spiritual teachers—some in the flesh and many in their writings (and one film). Here is a list ordered by when (more or less) they appeared in my life.

I am grateful to you all.

Sylvia and Alfred Gottlieb
Ray Bradbury, *Dandelion Wine*
Thoreau, *Walden*
The stories of I. L. Peretz
Dostoyevsky, *The Brothers Karamazov*
Tolstoy, *Anna Karenina and The Death of Ivan Ilych*
Søren Kierkegaard, *Fear and Trembling and*
The Concluding Unscientific Postscript

Paul Reps, *Zen Mind, Beginner's Mind*
Swami Sivananda on yoga
Kundalini Yoga
Miriam Greenspan
Jacob and Aidla Greenspan
Herman Hesse, *Siddhartha*
Edward Conze on Buddhism
Bagavad Gita
Harold and Maude
Womancraft
Rabbi Lev Friedman
B'nai Or of Boston
Chogyam Trungpa, *Cutting through Spiritual Materialism*
Tao Te Ching
Aaron Michael Gottlieb
Elie Wiesel
The *Siddur* (traditional Jewish prayer book)
Mantak Chia
Idries Shah on Sufism
Rabbi Abraham Joshua Heschel
Anna Gottlieb
Rebbe Nachman of Bratzlav
Rebbe Levi Yitzchak of Berditchev
Esther Greenspan
Temple Israel of Boston
Joanna Macy
Mohandas Gandhi
Reverend Martin Luther King Jr.
Rowan Williams, *Dostoevsky*

Notes

PREFACE

1. Henry David Thoreau, *Walden*, Chapter 1. http://thoreau.eserver.org/walden1a.html
2. Thoreau, *Walden*, Chapter 2. http://thoreau.eserver.org/walden02.html.

INTRODUCTION

1. William James, *The Varieties of Religious Experience* (Cambridge, MA: Harvard University Press, 1985), 399.
2. John Blake, "Are There Dangers in Being 'Spiritual but Not Religious'?" CNN Web site, June 3, 2010; http://articles.cnn.com/2010–06–03/living/spiritual. but.not.religious_1_spiritual-community-religious-god?_s=PM:LIVING.
3. Paulist Press, Classics of Western Spirituality.
4. www.findthedivine.com/retreatcenter/holytrinity/home.html.
5. www.stillpointlodge.com/index.html.
6. Ray Bradbury, *Dandelion Wine* (New York: Bantam, 1976).
7. It is said seventeenth-century French philosopher and mathematician Blaise Pascal had a powerful mystical experience and sewed a cloth star into his pants as a reminder.

PART I

1. Kabir, *Ecstatic Poems*, trans. Robert Bly (Boston: Beacon, 2004), 43.
2. References are in the notes, along with occasional discussions of intellectual or scholarly issues that arise.

CHAPTER 1

1. Quoted in Llewellyn Vaughan-Lee, ed., *Travelling the Path of Love: Sayings of the Sufi Masters* (Inverness, CA: Golden Sufi Center, 1995), p. 3.

2. In Robert Ellsberg, ed., *Modern Spiritual Masters: Writings on Contemplation and Compassion* (Maryknoll, NY: Orbis, 2008), p.11.

3. From the Special Peace Corps (people with disabilities serving the community) Creed: www.old.peaceabbey.org/education/education_corps.htm. Originally from prayers by St. Francis.

4. A comment from my wife when I told her I'd run my usual route 45 seconds faster.

5. Outside of the more extreme forms of immorality connected to violence, oppression, or exploitation, I personally have manifested virtually all of the neurotic forms of *unspiritual* behavior described in this book. That's one reason I'm writing it.

6. Sixty-five percent of runners are injured in an average year, one running injury occurs for about every 100 hours of running, and runners miss about 5–10 percent of their workouts due to injury. See W. C. Byrnes, P. McCullagh, A. Dickinson, and J. Noble, "Incidence and Severity of Injury Following Aerobic Training Programs Emphasizing Running, Racewalking, or Step Aerobics," *Medicine and Science in Sports and Exercise* 25, no. 5 (1993): S81; www.pponline. co.uk/encyc/0123.htm. The day after I wrote this passage, a front-page story in the *Boston Globe* headlined "Teens Training Too Hard, Too Often: Athletes' Injuries Concern Doctors" (June 1, 2010). Numerous athletic problems from overtraining are leading to surgeries in the present and greater risk of arthritis in later life.

7. German philosopher Hegel (1770–1831) called this tension between desired enlightenment and a deeply flawed reality the "unhappy consciousness." See G. W. F. Hegel, *Phenomenology of Spirit* (Princeton, NJ: Princeton University Press, 2005).

8. Dorothy Soelle, *The Silent Cry: Mysticism and Resistance* (Minneapolis, MN: Fortress, 2001), chapter 1.

9. The delightful film *I Heart Huckabees* displays this beautifully.

10. Viktor E. Frankl, in L. Vardey, ed., *God in All Worlds: An Anthology of Contemporary Spiritual Writing* (New York: Vintage, 1996), p. 339.

11. Frederic Brussat and Mary Ann Brussat, *Spiritual Literacy: Reading the Sacred in Everyday Life* (New York: Touchstone, 1996), p. 37.

12. I've seen this in many places, including some Jewish prayer books (e.g., *Siddur Hadash* (Bridgeport, CT: Media Judaica, n.d.), p. 80, but have yet to find the original source.

13. Leo Tolstoy, *The Death of Ivan Ilych*, Literature Network: www.online-literature. com/tolstoy/death-of-ivan-ilych/12/.

14. Lewis Randa, director of the Peace Abbey of Sherborn, Massachusetts, in a public lecture, June, 2000, I attended.

15. Leonard Cohen, "Anthem," www.azlyrics.com/lyrics/leonardcohen/anthem. html.

16. Thich Nhat Hanh, *The Miracle of Mindfulness* (Boston: Beacon, 1999), p. 4.

17. Guru Nanek, founder of Sikh tradition, in the "Peace Prayers of the World's Twelve Major Religions," from the Community of St. Francis Web site: www. worldcommunityofsaintfrancis.com/Peace_Prayers.html.

18. Ahmad Jam, "True Destination," in Mahmood Jamal, ed., *Islamic Mystical Poetry: Sufi Verse from the Early Mystics to Rumi* (New York: Penguin, 2009), p. 53.

19. J. Krishnamurti, *Freedom from the Known* (New York: Harper and Row, 1969), pp. 34–35.

20. Thomas Merton, quoted in Ellsberg, *Modern Spiritual Masters*, p. 12.

21. An old story I heard years ago. I've forgotten the source.

22. *Ashtavakra Gita*, 5.4., Realization Web site: www.realization.org/page/doc0/doc0004.htm.

23. *Chuang Tzu*, chapter 6, http://nothingistic.org/library/chuangtzu/chuang15.html.

24. Krishnamurti, *Freedom*, pp. 60–61. 60–61

25. *Bagavad Gita*, chapter 5. The date of its composition is the subject of much dispute, ranging from the fifth century B.C.E. to a few centuries into the Common Era.

26. Søren Kierkegaard, *Concluding Unscientific Postscript* (Princeton, NJ: Princeton University Press, 1974), p. 121.

27. My much longer answer to this question is contained in *A Spirituality of Resistance: Finding a Peaceful Heart and Protecting the Earth* (Lanham, MD: Rowman and Littlefield, 2003).

28. The Dalai Lama and Howard C. Cutler, *The Art of Happiness: A Handbook for Living* (New York: Riverhead, 1998), p. 257.

29. Joanna Macy, *World as Lover, World as Self* (San Francisco, CA: Parallax, 2007).

30. Paul Heelas and Linda Woodhead, *Spiritual Revolution: Why Religion Is Giving Way to Spirituality* (Malden, MA: Blackwell, 2005), p. 2.

31. Jeremy Carrette and Richard King, *Selling Spirituality: The Silent Takeover of Religion* (London: Routledge, 2005), pp. 1, 3.

32. Paul Heelas, *Spiritualties of Life: New Age Romanticism and Consumptive Capitalism* (Malden, MA: Blackwell, 2008), p. 167.

33. James Martin, Jesuit author, quoted in John Blake, "Are There Dangers in Being 'Spiritual' but Not 'Religious'?" CNN Web site, June 3, 2010: http://articles.cnn.com/2010–06–03/living/spiritual.but.not.religious_1_spiritual-community-religious-god?_s=PM:LIVING.

34. Eugene H. Peterson, "In the Word: What's Wrong with Spirituality?" *Christianity Today* Web site, June 16, 2011: www.christianitytoday.com/ct/1998/july13/8t8051.html?start=6.

35. One version of this history is in Roger S. Gottlieb, *Marxism 1844–1990: Origins, Betrayal, Rebirth* (New York: Routledge, 1992).

36. Friedrich Nietzsche, *Genealogy of Morals*, part 1. Ayn Rand, *Atlas Shrugged* (New York: Signet, 1966). Nietzsche adds that the delighted Christian expectation of witnessing the torments of the damned indicate the hidden aggressive motives

beneath the loving façade. Compare on this point St. Benedict: "All who despise God will burn in hell for their sins, and all who reverence God have everlasting life awaiting them." Quoted in Joan Chittister, *The Rule of Benedict: A Spirituality for the 21st Century* (New York: Crossroad, 1992), p. 79.

37. Nietzsche, a much subtler thinker than Rand, sees that ascetic disciplines give practitioners a kind of power (*Genealogy*, part 3). Extreme forms of self-control embody, he argued, a great deal of the "will to power": the universal psychic impulse to increase our strengths and abilities. To see how acceptance and control connect, compare this quote from Zen teacher Shunryu Suzuki: "We say concentration, but to concentrate your mind on something is not the true purpose of Zen. The true purpose is to see things as they are, to observe things as they are, and to let everything go as it goes. This is to put everything under control in its widest sense" (*Zen Mind, Beginner's Mind: Informal Talks on Zen Meditation and Practice* [New York: Weatherhill, 1970], p. 33).

38. See chapter 10 for more details.

39. Although mindfulness is the best known, Buddhism teaches many different types of meditation. For a scholarly overview, see Paul J. Griffiths, "Indian Buddhist Meditation," in Takeuchi Yoshinori, ed., *Buddhist Spirituality: Indian, Southeast Asian, Tibetan, Early Chinese* (New York: Crossroad, 1993). Two widely read contemporary Buddhist treatments of meditation are Suzuki, *Zen Mind*, and Joseph Goldstein and Jack Kornfield, *Seeking the Heart of Wisdom: The Path of Insight Meditation* (Boston: Shambhala, 1987).

40. Goldstein and Kornfield, *Seeking*, p. 19.

41. Samyutta-Nikaya, 5:307.

42. *Dhammapada*, chapter 1, verse 16.

43. David Steindl-Rast, *Gratitude Is the Heart of Prayer* (Mahwah, NJ: Paulist, 1984). The Eckhart quote I've seen in many places but have yet to locate the source.

44. Talmud, *Pirke Avot*, chapter 4, #1.

45. Samuel Dresner, ed., *Abraham Joshua Heschel, I Asked for Wonder: A Spiritual Anthology* (New York: Crossroad, 1990), p. 22.

46. Aldous Huxley, *Themes and Variations* (New York: Harper, 1950), p. 69.

47. "Dina-I Mainog-I Khirad (Spirit of Wisdom)" in Raghavan Iyer, ed., *The Jewel in the Lotus* (New York: Concord Grove, 1983), p. 575.

CHAPTER 2

1. "Thirty-Six Aphorisms of the Baal Shem Tov": www.chabad.org/library/article_cdo/aid/3073/jewish/36-Aphorisms-of-the-Baal-Shem-Tov.htm.

2. Sharafuddin Maneri, *The Hundred Letters* (New York: Paulist, 1980), p. 16.

3. Suzuki, *Zen Mind*, 46–49.

4. Chogyam Trungpa, *Cutting through Spiritual Materialism* (Berkeley, CA: Shambala, 1973), 13–14.

5. Martin Laird, *A Sunlit Absence: Silence, Awareness, and Contemplation* (New York: Oxford University Press, 2011), 9.

6. Thomas Merton, quoted in Robert Ellsberg, *Modern Spiritual Masters*, 14.

7. Philip Goodman, ed., *The Yom Kippur Anthology* (New York: Jewish Publications Society, 1971), 115.

8. Søren Kierkegaard, *Postscript*, 147.

9. Contemporary Buddhist David Loy describes this problem in the context of modern philosophy and psychology in *Lack and Transcendence: The Problem of Death and Life in Psychotherapy, Existentialism, and Buddhism* (Amherst, NY: Humanity Books, 1996).

10. For example, the 12-step commitment to make "a decision to turn our will and our lives over to the care of God" and the often used phrase, originating in the Gospels, that asks God to fulfill not our will but God's.

11. *Bagavad Gita*, 2.55–57.

12. Brain scans of long-term, serious meditators suggest that extended meditation may actually change the structure of the brain. See Jon Kabat-Zinn, *Coming to Our Senses: Healing Ourselves and the World through Mindfulness* (New York: Hyperion, 2005), 371. There is some indication that significant physiological effects can occur much more quickly; see "Seven Hours to Lower Anxiety," *Spirituality and Health*, September–October 2011, 31.

13. I heard this a long time ago, and although I remember it (I tell myself) accurately, I have no idea where it came from.

14. Laird, *Sunlit*, 84.

15. Suzuki, *Zen Mind*, 80–81.

16. A classic teaching. See www.dharmaweb.org/index.php/The_Zen_Concept_of_Emptiness,_or_Mu.

17. Samuel Dresner, ed., *Abraham Joshua Heschel, I Asked for Wonder*, 20.

18. Dietrich Bonhoffer, *Letters and Papers from Prison* (New York: Macmillan, 1971).

19. For example, Rick Fields, with Peggy Taylor and Rex Weylar, *Chop Wood, Carry Water: A Guide to Finding Spiritual Fulfillment in Everyday Life* (New York: Tarcher, 1984); and Brussat and Brussat, *Spiritual Literacy*. And at least 10 other titles at Amazon.

20. Kabir, *Ecstatic Poems* (Boston: Beacon Press, 2007), 8.

21. Gerard Manley Hopkins, "God's Grandeur." Poetry Foundation Website: www.poetryfoundation.org/poem/173660.

22. Xavier Leon-Dufour, quoted in Gregory Boyle, *Tattoos on the Heart: The Power of Boundless Compassion* (New York: Free Press, 2010), 158.

23. Goldstein and Kornfield, *Seeking the Heart of Wisdom*, 99.

24. Brussat and Brussat, *Spiritual Literacy*, 42.

25. Robert Ellsberg, *The Saints' Guide to Happiness: Practical Lessons in the Life of the Spirit* (New York: Doubleday: 2003), 126.

26. I heard this version many several years ago, but I have no idea where. A slightly different wording can be found in Teresa's *Mother Teresa of Calcutta, A Gift for God* (New York: HarperCollins, 1975), 24–25.

27. Thomas à Kempis, *The Imitation of Christ* (New York: Alba House, 1983), chapter 1, paragraph 1.

28. This question of the role of belief and the distinct concept of spiritual "truth" will return a number of times in this book, especially in an extended discussion in chapter 5.

29. See Rumi's version, "Elephant in the Dark," in *The Essential Rumi*, trans. Coleman Barks (San Francisco, CA: HarperSanFrancisco, 1995), 252. The accuracy of Barks's translations is a matter of some dispute, but the value of the thought remains, whether it is Rumi's or not.

30. St. Augustine, *Super Boethium De Trinitate*, Priory of the Immaculate Conception Web site: http://dhspriory.org/thomas/BoethiusDeTr.htm#11.

31. *Chuang Tzu*, in Timothy Freke, *The Illustrated Book of Sacred Scriptures* (Wheaton, IL: Quest, 1988), 59.

32. Another story whose source escapes me.

33. Suzuki, *Zen Mind*, 54–55.

34. Waskow is a major voice in Jewish Renewal, a "spiritually" oriented contemporary form of Judaism. For his writings and blog, see The Shalom Center: www.theshalomcenter.org/. Thich Nhat Hanh is a Vietnamese Zen Buddhist, widely known in the west for his teaching of the socially oriented "Engaged Buddhism." Of his many writings, one might begin with *Being Peace* (San Francisco, CA: Parallax, 1987).

35. Rabbi Dovid Gottlieb (author's brother), *The Informed Soul* (New York: ArtScroll, 1990). For a comparable recent effort, see Michael Coren, *Why Catholics Are Right* (Toronto: McClelland & Stewart, 2011). On Benedict's decision, see "Pope Won't Allow Joint Prayer at Pilgrimage," *Boston Globe*, October 19, 2011, A3.

36. In Pat Rodegast and Judith Stanton, *Emmanuel's Book: A Manual for Living Comfortably in the Cosmos* (New York: Friend's Press, 1985), xviii.

37. Lisa Jones, *Broken: A Love Story* (New York: Scribner, 2009).

38. Kaethe Weingarten, *Common Shock: Witnessing Violence Every Day—How We Are Harmed, How We Can Heal* (New York: Dutton, 2003).

39. Boyle, *Tattoos*, 67.

40. Boyle, *Tattoos*, 75.

41. Rowan Williams, *Dostoyevsky: Language, Truth and Fiction* (Waco, TX: Baylor University Press, 2008). This book is a profound meditation on spiritual relationships. The understanding of compassion it offers is a kind of fusion between Williams and Dostoevsky.

42. Kierkegaard puts it this way: "If there were no eternal consciousness in a man, if at the foundation of all there lay only a wildly seething power which writhing with obscure passions produced everything that is great and everything that is

insignificant, if a bottomless void never satiated lay hidden beneath all—what then would life be but despair?" (Søren Kierkegaard, *Fear and Trembling*, trans. Walter Lowrie [Princeton, NJ: Princeton University Press, 1941], 30).

43. Drug experiences may suddenly launch us up to mystical realities but tend to bring us down from them just as quickly. At best, hallucinogenics can prompt the pursuit of a serious—sober—spiritual practice.

44. *The Sayings of Lao Tsu*: www.freehealingbooks.com/user/image/sayings_of_lao_tzu_l_giles.pdf.

45. Sutta Nipata, vol. I, sutra 8. In Thich Nhat Hanh, *Teachings on Love* (Berkeley, CA: Parallax, 1998), 12.

46. The online *Stanford Encyclopedia of Philosophy* has excellent entries on the varieties of moral theory: http://plato.stanford.edu/.

47. Thich Nhat Hanh, for example, emphasizes that a Buddhist sage seeks joy for everyone, including himself or herself. There is no element of self-sacrifice. See *Teachings on Love*, 4–8. As well, the dissolution of a sense of separate selfhood, which is often posed as the goal of spiritual practice, leaves no room for the self-righteousness and judgmentalism that may accompany standard forms of morality. Consider fourteenth-century Sufi teacher Sharafuddin Maneri's comment: "When the 'I' and the 'You' have passed away, God alone will remain" (*The Hundred Letters* [New York: Paulist, 1980], 4).

48. From a wonderful book that includes dozens of first-person narratives with instructive spiritual commentary written by the eclectic teacher Ram Dass and the Christian Paul Gorman: "At times, helping happens simply in the way of things. It's not something we really think about, merely the instinctive response of an open heart.... You live, you help. When we join together in this spirit, action comes more effortlessly, and everybody ends up nourished" (*How Can I Help: Stories and Reflections on Service* [New York: Knopf, 1985], 5).

49. Adapted by Raymond M. Smullyan, quoted and commented on by Douglas Hofstadter and Daniel Dennet in an online version of *The Mind's I*: http://themindi.blogspot.com/2007/02/chapter-20-is-god-taoist.html. There are many similar criticisms of priggish morality and religious literalism in Sufi poet Hafiz, in what one commentator calls his "anti-clericalism." See Leonard Lewisohn, "The Religion of Love and the Puritans of Islam: Sufi Sources of Hafiz's Anti-Clericalism," in Leonard Lewisohn, ed., *Hafiz and the Religion of Love in Classical Persian Poetry* (London: I. B. Tauris, 2010).

50. Excerpted from "We Are One" by Frederic Brussat and Mary Ann Brussat: www.spiritualityandpractice.com/practices/features.php?id=19952. In the fashion of contemporary eclectic spirituality, this prayer was composed by Christian ministers and modeled after similar compositions by Zen Buddhist Thich Nhat Hanh.

51. There is also the point that while morality principally regulates relations among people (and perhaps between nature and people as well), some spiritual

questions are essentially individual: the meaning of our lives, how we are to face death, and the clarity of our own relation to God or ultimate truth. A spiritual life may even require that we spend some time in seclusion reflecting on that relation, temporarily suspending all our moral relations with other people. These needs are simply not recognized in the vast majority of secular ethical perspectives.

52. Whether what they share constitutes the core or essence of their respective traditions is a thorny issue, on which I'm not taking a position. But the commonalities, I would argue, are indisputable, whether the differences are comparatively trivial or absolutely central as well.

53. There are countless works on Francis. Here is a useful and short summary: Patrick F. O'Connell: "St. Francis of Assisi: The Spirituality of Conformation," *Spirituality Today* 38 (Winter 1986); www.spiritualitytoday.org/spir2day/8638420connell. html.

54. Christin M. Bochen, ed., *Thomas Merton: Essential Writings* (Maryknoll, NY: Orbis, 2000), 37–39,

55. Web site of Byron Katie, "The Work": www.thework.com/byronkatie.php.

56. Starhawk, *The Spiral Dance* (New York: Harper & Row, 1979), 104–105.

57. *Shambhala: The Sacred Path of the Warrior* (New York: Bantam: 1984), 23–25, 42, 46.

58. Reported many places, including this online *New World Encyclopedia*: www.new-worldencyclopedia.org/entry/Dazu_Huike.

59. St. John of the Cross, *Dark Night of the Soul* (Mineola, NY: Dover, 2003).

60. Mother Teresa to the Rev. Michael Van Der Peet, September 1979; quoted in David Van Biema, "Mother Teresa's Crisis of Faith," *Time*, August 23, 2007; www.time.com/time/world/article/0,8599,1655415,00.html.

CHAPTER 3

1. The Persian Sufi mystic Rumi's masterpiece *Masnavi* is translated as "spiritual couplets." Sixteenth-century Spanish Franciscan mystic Francisco de Osuna titled one of his works *The Third Spiritual Alphabet*. The fourth-century Syrian monk Pseudo-macarius authored *The Fifty Spiritual Homilies*. One could argue that *spiritual* is not the best word to use to translate these writings or that it had a very different meaning in other times and cultures, but the term is used by dozens of contemporary scholars to translate and refer to the works of traditional writers. See Crossroad Publishing's scholarly oriented and multivolume *World Spirituality: An Encyclopedic History of the Religious Quest*.

2. This process will be explained in detail in the following two chapters.

3. I describe what I find to be the wisest teachings from traditional sources. I am making no statement about the current spiritual development of any particular Mahayana Buddhist, Sufi, Catholic, or Hasid.

4. Despite a considerable amount of historical vagueness, one scholar tells us: "Aśoka stands out prominently as a man of peace and non-violence, a denouncer of war and an exemplary ruler devoted to the welfare of the people and dedicated to their moral regeneration." See Ananda Guruge, "Emperor Aśoka's Place in History: A Review of Prevalent Opinions," in Nuradha Seneviratna, ed., *King Asoka and Buddhism: Literary and Historical Studies* (Sri Lanka: Buddhist Publication Society, 1994), 204; www.buddhanet.net/pdf_file/king_asoka.pdf.

5. Edward Conze, *Buddhism: Its Essence and Development* (New York: Harper, 1959), 127.

6. E. A. Burtt, ed., *The Teachings of the Compassionate Buddha* (New York: Mentor, 1955), 130.

7. D. T. Suzuki, "Commentary on the 'Gandavyuha,'" in Edward Conze, ed., *On Indian Mahayana Buddhism* (New York: Harper, 1968), 164.

8. The "Four Unlimited" of the Bodhisattva are friendliness, compassion, sympathetic joy, and even mindedness.

9. *Abhidarmakosa* II, in Edward Conze, *Buddhism: Its Essence and Development*, 191–192.

10. Quoted in Andrew Harvey, *The Essential Mystics* (San Francisco, CA: Harper SanFranscico, 1996), 75.

11. Burtt, *Teachings*, 133.

12. Some might suggest that conventionally socialized women are already trained to put others' needs before their own. However, that form of codependence is not the Bodhisattva's universal compassion, but rather another form of ego that receives its identity through relationship and is dependent, often in self-destructive ways, on relationships.

13. Burtt, *Teachings*, 174.

14. "The Heart Sutra," Buddhist Dharma Education Association: www.buddhanet. net/e-learning/harttr.htm.

15. Edward Conze, *Buddhist Thought in India: Three Phases of Buddhist Philosophy* (Ann Arbor: University of Michigan Press, 1967), 213.

16. The term *Zen* is simply a Japanese translation of the Chinese word *Chan*, which is itself a rendering of the Sanskrit *dhyana*, which in turn simply means "meditation." Zen Buddhism is just meditation Buddhism, at least literally.

17. These are from a classic Zen collection, *The Gateless Gate*: www.ibiblio.org/zen/cgi-bin/koan-index.pl.

18. From Paul Reps, *Zen Flesh, Zen Bones*:http://www.101zenstories.com/http://gyanpedia.in/tft/Resources/books/zen.pdf.

19. Rodney Stark, *One True God: Historical Consequences of Monotheism* (Princeton, NJ: Princeton University Press, 2001).

20. Many thanks to Richard Foltz for helpful corrections to this section.

21. One view is that Arabic mystics spread throughout the early Islamic empire and connected to Hindu, Buddhist, Shamanic, Jewish, and Christian teachers

with similar concerns. The resulting synthesis, rooted in the Islamic world, was Sufism. See Idries Shah, *The Sufis* (New York: Doubleday, 1964).

22. Many of the sentiments of the few teachers discussed here are echoed by a much larger number in Jamal, *Islamic Mystical*.

23. Khalid Duran, quoted in Stephen Schwartz, *The Other Islam: Sufism and the Road to Global Harmony* (New York: Doubleday, 2008), 40.

24. Rumi is undoubtedly the world's best known Sufi writer. His major work *Masnavi* is described by one Rumi scholar as "a kind of Koran commentary," which "concentrates on the spiritual message of scripture," describing a path "that leads the soul back home to its heavenly abode." See Franklin D. Lewis, *Rumi: Past and Present, East and West* (Oxford: One World, 2000), 399. Lewis's extremely detailed account of Rumi's life and ideas supports the general perspective of this section.

25. Sufis refer to practices like meditation, prayer, or movement (the "whirling" in the "whirling dervish") as *dhkr*—which is etymologically almost identical to the Hebrew root of the word for remembrance (*zkr*).

26. Schwartz, *The Other Islam*, 38.

27. Schwartz, *The Other Islam*, 38.

28. "Paradise Face," in *Drunk on the Wine of the Beloved: 100 Poems of Hafiz*, trans. Thomas Rain Crowe (Boston: Shambhala, 2001), 16.

29. "In the School of Truth," in *Drunk*, 18.

30. A common game in Iran, and indeed throughout the Persian world from the Balkans to China, is the *musha'era*, which begins with someone reciting a line of poetry, often of Rumi, to be answered by another who would take the ending of the first line as the beginning of another quotation.

31. Mevlevi order of the United States: www.hayatidede.org/index.htm.

32. James Fadiman and Robert Frager, eds., *Essential Sufism* (San Francisco, CA: HarperSanFrancisco, 1997), 15.

33. Schwartz, *The Other Islam*, 46.

34. Schwartz, *The Other Islam*, 88.

35. Schwartz, *The Other Islam*, 97–98.

36. Kabir Helminski, *The Knowing Heart: A Sufi Path of Transformation* (Boston: Shambhala, 1999), 9.

37. Fadiman and Frager, *Essential Sufism*, 86.

38. Schwartz, *The Other Islam*, 71. Consider also this Ibn Arabi statement: "It is He who is revealed in every face, sought in every sign, gazed upon by every eye, worshipped in every object of worship, and pursued in the unseen and the visible. Not a single one of His creatures can fail to find Him in its primordial and original nature." See the Muhyiddin Ibn Arabi Society: www.ibnarabisociety. org/articles/twinch.html.

39. Fadiman and Frager, *Essential Sufism*, 13.

40. Helminksi, *The Knowing Heart*, 10.

41. Hafiz, "So Many Gifts," in *The Gift: Poems by Hafiz The Great Sufi Master*, trans. Daniel Ladinsky (New York: Penguin, 1999), 67. The reliability of Ladinsky's translations have been questioned by scholars.

42. Lewisohn, "Religion of Love."

43. Maria Jaoudi, *Christian and Islamic Spirituality: Sharing a Journey* (Mahweh, NJ: Paulist, 1993).

44. For example, Christian thinkers affected by ecumenism or modern political movements like the New Left, feminism, or environmentalism; for example, Thomas Merton, Matthew Fox, Rosemary Radford Ruether, John B. Cobb, and Thomas Berry.

45. The Classics of Western Spirituality series has many, from a wide range of periods and settings.

46. "With the exception of the Bible, it is perhaps the most widely read spiritual book in the world," claims *The Catholic Encyclopedia*: www.newadvent.org/cathen/07674c.htm. Saint Ignatius, founder of the Jesuits, recommends *The Imitation of Christ. The Spiritual Exercises of Saint Ignatius* (New York: Doubleday, 1964), 68. While I will reference a published edition, the text is easily available online.

47. Thomas à Kempis, *The Imitation of Christ* (New York: Alba House, 1983), 23, I. Chapter 2, par. 4

48. Thomas à Kempis, *The Imitation of Christ*, 26. I. chapter 3, par. 3.

49. Thomas à Kempis, *The Imitation of Christ*, 107. II. chapter 3, par. 2.

50. Thomas à Kempis, *The Imitation of Christ*, 56. I. chapter 16, par. 4. I first saw this passage from Kempis in a collection of brief spiritual quotations some 30 years ago. I was immediately struck by its wisdom and how much better life would be for all of us if we took that wisdom in. The biblical passage Kempis refers to "Brothers, if someone is caught in a sin, you who are spiritual should restore him gently. But watch yourself, or you also may be tempted. Carry each other's burdens, and in this way you will fulfill the law of Christ" (Galatians 6:1–2).

51. There is a Jewish legend that the fate of the world at any given time depends on the spiritual merit of the "lamad-vavniks"—36 usually hidden, unrecognized, but unusually righteous men. It is based in the Talmudic claim that in every generation 36 men greet the "divine presence" (*Schechinah*). Tractate Sanhedrin 97b; Tractate Sukkah 45b.

52. Maurice Samuel, *Prince of the Ghetto* (New York: Knopf, 1948), 198.

53. For the historical background, see Paul Johnson, *A History of the Jews* (New York: Harper, 1987), part 4.

54. Elie Wiesel, *Souls on Fire* (New York: Simon and Schuster, 1984), 25–26.

55. The story is widely circulated. Here is one source: www.story-lovers.com/lists-shepherdsprayer.html.

56. Yaffa Eliach, *Hasidic Tales of the Holocaust* (New York: Vintage, 1988).

57. Martin Buber, *Tales of the Hasidim: Early Masters* (New York: Schocken, 1986), 3.

58. Medieval India saw the rise of the Bhakti movement, with a similar emphasis on religious joy and a similar movement away from the expertise of highly trained priests in favor of the daily language and value of common people. Two of the movement's best known representatives are the poets Kabir and Mirabai.

CHAPTER 4

1. Holy Yoga Foundation, guided by "the intentional practice of connecting our entire being; body, mind and spirit with God; the Father, Son and Holy Spirit," has trained over 400 yoga teachers: http://holyyogafoundation.com/.

2. Boyle, *Tattoos.*

3. A historian of religion tells us that even in the sixteenth century Roman Catholics and Lutherans (despite disagreements about method) "have the same focus" for their spiritual lives. What is striking is how much blood was shed before this contemporary insight could even be conceptualized. See Jill Raitt, "Saints and Sinners: Roman Catholic and Protestant Spirituality in the Sixteenth Century," in Jill Raitt, ed., *Christian Spirituality: High Middle Ages and Reformation* (New York: Crossroad, 1989), 460.

4. John Locke, *A Letter Concerning Toleration.* See Constitution Society: www.consti-tution.org/jl/tolerati.htm.

5. Douglas V. Steere, *Quaker Spirituality: Selected Writings* (Mahwah, NJ: Paulist, 1984); Sheila Rowbotham, *Women, Resistance, and Revolution* (New York: Penguin, 1974), chapter 1.

6. Talmud, Arachin 15b.

7. Itself an account of the teaching of Indian Buddhist Atisha Dipankara Shrijnana, who came to instruct Tibetan Buddhists in the eleventh century. See editor's "Forward," in Chogyam Trungpa, *Training the Mind: And Cultivating Loving-Kindness* (Boston: Shambhala 1993), xiii–xiv, 173–174.

8. The *Tara Tantra*, quoted in Tsultrim Alliione, "Tara, the First Feminist," *Buddhadharma,* Winter 2010, 33.

9. For example, Yin Yoga, which stresses holding each pose for three to five minutes, describes the effects of the poses in the terminology of Chinese medicine (meridians, organs, etc.). See www.yinyoga.com/ys2_2.1_asanas.php.

10. Roger Walsh, Robin Bitner, Bruce Victor, and Lorena Hillman, "Medicate or Meditate," *Buddhadharma: The Practitioner's Quarterly,* Spring 2009: http://archive.thebuddhadharma.com/issues/2009/spring/medicate.php.

11. The Dalai Lama about himself, *Toward a True Kinship of Faiths* (New York: Harmony, 2010), 1, ix.

12. Adapted from Kierkegaard, *Postscript,* 49.

13. While some versions use other terms (trial, temptation), an informal survey of Christian and Jewish sources has "test" as the most frequent translation.

14. Kierkegaard's answer to the question of Abraham's greatness has two sides, only one of which I will examine. I will ignore the ethical question of whether faith makes it a holy act to be willing to murder your son. Kierkegaard examines and rejects a number of answers: that Abraham was special, that it only had to happen once, that after all everything worked out. His own answer is that under certain circumstances we are justified in suspending our moral relations to people to serve God. It is a bold, controversial, and—given the number of crazy people who tell us that the Lord has commanded them to violence—frightening interpretation.

15. Kierkegaard explores these possibilities in a series of imaginative retellings and additions to the biblical narrative. In Jewish tradition, such imaginative additions and retellings of scripture are called "midrash." There are an enormous number of them, some of which contain Judaism's richest spiritual insights.

16. The "I" here is not Kierkegaard, but a pseudonym. His philosophical works were published under a series of pseudonyms, which he used to distance himself from his own positions. His goal was to represent the different stages of a person's approach to authentic Christianity, not just by describing those stages but by embodying them in different authorial voices. However, it is clear from his journals that Kierkegaard believed that he himself was not capable of Abraham's level of faith.

17. Kierkegaard, *Fear and Trembling*, 49–51, my emphasis.

18. Kierkegaard did not consider Abraham Christian but did believe that his extreme form of faith was a necessary condition for Christianity. And clearly for Kierkegaard Abraham represents an aspect or dimension of Christian faith.

19. See reference to Steindl-Rast in chapters 1 and 2; Marcia Praeger, *The Path of Blessing* (Woodstock, VT: Jewish Lights, 2003).

20. Louis Jacobs, *Hasidic Prayer* (New York: Schocken, 1987), 30.

21. On Deep Ecology and its similarities to religion, see David Barnhill and Roger S. Gottlieb, eds., *Deep Ecology and World Religions* (Albany: State University of New York Press, 2001).

22. Of many sources, see, e.g., Shamara Shantu Riley, "Ecology Is a Sistah's Issue Too," in Roger S. Gottlieb, ed., *Liberating Faith: Religious Voices for Justice, Peace, and Ecological Wisdom* (Lanham, MD: Rowman and Littlefield, 2003), 398–410

23. Kabir, *Ecstatic Poems*, 70.

24. Abraham Joshua Heschel, *A Passion for Truth* (Woodstock, VT: Jewish Lights, 1995).

25. Kierkegaard, *Postscript*, 171.

26. Kierkegaard, *Postscript*, 178.

27. Kierkegaard, *Postscript*, 179–180, my emphasis.

CHAPTER 5

1. See Best Spirituality: www.bestspirituality.com/quotes-1/nf/DalaI_Lama.htm.
2. Paul Heelas and Linda Woodhead, *Spiritual Revolution: Why Religion Is Giving Way to Spirituality* (Malden, MA: Blackwell, 2005), 1. This description, one researcher suggests, may refer to 15 to 20 percent of the United States. See Carl E. Thoresen, "Spirituality, Religion, and Health: What's the Deal?" in Thomas G. Plante and Carl E. Thoresen, *Spirit, Science, and Health: How the Spiritual Mind Fuels Physical Wellness* (Westport, CT: Praeger, 2007).
3. As novelist Vladimir Nabakov summarized, "The Tolstoyan formula is: Ivan lived a bad life and since the bad life is nothing but the death of the soul, then Ivan lived a living death; and since beyond death is God's living light, then Ivan died into a new life." See Vladimir Nabokov, *Lectures on Russian Literature* (New York: Harcourt, 1981), 237.
4. A decade ago, one scholar estimated the designation might apply to as many as a fifth of Americans. See Robert Fuller, *Spiritual but Not Religious: Understanding Unchurched America* (New York: Oxford University Press, 2001), 5. Fuller's book provides a useful account of the self-descriptions of this group.
5. Noted religious historian Catherine L. Albanese, *American Spiritualities: A Reader* (Bloomington: Indiana University Press, 2000), 11.
6. "Why Angels Have Wings," *Spirituality and Health* 13, no. 1 (2010), 51.
7. Brad Hirschfield, *You Don't Have to Be Wrong for Me to Be Right: Finding Faith without Fanaticism* (New York: Harmony, 2007).
8. How this usage of truth is related to the first one is a fascinating question but would take us too far afield.
9. As Edward Conze, a leading American scholar of Buddhism put it, Buddhist doctrines do not "aim at terminating controversy but are designed to act as a rallying point for meditation." See Edward Conze, ed., *Buddhist Scriptures* (New York: Penguin, 1959), 181.
10. Matthew Fox served as a Dominican priest for 34 years and then was expelled from the order for his teaching about the importance of creation as opposed to sin, equality of women, and social activism. He subsequently became an Episcopal priest. See www.matthewfox.org/. European-born Schachter-Shalomi was a traditionally trained Lubavitch rabbi who was influenced by the spiritual upheavals of the 1960s and has become a leading figure in the Jewish Renewal movement and Reconstructionist Judaism. See the Reb Zalman legacy project: www.rzlp.org/.
11. Such positions, though rarely, are found in much earlier religious writings as well. See Lewisohn, "Hafiz and the Religion of Love."
12. Jesus is often referred to as "rabbi," which can be translated quite comfortably as "teacher."
13. Nachshon, Aaron's brother-in-law, supposedly went into the water before God opened up the sea. *Mechilta d'Rebbi Yishmael, Beshalach, parsha 5.* Midrash

on relation between courage and miracle is from Anna Gottlieb (author's daughter).

14. Henri Nouwen, "The Selfless Way of Christ," in Ellsberg, *Spiritual Masters*, 146.

15. At least in the northern hemisphere!

16. A similar spiritual reading of the metaphysical claims of the yoga system (Kundalini energy coiled at the base of the spine, channels [*nadis*] through which energy [*prana*] circulates, etc.) is offered by contemporary American yoga teacher Richard Freeman, who cautions against "taking the metaphors that describe the yogic process too literally": *The Mirror of Yoga: Awakening the Intelligence of Body and Mind* (Boston: Shambhala, 2010), 46. For Latin American nun Ivone Gebara, Christians need to interpret the Trinity spiritually: "The Trinity, then, is not three separate persons living in a heaven we cannot locate. The Father, Son, and Holy Spirit ... are *relationships* ... relationships we human beings experience. The relationships are expressed in anthropomorphic style, but the expression is metaphorical and not primary metaphysical." See her "The Trinity and Human Experience: An Ecofeminist Approach," in Gottlieb, *Liberating Faith*, 574.

17. Kierkegaard, *Postscript*, 25–48.

18. If we are told that it is only God's grace that will give you spiritual comfort or that a fulfilled life is only possible through God's grace, then the conversation might have reached a kind of dead end. Unless one replies: what do you have to do to be the kind of person who lets in God's grace, rather than shuts it out?

19. G. K. Chesterton, *Orthodoxy* (London: Bodley Head, 1909), 136, 138.

20. Eugene H. Peterson, "In the Word: What's Wrong with Spirituality?" *Christianity Today*, June 16, 2011: www.christianitytoday.com/ct/1998/july13/8t8051.html?start=6. Interestingly, Peterson uses the word *spirituality* in a positive sense several times in his essay. Even more interesting would be his answer to the question: how we can ever dispense with the self when we look at God—who, after all, is doing the looking? In my version, the heart of spirituality is making sure we are the kind of people who can see clearly. What we are looking at will take care of itself.

21. Lesser, *Guide*, 59.

22. Helen Schucman, *A Course in Miracles* (Mill Valley, CA: Foundation for Inner Peace, 2007).

23. Rabbi Isser Zalman Meltzer, quoted in Alan Morinis, *Every Day Holiness: The Jewish Spiritual Path of Mussar* (Boston: Trumpeter, 2009), 127. C. S. Lewis, *Surprised by Joy* (London: Geoffrey Bles, 1955), 22.

24. Neil MacFarquahar, "Royal Fund Buys Saudi Peace," *Boston Globe*, June 9, 2011. In return, the religious establishment received $200 million from the government.

25. There are, sadly, many instances of self-defined contemporary spiritual groups manifesting serious moral flaws. For one example, there is the role of sexual and financial misconduct in the breakup of the influential

San Francisco Zen Center: Michael Downing, *Shoes outside the Door: Desire, Devotion, and Excess at San Francisco Zen Center* (Berkeley, CA: Counterpoint, 2002).

26. In what is in all probability an unintended irony, Pope Benedict has asked that the Catholic Church be judged by the "same standards" as other societal institutions in regard to sex abuse. One would think, given the supposed special qualities of the church, that it would be held (to say the least) to higher standards that those applied to college football programs, bowling leagues, or the Boy Scouts. See Frances D'Emillio, "Pope Says Sex Abuse Not Just Church Issue," Boston *Sunday Globe*, November 27, 2011, A16.

27. M. Juergensmeyer and M. Kitts, "Introduction," in *Princeton Readings in Religion and Violence* (Princeton, NJ: Princeton University Press, 2011), 1. Some argue that since it offers believers the rewards of an all-powerful divine personality, monotheism has a unique power to motivate, compared to more philosophical creeds like Buddhism and Taoism. This leads to monotheism's greater amount of missionizing, religious violence, or (in the case of Judaism) ability to persevere. Rodney Stark, *One True God: Historical Consequences of Monotheism* (Princeton, NJ: Princeton University Press, 2001). Expansionist Confucian or Taoist Chinese emperors, aggressive indigenous tribes, and violent modern Hindu nationalism cast doubt on Stark's thesis.

28. Roof, *Generation*, 217–223, offers data on how seriously a large number of women, even conservative women, respond to traditional religion's sexism.

29. Richard Dawkins, *The God Delusion* (New York: Mariner, 2008); Sam Harris, *The End of Faith: Religion, Terror, and the Future of Reason* (New York: W. W. Norton, 2005).

30. Chittister is prolific, but perhaps begin with *Called to Question: A Spiritual Memoir* (Lanham, MD: Sheed and Ward, 2009).

31. Greek philosophy is very much oriented toward the virtues and thus has some real affinities to spiritual teaching. However, it also accepts many of the essential features of normal social life. For the role of the virtues in moral theory, see the groundbreaking work of Alasdair MacIntyre.

CHAPTER 6

1. Suzuki, *Zen Mind*, 37.

2. In *The Sun* magazine: www.thesunmagazine.org/issues/376/sunbeams.

3. Idries Shah, *The Sufis* (New York: Doubleday, 1964), xxviii.

4. Thus Mantak Chia, one of the first contemporary teachers of Chinese forms of meditation in the west, termed his system "Taoist esoteric yoga." Tibetan Buddhist writings and the (Hindu) *Bagavad Gita* often refer to any accomplished spiritual seeker as a "yogi."

5. Patanjali, *Yoga Sutras*. This is available online and in many modern translations.

6. The image often used to explain this is a coil of powerful energy (*kundalini*), which is located at the base of the spine. The more balanced and integrated our energies, the more powerful and liberated the kundalini becomes. As it rises, it passes through successive chakras or energy centers—from the perineum to the genitals, abdomen, heart, throat, forehead (the "third eye"), and out the top of the head. When the kundalini completes this journey, *samadhi*, or "enlightenment," results.

7. How much of the current stress on asana practice is dependent on late-nineteenth- to early-twentieth-century adaptations of and to European culture, as Mark Singleton (*Yoga Body: The Origins of Modern Posture Practice* [New York: Oxford University Press, 2010]) argues, and how much is actually centuries to millennia old is a question I will not explore. The nearly 2,000-year-old Patanjali *Yoga Sutras* includes asana as one of its essential eight aspects (limbs) of yoga, so clearly the idea of some kind of postural practice has been part of the system for a long time, although probably not stressed nearly as much as in modern western practice (and given the comparative lack of overeating, sedentary lifestyle, and media distractions in premodern times, probably not as necessary either). As well, several contemporary classics of what Singleton calls "postural yoga" include brief sections on practices like nostril cleaning and muscle locks (e.g., of the perineum [*mool bandha*] and the abdomen [*uddiyna bandha*]) that are described in texts at least five centuries old. For a helpful overview of the conceptual complexities of yoga, see a review of Singleton: Wendy Doniger, "Assume the Position," *Times Literary Supplement*, March 4, 2011, 10–11.

8. Estimates for the United States alone range from 15 million to 25 million.

9. With the rise of more vigorous forms of yoga practice—power yoga," ashtanga, and Bikram—there has been a corresponding rise in injuries from yoga practice.

10. B. K. S. Iyengar, *The Tree of Yoga* (Boston: Shambhala, 1988), 54, my emphasis.

11. B. K. S Iyengar, *Light on Yoga*, rev. ed. (New York: Schocken, 1976), 443.

12. Many forms of Buddhist meditation focus on the breath. Chi kung, which in some ways is a Chinese analogue to Hatha Yoga and *pranayama*, teaches some remarkably similar breathing exercises.

13. Swami Sivananda Rada, *Hatha Yoga: The Hidden Language* (Porthill, ID: Timeless Books, 1987), 43–47. Similarly, Donald Moyers presents a wide-ranging analysis of *vrksasana*—the tree pose—in which a person balances on one leg. Moyers's account draws on ancient Hindu mythology of trees and tree goddesses, more recent Indian teachers who meditated in trees, and the essential yogic practice of asceticism to "burn away impurities." When one's balance and strength have developed, says Moyers, "we may achieve the full experience of the pose, in Jung's phrase, like a cosmic tree" "rooted in this world and growing up to heaven." See Donald Moyers, "Vrksasana: The Tree Pose," *Yoga Journal*, January–February 1989.

14. John Friend, *Anusara Yoga Teacher Training Manual*, 12th ed. (The Woodlands, TX: Anusara, 2009), 106.

15. Michael Stone, "Practice Maps of the Great Yogis," in Michael Stone, ed., *Freeing the Body: Freeing the Mind: Writings on the Connections between Yoga and Buddhism* (Boston: Shambhala, 2010), 218; Christopher Key Chapple, *Yoga and the Luminous* (Albany, NY: State University of New York Press, 2010), 49–60.

16. Fred Rohe, *The Zen of Running* (New York: Random House, 1974).

17. T. K. Desikachar quoted in Rodney Yee, *Moving toward Balance* (Emmaus, PA: Rodale, 2004), ix. My emphasis.

18. By the leading Indian teachers who brought modern yoga to the west: B. K. S. Iyengar, *Light on Yoga* (New York: Schocken, 1979); Swami Satchitananda, *Integral Hatha Yoga* (New York: Integral Yoga, 1970); and Swami Vishnudevanada, *Complete Illustrated Book of Yoga*, reprint ed. (New York: Three Rivers, 1995). By well-known Americans: Beryl Bender Birch, *Power Yoga: The Total Strength and Flexibility Workout* (New York: Touchstone, 1995); and Rodney Yee with Nina Zolotow, *Moving toward Balance: Eight Weeks of Yoga with Rodney Yee* (Emmaus, PA: Rodale, 2004). Yee, one of the most popular of the teachers on the *Yoga Journal* circuit, begins his several hundred pages of asana instruction with short paragraphs on topics like being present, opening to vulnerability, allowing receptivity, and turning inward (xii–xiii).

19. At 300,000 subscribers, the world's leading publication.

20. Green Yoga: www.greenyoga.org/. Off the mat into the world: www.offthematin-totheworld.org/. The film is *Yogawoman*: www.yogawoman.tv/.

21. Quoted in Zalman Schachter Shalomi, *Wrapped in a Holy Flame: Teachings and Tales of the Hasidic Masters* (San Francisco, CA: Jossey-Bass, 2003), 78.

22. Much of what I say here about emotions is based in the work of Miriam Greenspan, *Healing through the Dark Emotions: The Wisdom of Grief, Fear, and Despair* (Boston: Shambhala, 2004), as well as many personal conversations with Greenspan (full disclosure: we are married). See also the groundbreaking work of Joanna Macy: www.joannamacy.net.

23. So few people are these days.

24. Kierkegaard, *Postscript*, 175.

25. There are obvious similarities between this understanding of the *sh'ma* and the Tonglen meditation discussed later.

26. Kierkegaard, *Postscript*, 145. See his brilliant account of prayers of gratitude, 158–160.

27. Similar issues, including searching reflections on the Lord's Prayer, are found in C. S. Lewis, *Letters to Malcolm* (New York: Mariner, 2002).

28. Adin Steinsaltz, *A Guide to Jewish Prayer* (New York: Schocken, 2000), 8.

29. Sayyed Hossein Nasr, "The Long Journey," in William C. Chittick, ed., *The Inner Journey: Views from the Islamic Tradition* (Sandpoint, ID: Morning Light, 2007), 219.

30. Described in chapter 1.

31. Praeger, *Path*.

32. Mantak Chia, *Fusion of the Five Elements I: Basic and Advanced Meditations for Transforming Negative Emotions* (Huntington, NY: Healing Tao, 1989).

33. See Aryeh Kaplan, *Jewish Mediation: A Practical Guide* (New York: Schocken, 1995); James Finley, *Christian Meditation: Experiencing the Presence of God* (New York: HarperOne, 2005).

34. Trungpa, *Training*, 46–51, my emphasis.

35. Sarah Harding, ed., *Machik's Complete Explanation: Clarifying the Meaning of Chöd* (Ithaca, NY: Snow Lion, 2003).

36. A View on Buddhism Web site: http://viewonbuddhism.org/mind.html.

37. According to the CDC, nearly 10 percent of U.S children age 4 to 17 have ADHD. www.cdc.gov/ncbddd/adhd/data.html. On multitasking: Dave Crenshaw, *The Myth of Multitasking: How "Doing It All" Gets Nothing Done* (New York: Jossey-Bass, 2008).

38. Jenny Phillips, *The Dhamma Brothers* (Onalaska, WA: Pariyatti, 2008), 61.

39. Phillips, *Brothers*, 55.

40. Phillips, *Brothers*, 37.

41. *Changing from the Inside* and *Doing Time, Doing Vipassana*.

42. Phillips, *Brothers*, 182.

43. Phillips, *Brothers*, 209. See also the Web site of the North American Vipassana Prison Project: www.prison.dhamma.org/en/na/project-overview.html.

44. Anatta-lakkhana Sutta: The Discourse on the Not-Self Characteristic: www.accesstoinsight.org/tipitaka/sn/sn22/sn22.059.mend.html.

45. www.learntarot.com/less1.htm. My emphasis.

CHAPTER 7

1. He adds: "Theology cannot escape this tendency if it is to be a serious mode of contemporary thought." Paul Van Buren, *The Secular Meaning of the Gospel* (New York: Macmillan, 1963), 198. Clearly, there are many people for whom this is not true. The point, however, is that there are many for whom it is.

2. Charles Taylor, *The Ethics of Authenticity* (Cambridge, MA: Harvard University Press, 1991), 26.

3. Paul Heelas and Linda Woodhead, *Spiritual Revolution: Why Religion Is Giving Way to Spirituality* (Malden, MA: Blackwell, 2005), 130.

4. Monika Bauerlein and Clara Jeffrey, "The Speedup," *Mother Jones*, July–August 2011.

5. Reviewing much social science literature, David G. Blanchflower and Andrew Oswald assert that "in the United States the well-being of successive birth-cohorts has gradually fallen through time." See their "Is Well-Being U-Shaped over the Life Cycle?" National Bureau of Economic Research Web site: www.nber.org/papers/w12935. Similarly, Betsy Stevenson and Justin Wolfers state: "It is

now widely understood that average levels of happiness have failed to grow in the United States, despite ongoing economic growth." See their "Happiness Inequality in the United States," Wharton School of Business, University of Pennsylvania: http://bpp.wharton.upenn.edu/betseys/papers/Happiness%20 Inequality.pdf. The National Institute of Mental Health claims: "Mental disorders are common in the United States, and in a given year approximately one quarter of adults are diagnosable for one or more disorders": www.nimh.nih. gov/statistics/1ANYDIS_ADULT.shtml.

6. "Mental Health: Depression": www.who.int/mental_health/management/depression/definition/en/index.html. On China, see *Wall Street Journal*, "China's Changing View of Mental Illness": http://blogs.wsj.com/chinarealtime/2010/06/22/china %E2%80%99s-changing-view-on-mental-illness/.

7. Bill McKibben, *Deep Economy: The Wealth of Communities and the Durable Future* (New York: St. Martins, 2008).

8. On the negative aspects of globalization: Arundhati Roy, *Power Politics* (Boston: South End, 2001); William F. Fisher and Thomas Ponniah, eds., *Another World Is Possible: Popular Alternatives to Globalization at the World Social Forum* (London: Zed, 2003).

9. Ronald Inglehart's *Culture Shift in Advanced Industrial Society* (Princeton, NJ: Princeton University Press, 1990) was a pioneering effort to document the change "from an overwhelming emphasis on material well-being and physical security toward greater emphasis on the quality of life" (5).

10. Juliet Schor, *True Wealth* (New York: Penguin, 2010); Charlene Spretnak, *Relational Reality* (Topsham, ME: Green Horizon, 2011).

11. For example, we replace heroin addicts with methadone addicts, childhood ADD with Adderall dependence. Subsidies for ethanol production lead to severe increases in global food prices. And so on.

12. For instance, there is the track record of many of the miracle antidepressants. See Joanna Moncrieff, *The Myth of the Chemical Cure: A Critique of Psychiatric Drug Treatment* (London: Palgrave Macmillan, 2009); Irving Kirsch, *The Emperor's New Drugs: Exploding the Antidepressant Myth* (New York: Basic Books, 2010).

13. Martin E. P. Seligman and Mihaly Csikszentmihalyi, "Positive Psychology: An Introduction," *American Psychologist*, January 2002, 1.

14. John Brueggemann, *Rich, Free, and Miserable: The Failure of Success in America* (Lanham, MD, Rowman and Littlefield, 2010), 9–10.

15. One striking example: following a strong Vatican rejection of women priests, American Catholic support of women clergy rose rather than fell. See Rosemary Ruether, "Entering the Sanctuary: The Roman Catholic Story," in Rosemary Ruether and Eleanor McLaughlin, eds., *Women of Spirit: Female Leadership in the Jewish and Christian Traditions* (New York: Simon and Schuster, 1979), 381.

16. For a general account of the compatibility of religion and left politics, see my *Joining Hands: Politics and Religion Together for Social Change* (Cambridge, MA: Westview, 2002).

17. See the work of religious writer-activists like Rabbi Michael Lerner and Protestant Jim Wallis.

18. Robert Wuthnow, *America and the Challenges of Religious Diversity* (Princeton, NJ: Princeton University Press, 2005), 150. See Peter Berger on the insight that "pluralism undermines the taken-for-grantedness of beliefs and values" in "Protestantism and the Quest for Certainty," *Christian Century*, August 26–September 2, 1998, 782. Also Edwin Gaustad and Leigh Schmidt, *The Religious History of America: The Heart of the American Story from Colonial Times to Today* (New York: HarperCollins, 2002), 426.

19. Robert Wuthnow, *After Heaven: Spirituality in America since the 1950s* (Berkeley: University of California Press, 1998). Other scholars (e.g, Gaustad and Schmidt, *Religious History*, 425–426) echo Wuthnow, describing ours as a "quest" culture in search of "wholeness" and "meaning." Wade Clark Roof reflects the critical, searching attitude of baby boom spiritual seekers in a chapter titled "It's Hard to Find a Religion You Can Totally Believe In," in *A Generation of Seekers: The Spiritual Journeys of the Baby Boom Generation* (San Francisco, CA: HarperSanFrancisco, 1993).

20. Heelas and Woodhead, *Spiritual Revolution*, 61, 67.

CHAPTER 8

1. Mayoclinic.com, "Psoriasis": www.mayoclinic.com/health/psoriasis/DS00193/DSECTION=treatments-and-drugs.

2. Kabat-Zinn, *Coming to Our Senses*, 363.

3. Yoga for Vets: http://www.yogaforvets.com/testimonials.

4. Paul Zipes, interview, December 9, 2010.

5. Tom Boyle, quoted at Central Mass Yoga: www.centralmassyoga.com/veterans.htm.

6. Neal Pollack, "Warriors at Peace," *Yoga Journal*, August 2010.

7. Thomas Moore, *Care of the Soul in Medicine: Healing Guidance for Patients, Families, and the People Who Care for Them* (Carlsbad, CA: Hay House, 2010), 182.

8. I am the husband in this story.

9. Consortium of Academic Centers for Integrative Medicine. "Curriculum in Integrative Medicine: A Guide for Educators": www.imconsortium.org/prod/groups/ahc/@pub/@ahc/documents/asset/ahc_58948.pdf.

10. Noah St. John, Duke Integrative Medicine: www.dukeintegrativemedicine.org/index.php/2009011919/about-us/our-physicians-providers-and-staff.html#st_john.

11. I will avoid the complicated question of whether techniques like acupuncture, message, or chiropractic are more spiritual than surgery or prescribed medications. In practice, patients of these techniques may be as passive about and ignorant of what is going on, and the practitioner as detached, distant, and authoritarian, as anything in conventional western medicine.

12. Shauna L. Shapiro, Roger Walsh, "Meditation: Exploring the Farther Reaches," in Thomas G. Plante and Carl E. Thoresen, eds., *Spirit, Science, and Health: How the Spiritual Mind Fuels Physical Wellness* (Westport CT: Praeger, 2007), 60. For a detailed list of mind-body interventions, listed by condition, see Herbert Benson and William Proctor, *Relaxation Revolution: Enhancing Your Personal Health through the Science and Genetics of Mind Body Healing* (New York: Scribner, 2010).

13. See the overview in Timothy McCall, *Yoga as Medicine: The Yogic Prescription for Health and Healing* (New York: Bantam, 2007); and J. Vogel and M. Krucoff, "ACC CAM Consensus Statement," *Journal of the American College of Cardiology* 46 (2005):184–221. Recent studies have also looked at chronic low-back pain, chronic obstructive pulmonary disease, diabetes risk, HIV, immune function, inflammatory arthritis and knee osteoarthritis, multiple sclerosis, and smoking cessation. See National Institute of Health, National Center for Complementary and Alternative Medicine: http://nccam.nih.gov/health/yoga/introduction.htm#keypoints. For another detailed summary, including physiological effects in terms of heart rate and biochemical shifts in the blood, see Trish Lamb, "Health Benefits of Yoga," International Association of Yoga Therapists: www.iayt.org/site_Vx2/publications/articles/hlthbenefits.aspx.

14. The author is a yoga therapist who treats MS patients. Roger Nolan, "Yoga for MS": www.yogasite.com/ms.htm.

15. Donna Eden, *Energy Medicine: Balance Your Body's Energies for Optimum Health, Joy, and Vitality* (New York: Putnam, 1998), 88.

16. Allen Hamilton, *The Scalpel and the Soul: Encounters with Surgery, the Supernatural and the Healing Power of Hope* (New York: Tarcher/Putnam, 2009), 229–230.

17. Esther M. Sternberg, *The Balance Within: The Science Connecting Heath and Emotions* (New York: W. H. Freeman, 2001). See also B. Alan Wallace, *Mind in the Balance: Meditation in Science, Buddhism, and Christianity* (New York: Columbia University Press, 2009).

18. J. Vogel and C. Krucoff, "ACC CAM Consensus Statement," *Journal of the American College of Cardiology* 46 (2005):184–221; http://circ.ahajournals.org/cgi/content/full/116/1/77/FIG4184560.

19. Dacher Keltner, *Born to Be Good: The Science of a Meaningful Life* (New York: Norton, 2009), 249.

20. Helen Riess, director of empathy research at Massachusetts General Hospital, quoted in Karen Weintraub, "Giving to Others Just Might Help People in the Treatment of Their Own Aches and Anxieties," *Boston Globe*, November 29, 2010.

21. Candace Pert, *Molecules of Emotion: Why You Feel the Way You Feel* (New York: Scribner, 1997), 307.

22. Pert, *Molecules*, 230.

23. Kabat-Zinn, *Senses*, 371. See also Emma Seppala, "Shift Your Body, Change Your Mind," *Spirituality and Health*, September–October 2010; Richard J. Davidson et al., "Alterations in Brain and Immune Function Produced by Mindfulness Meditation," *Psychosomatic Medicine* 65, no. 4(2003): 564–570; Wallace, *Mind in the Balance*, 27.

24. Jeffery A. Dusek, Hasan H. Out, Ann L. Wohlhueter, Manoj Bhasin, Luiz F. Zerbini, Marie G. Joseph, Herbert Benson, and Towia A. Libermann, "Genomic Counter-Stress Changes Induced by the Relaxation Response," PLoS ONE 3, no. 7(2008): e2576; doi:10.1371/journal.pone.0002576

25. Seppala, "Shift Your Body."

26. Carol Krucoff, interview, December 20, 2010.

27. Sat Bir Singh Khalsa, interview, December 21, 2010.

28. Jean van Gemert, interview, December 21, 2010.

29. Center for Mindfulness in Medicine, Health Care, and Society: www.umassmed.edu/cfm/oasis/index.aspx

30. The same question has been posed about yoga therapy's application of asanas to specific illnesses or injuries. See Julie Deife, "Is Yoga Medicine? Yoga Therapy Enters the Arena," *LA Yoga, Ayurveda and Health*, March 2007. Deife asks: When yoga becomes "medicine" do we necessarily ignore the overall goal of connecting the personal soul to God which is the theme of traditional yoga? Common Ground Yoga: http://commongroundyoga.com/wp-content/uploads/2008/12/is-1.pdf. Or see this comment by the head of the Himalayan Institute yoga center: "The lack of a grounding Yoga philosophy has shrunk Yoga practices to asana. People who regard asana practice as a beautiful set of exercises are definitely benefiting, but only in proportion to what they think asana is all about. . . . Yoga Philosophy . . . tells them that a human being . . . is body and mind together and that our core is pure consciousness and. . . . Yoga practices are designed to lead us to that core." Natalya Podgorny, "Inward Bound: An Interview with Pandit Rajmani Tigunait," *Yoga International*, Fall 2010, 34.

31. Yoga for Vets: www.yogaforvets.org/testimonials.

32. Interview in *Yoga International*, April–May 2002.

33. Some material in this and the following section is based in chapter 8 of Gottlieb, *Joining Hands.*

34. Mircea Eliade, *Journals*, vol. 3, 1970–1978 (Chicago: University of Chicago Press, 1989), 178.

35. Philip Martin, *The Zen Path through Depression* (San Francisco, CA: HarperSanFrancisco, 2000), xii.

36. Hamilton, *Scalpel*, 213.

37. Nedda Hobbs, interview, December 20, 2010.

38. Quoted at Good Reads: www.goodreads.com/author/quotes/4169.Stephen_Levine.

39. Another story whose source I cannot remember.

40. I have no idea where I heard this.

41. Susan Kenner, Carol Osborn, Linda Quigley, and Karen Stroup, *Speak the Language of Healing: Living with Breast Cancer without Going to War* (Berkeley, CA: Conari, 1999), 157–159.

42. Kenner et al., *Speak*, 40.

43. Kenner et al., *Speak*, 165–167.

44. Michael Ignatieff, quoted in Vardey, *God in All Worlds*, 347.

45. Susan Wendell, *The Rejected Body* (New York: Routledge, 1996), 63.

46. Wendell, *Rejected*, 175.

47. For a useful selection of Hauerwas's writings on this topic, as well as several interesting responses, see John Swinton, ed., *Critical Reflections on Stanley Hauerwas' Theology of Disability: Disabling Society, Enabling Theology* (Binghamton, NY: Haworth Pastoral, 2004).

48. Kierkegaard, *Postscript*, 115–159. Talmud: Sanhedrin 37a.

49. Paula Ickes, "Grandma Knows Best," in C. Dowling, N. Nicoll, and B. Thomas, eds., *A Different Kind of Perfect: Writings by Parents on Raising a Child with Special Needs* (Boston: Shambhala, 2004), 39.

50. Cindy Dowling, "Everything and Nothing at All," in Dowling et al., *Different Kind of Perfect*, 8.

51. Kittay, *Labor*, 147–161.

52. Michael Berube, *Life as We Know It: A Father, a Family, and an Exceptional Child* (New York: Pantheon, 1996).

53. Dowling et al., *Different Kind of Perfect*; Stanley D. Klein and Kim Schive, eds., *You Will Dream New Dreams* (New York: Kensington, 1999).

54. Kimberly Nava, "To Love and Be Loved," in Dowling et al., *A Different Kind of Perfect*, 217.

55. Greenspan (Esther's mother), *Healing*.

56. Robert A. Naseef, "The Rudest Awakening," in Klein and Schive, *You Will Dream New Dreams*, 209.

57. Jillian K. Welch, "The Journey," in Klein and Schive, *You Will Dream New Dreams*, 198–199.

58. Trungpa, *Training the Mind*, 89–90.

59. C. S. Lewis, *A Grief Observed* (San Francisco, CA: Harper SanFrancisco, 1994).

CHAPTER 9

1. Dennis Wall and Virgil Masayesva, "People of the Corn: Teachings in Hopi Traditional Agriculture Spirituality and Sustainability," in Roger S. Gottlieb, ed., *Religion and the Environment* (New York: Routledge, 2010), 2:310.

2. Chapter 5 of *Walden*.

3. Quoted at Azamra: www.azamra.org/Earth/field-05.html.

4. Clearly nothing humans can do will alter the laws governing motion, chemical interaction, or the structures of atom. Throw my body off the roof, and it will fall at the same rate as a raccoon or a maple tree. And just like a hawk or a halibut, my DNA code evolved. Yet even if we totally abandon the nature-human distinction, the distinct features of our species will still require some kind of recognition. Nowhere else in nature are history, self-consciousness, culture, and technology so important or the capacity to produce ecosystem-damaging substances so significant.

5. The phrase "nature deficit disorder" was coined by Richard Louv, *Last Child in the Woods* (New York: Algonquin, 1995). See also the idea that an absence of contact with nature is diminishing humanity's mental health in Paul Shepard, *Nature and Madness* (San Francisco, CA: Sierra Club, 1982). There is now an entire discipline, ecopsychology, that focuses on such questions.

6. James William Gibson, *A Reenchanted World: The Quest for a New Kinship with Nature* (New York: Holt, 2009).

7. Bron Taylor, *Dark Green Religion: Nature Spirituality and the Planetary Future* (Berkeley: University of California Press, 2009).

8. See Roger S. Gottlieb, ed., *The Oxford Handbook of Religion and Ecology* (New York: Oxford University Press, 2006).

9. Christopher Childs, *The Spirit's Terrain: Creativity, Activism, and Transformation* (Boston: Beacon, 1999), 50. This overlap between spirituality and environmentalism is examined in detail in chapter 5 of Roger S. Gottlieb, *A Greener Faith: Religious Environmentalism and Our Planet's Future* (New York: Oxford University Press, 2006).

10. In many publications, including Roger S. Gottlieb, ed., *This Sacred Earth* (New York: Routledge, 2003), 729–730; and at Resources for Environmental Justice Activists: www.ejnet.org/ej/principles.html.

11. In Elizabeth Roberts and Elias Amidon, eds., *Earth Prayers* (San Francisco, CA: HarperSanFrancisco, 1990), 251.

12. "The Goddess," in Roger S. Gottlieb, ed., *A New Creation: America's Contemporary Spiritual Voices* (New York: Crossroad, 1990), 213.

13. John Muir, *Our National Parks* (San Francisco, CA: Sierra Club, 1991), 56.

14. "The Ecology of Magic," in Peter Sauer, ed., *Finding Home: Writing on Nature and Culture from Orion Magazine* (Boston: Beacon, 1992), 183.

15. Brenda Peterson, "Killing Our Elders," in *Finding Home*, 56.

16. Deborah Bird Rose, "Indigenous Traditions–Australia," and Melissa K. Nelson, "Indigenous Traditions–Native America," both in Willis Jenkins, ed., *Encyclopedia of Sustainability, Volume 1: The Spirit of Sustainability* (Great Barrington, MA: Berkshire, 2010), 222–228.

17. Eliot Cowan, *Plant, Spirit, Medicine* (Columbus, NC: Swan Raven, 1995), 19.

18. Letter to Hubert W. Pelt, New York City, February 24, 1930.

19. Thomas Berry, *The Dream of the Earth* (San Francisco, CA: Sierra Club, 2006); John Hart, *Sacramental Commons: Christian Ecological Ethics* (Lanham, MD: Rowman and Littlefield, 2006).

20. William Hazlitt, "Walking," in Gottlieb, *This Sacred Earth*, 27.

21. Quoted in Linda Lear, *Rachel Carson: Witness for Nature* (New York: Holt, 1997), 86.

22. The modern ego is defined by independence of judgment, individual moral freedom, and economic and ideological liberty. This is clear in philosophers from Locke to John Rawls and in a great deal of psychological theory as well.

23. John C. H. Wu, *The Golden Age of Zen* (Bloomington, IN: World Wisdom, 1986), 286.

24. Rumi, "A Great Wagon," in *The Essential Rumi*, 36.

25. Shepard Krech III, *The Ecological Indian: Myth and History* (New York: W. W. Norton, 2000).

26. Overirrigation destroyed Babylonian agriculture by raising the level of salt in the fields. The Roman siege of Jerusalem led to a clear-cutting of the forests around the city, leaving barren hillsides that continue to the present.

27. Joseph Bruchac, "The Circle Is the Way to See," in Inter Press Service, ed., *Story Earth: Native Voices on the Environment* (San Francisco, CA: Mercury House, 1993), 4–5.

28. Marcos Terena, "Sing the Song of the Voice of the Forest," in *Story Earth*, 41.

29. Terena, "Sing the Song," in *Story Earth*, 32.

30. Quoted in Frederic Lehrman, *The Sacred Landscape* (Berkeley, CA: Celestial Arts, 1988), 25.

31. While most of spirituality has been in conflict with the dominant society, indigenous spirituality seems to actually have been the norm.

32. Rachel Carson, *Silent Spring* (Boston: Houghton Mifflin, 1962), 297. The earlier book is *The Sea around Us* (New York: Oxford University Press, 1951).

33. For one compelling example, consider how the Menominee tribe has managed its 220,000-acre Wisconsin forest for 150 years, taking out 2 billion board feet of lumber yet increasing total wood mass and biodiversity. See Paula Rogers Hugg and Marshall Pecore, "Menominee Tribal Enterprises": www.menominee.edu/sdi/csstdy.htm#A. http://www.epa.gov/ecopage/upland/menominee/forestkeepers.pdf

34. Bill McKibben, *The Age of Missing Information* (New York: Plume, 1993).

35. Andy Fisher, *Radical Ecopsychology: Psychology in the Service of Life* (Albany: State University of New York Press, 2002), 10.

36. Fisher, *Radical Ecopsychology*, 97–98.

37. John McPhee, *Encounters with the Archdruid* (New York: Farrar, Straus and Giroux, 1980).

38. David Brower, *Let the Mountains Talk, Let the Rivers Run* (Gabriola Island, BC: New Society, 2000), 139.

39. Barry Lopez, *Arctic Dreams* (New York: Scribner's, 1986), 228. For a concentrated and knowledgeable account of this element in the Bible, see chapter 7 of Richard Bauckham, *Living with Other Creatures: Green Exegesis and Theology* (Waco, TX: Baylor University Press, 2011).

40. Berry quoted in Jay Wallijasper, ed., *Visionaries: People and Ideas to Change Your Life* (Gabriola Island, BC: New Society, 2001), 5.

41. W. H. Auden, "Precious Five," in *Collected Poems* (London: Faber, 1976), 447.

42. Jim Nollman, *The Man Who Talks to Whales* (Boulder, CO: Sentient, 2002), 150–156.

43. Evelyn Fox Keller, *A Feeling for the Organism: The Life and Work of Barbara McClintock* (New York: W. H. Freeman, 1983).

44. Judaism is complicated in this area. It is certainly hierarchical in privileging mind and soul over body, but it also has a strong earthly side in its celebration of (religious-monitored) pleasures, including sexuality.

45. Patanjali, "Yoga Sutras," in Chapple, *Yoga and the Luminous*, 124, 133.

46. For example, the "Fire Sermon," in which every sense and sensory experience is represented as being "on fire."

47. Grace Paley, in Irene Diamond and Gloria Orenstein, eds., *Reweaving the World: The Emergence of Ecofeminism* (San Francisco, CA: Sierra Club, 2000), iii.

48. Charlene Spretnak, "Ecofeminism: Our Roots and Flowering," in Diamond and Orenstein, *Reweaving*, 7–8.

49. Of the many important ecofeminist writings, none is more eloquent than Susan Griffin's *Women and Nature: The Roaring inside Her* (San Francisco, CA: Sierra Club, 2000).

50. Carol Christ, "Rethinking Theology and Nature," in Carol Christ and Judith Plaskow, *Weaving the Visions: New Patterns in Feminist Spirituality* (New York: Harper, 1989), 322–323.

51. Delores S. Williams, "Sin, Nature, and Black Women's Bodies," in Carol J. Adams, ed., *Ecofeminism and the Sacred* (New York: Continuum, 1993), 25. Williams is particularly concerned with black women in this essay, but the point is true, in varying degrees, for all women in patriarchal societies. A similar analysis is made by many authors.

52. Philosopher Martha Nussbaum argues that human dignity "just is the dignity of a certain kind of animal" and that morality and rationality are "thoroughly material and animal." See Martha Nussbaum, *Frontiers of Justice: Nationality, Disability, Species Membership* (Cambridge, MA: Harvard University Press, 2006), 132–133.

53. David Suzuki, *The Sacred Balance: Rediscovering Our Place in Nature* (Vancouver, BC: Greystone, 2007), 209.

54. Howard Zahniser, "The Need for Wilderness," quoted at the Wilderness Society: www.wilderness.org/.

55. In Alon Tal, *Speaking of Earth: Environmental Speeches That Moved the World* (Piscataway, NJ: Rutgers University Press, 2006), 252.

56. Rick Bass, "The Turtle," *Shambhala Sun*, May 2009: http://shambhalasun.com/index.php?option=content&task=view&id=3354&Itemid=244&limit=1&limitsta rt=1.

57. See, e.g., Mark Plotkin, *Tales of a Shaman's Apprentice* (New York: Viking, 1993).

58. Macy, *World as Lover*.

59. See historian William Cronin's polemic, "The Trouble with Wilderness," at www. williamcronon.net/writing/Trouble_with_Wilderness_Main.html. For a non-western perspective, see Indian environmental historian Ramachandra Guha's widely read "Radical American Environmentalism and Wilderness Preservation: A Third World Critique," in Lori Gruen and Dale Jamieson, eds., *Reflecting on Nature: Readings in Environmental Philosophy* (New York: Oxford University Press, 1994).

60. The base price of the Chevy Volt, the new all-electric car, is around $35,000. And in any case the power it stores probably comes from a power plant burning coal or natural gas.

61. Michael Zimmerman, "Ecofascism: A Threat to American Environmentalism?" in Roger S. Gottlieb, ed., *The Ecological Community* (New York: Routledge, 1996).

62. It was the environmental justice movement that confronted and transformed the dominant environmental organizations on this issue. See, of many other works, Julian Agyeman, *Sustainable Communities and the Challenge of Environmental Justice* (New York: New York University Press, 2005).

CHAPTER 10

1. From Cesar Chavez, nonviolent Catholic union and environmental leader, in Catherine Ingram, *In the Footsteps of Gandhi: Conversations with Spiritual Social Activists* (Berkeley, CA: Parallax, 1990), 120.

2. Dorothy Day, "Our Brothers, the Communists," in Gottlieb, *Liberating Faith*, 252.

3. Andrew Harvey: www.andrewharvey.net/sacred_activism.php.

4. Aldo Leopold, *A Sand County Almanac* (New York: Ballantine, 1966), 197.

5. Access to which is remarkably easy these days. Here is a list of 100 useful sites: www.world.org/weo/environment.

6. Rabbi Michael Lerner calls this a rejection of the common sense of an oppressive and spiritually unfulfilling form of life.

7. Dorothy Soelle, *The Silent Cry: Mysticism and Resistance* (Minneapolis, MN: Fortress, 2001), 198.

8. Santikaro Bikku, "Buddhadasa Bikku: Life and Society through the Natural Eyes of Voidness," in Christopher S. Queen and Sallie King, eds., *Engaged Buddhism: Buddhist Liberation Movements in Asia* (Albany: State University of New York Press, 1996), 167.

9. For example, as wild areas for hunting by upper-class men. See Raymond Bonner, *At the Hands of Man: Peril and Hope for Africa's Wildlife* (New York: Simon and Schuster, 1994).

10. The violent and often genocidal expulsions are described in Mark Dowie's excellent *Conservation Refugees: The Hundred Year Conflict between Global Conservation and Native Peoples* (Cambridge, MA: MIT Press, 2009). Too often conservationism, when not motivated by simple greed, mistakenly took an urban and technological civilization as the norm and lacked the moral perspective of the ecojustice movement.

11. Leaders of China's Communist Party reserve for themselves the privilege of portable air purifiers, allowing them, but not China's masses, some respite from horrific air pollution. See Andrew Jacobs, "The Privileges of China's Elite Include Purified Air," *New York Times*, November 4, 2011: www.nytimes.com/2011/11/05/world/asia/the-privileges-of-chinas-elite-include-purified-air.html.

12. Germany's Green party and U.S. feminism are two significant examples.

13. The left's failure to understand the Israeli-Palestinian conflict is a glaring instance of this weakness.

14. Christopher S. Queen, "Introduction," in Christopher S. Queen, ed., *Engaged Buddhism in the West* (Boston: Wisdom, 2000), 1.

15. International Network of Engaged Buddhists: www.inebnetwork.org/#. For a recent effort by Engaged Buddhists on environmental concerns, see John Stanley, David R. Loy, and Gyurme Dorje, *A Buddhist Response to The Climate Emergency* (Somerville: MA, Wisdom, 2009).

16. Traditionally, these might include extremely limited food intake, celibacy, and spartan living conditions.

17. There are many sources, including Queen, *Engaged*; Arnold Kotler, ed., *Engaged Buddhist Reader* (San Francisco, CA: Parallax, 1999); International Network of Engaged Buddhists: www.inebnetwork.org/.

18. Nambaryn Enkhbayar, "Some Thoughts on Buddhist Philosophy and Economics," Alliance for Religions and Conservation: www.arcworld.org/projects.asp?projectID=186.

19. This discussion of Sarvodaya is partly based in *A Greener Faith*, 99–100.

20. Sarvodaya: http://sarvodaya.org/Introduction/sarvodayaover.html. http://www.sarvodaya.org/

21. Sarvodaya Web site.

22. Quoted in George D. Bond, *Buddhism at Work: Community Development, Social Empowerment, and the Sarvodaya Movement* (Bloomfield, CT: Kumarian, 2004), 16.

23. Detlef Kantowsky, *Sarvodaya: The Other Development* (New Delhi: Vikas, 1980), 166.

24. Sarvodaya: http://sarvodaya.org/Introduction/sarvodayaphilos.html. Quoted in *The Hindu: India's Online Newspaper*, March 9, 2003: http://www.rmaf.org.ph/madc/archive/files/article_the-compassionate-activist_ariyaratne_cf99939d2c.pdf.

25. Bond, *Buddhism at Work*, 50.

26. Bond, *Buddhism at Work*, 50.

27. Ingram, *Footsteps*, 133.

28. Thich Nhat Hanh, *Being Peace* (Berkeley, CA: Parallax, 1987), 79.

29. Thich Nhat Hanh, *Love in Action: Writings on Nonviolent Social Change* (Berkeley, CA: Parallax, 1993), 143–145. My emphasis.

30. See Joanna Macy's account: http://www.joannamacy.net/nuclearguardianship.html.

31. Kenneth Kraft, "Nuclear Ecology and Engaged Buddhism," in Mary Evelyn Tucker and Duncan Williams, eds., *Buddhism and Ecology: The Interconnection of Dharma and Deeds* (Cambridge, MA: Harvard University Press, 1997).

32. For example, Dalai Lama and Howard Cutler, *The Art of Happiness: A Handbook for Living* (New York: Riverhead, 1998), 2; Thich Nhat Hanh, *Love in Action*, 145.

33. Gottlieb, *Liberating Faith*, offers many examples of religious political activism.

34. Mary Daly, *Beyond God the Father* (Boston: Beacon, 1993), 19.

35. Rosemary Radford Ruether, *Sexism and God-Talk: Toward a Feminist theology* (Boston: Beacon, 1983), 173.

36. Rabbi Sandy Sasso quoted in Laura Geller, "From Equality to Transformation: The Challenge of Women's Rabbinic Leadership," in T. M. Rudavsky, ed., *Gender and Judaism: The Transformation of Tradition* (New York: New York University Press, 1995), 247.

37. One can certainly find relational men and hierarchical women. Yet common themes have emerged in the study of women in a variety of professional settings—from business managers to scientists. Given the cultural frameworks demanding that women above all be relational, sensitive, and caring about others—a "bitch" is a woman who doesn't do these things—these are hardly surprising findings.

38. See Lesser, *Seekers Guide*, 70–83, for a clear summary of these issues.

39. Charlene Spretnak, "Earthbody and Personal Body as Sacred," in Carol Adams, ed., *Ecofeminism and the Sacred* (London: Continuum, 1994), 272–273.

40. Carter Heyward, *Touching Our Strength: The Erotic as Power and the Love of God* (San Francisco, CA: Harper and Row, 1989).

41. The use of tradition for gender equality is theoretically possible. But as noted Protestant theologian John Cobb observed: "One can justify [gender] equality by using certain scriptures, but one is unlikely to do so if one is motivated only by conformation to the canon. Only when one accepts insights coming out of contemporary feminism is one likely to find that these are supported in scripture." See John B. Cobb Jr., *Reclaiming the Church* (Louisville, KY: Westminster John Knox, 1997), 65.

42. Orthodox Jewish feminist Blu Greenberg puts it slightly differently, responding to the charge that feminism is a "foreign body contamination" in Judaism: "Is there any religion in history, including Judaism, that has not borrowed from

the surrounding culture? The real question is: What do we do with what we borrow?" See her "The Theoretical Basis of Women's Equality in Judaism," in Gottlieb, *Creation*, 239.

43. Some of the material of these paragraphs is adapted from *Joining Hands*, 83–84.

44. Edward H. Carr, *The Bolshevik Revolution* (New York: Norton, 1985); Isaac Deutscher, *Trotsky: The Prophet Unarmed* (New York: Vintage, 1959); Robert Daniels, *A Documentary History of Communism*, vols. 1 and 2 (New York: Vintage, 1960).

45. Louis Fischer, *Gandhi: His Life and Message for the World* (New York: New American Library, 1991).

46. Stephen B. Oates, *Let the Trumpets Sound: A Life of Martin Luther King, Jr.* (New York: Harper, 1994), 218.

47. Oates, *Trumpets*, 236.

48. David Halberstam, *The Children* (New York: Ballantine, 1998), 139–140.

49. Student Nonviolent Coordinating Committee, "Founding Statement," in *Liberating Faith*, 463.

50. John Lewis, *Walking with the Wind: A Memoir of the Movement* (New York: Harcourt and Brace, 1998), 75.

51. Peter Litster, Interview, October 30, 2004.

52. See excellent accounts of pre-2000 struggles in Peter Ackerman, *A Force More Powerful* (New York: Palgrave, 2001). The ultimate results of the Arab Spring are still unknown.

53. Noted philosopher Richard Rorty offered a sophisticated version of this position in, for example, *Contingency, Irony, and Solidarity* (New York: Cambridge University Press, 1989). Philosophers Michael Sandel and Jeffrey Stout have offered alternative interpretations of the fundamental meanings of liberalism and democracy.

54. Quoted in Brussat and Brussat, *Spiritual Literacy*, 244: Martin Buber: "The beating heart of the universe is holy joy." Jesus: "These things have I spoken to you, that my joy may be in you, and that your joy may be full." Rebbe Nachman: "Joy is not incidental to your spiritual quest. It is vital." Julian of Norwich: "The fullness of joy is to behold God in everything."

55. Michael Lerner, *The Politics of Meaning: Restoring Hope and Possibility in an Age of Cynicism* (New York: Basic Books, 1989); and at Tikkun: www.tikkun.org.

56. Brueggemann, *Rich, Free, and Miserable*, 1.

57. Unfortunately positive psychology's interpretation of happiness, claims social analyst Barbara Ehrenreich, tends toward political passivity and conservatism. See her *Bright-Sided: How the Relentless Promotion of Positive Thinking Has Undermined America* (New York: Metropolitan, 2009), 147–176.

58. Talmud, Berachot 57b.

59. www.lightparty.com/Spirituality/Culture.html.

60. For another example, in Bangladesh, a combined spiritual and intensely practical attitude toward nature and agriculture animates the 60,000-strong organic farming association, Nayakrishi Andolan. See Bill McKibben, *Deep Economy* (New York: Macmillan, 2007), 200–209; and a brief account with associated links at the Think Forward website: http://iatp.typepad.com/thinkforward/2008/09/one-just-world. html http://tcdc.undp.org/sie/experiences/vol3/organic%20farming.pdf.

61. Dorothy Day, "Love Is the Measure," reprinted in *Liberating Faith*, 250–251.

CHAPTER 11

1. Ruth Stone, "Yes, Think" *Prairie Schooner* 71, no. 1 (1997).

2. Bill Marsh, "Into the Trash It Goes," *New York Times*: http://graphics8.nytimes. com/images/2008/05/18/weekinreview/0518MARTIN-1260x909.jpg.

3. North Korea alone is estimated to hold 200,000 in brutal, slavelike conditions. See "North Korea Holding 200,000 Political Prisoners," Reuters, May 3, 2011: www.reuters.com/article/2011/05/03/us-northkorea-prisons-idUSTRE74275D2 0110503.

4. "With every mistake, we must surely be learning." George Harrison, "While my guitar gently weeps."

Index